YOUR PERSONAL HOROSCOPE 2015

JOSEPH
POLANSKY

YOUR PERSONAL HOROSCOPE 2015

Month-by-month forecast for every sign

The only one-volume horoscope you'll ever need

HarperElement
An Imprint of HarperCollins*Publishers*
77–85 Fulham Palace Road,
Hammersmith, London W6 8JB

www.harpercollins.co.uk

and *HarperElement* are trademarks of
HarperCollins*Publishers* Ltd

Published by HarperElement 2014

1 3 5 7 9 10 8 6 4 2

© Star ★ Data, Inc. 2014

Star ★ Data assert the moral right to
be identified as the authors of this work

A catalogue record for this book is
available from the British Library

ISBN 978-0-00-754418-9

Printed and bound in Great Britain by
Clays Ltd, St Ives plc

MIX
Paper from
responsible sources
FSC **FSC™ C007454**

FSC™ is a non-profit international organisation established to promote
the responsible management of the world's forests. Products carrying the
FSC label are independently certified to assure consumers that they come
from forests that are managed to meet the social, economic and
ecological needs of present and future generations,
and other controlled sources.

Find out more about HarperCollins and the environment at
www.harpercollins.co.uk/green

The author is grateful to the people of STAR ★ DATA, who truly fathered this book and without whom it could not have been written.

Contents

Introduction

Welcome to the fascinating and intricate world of astrology!

For thousands of years the movements of the planets and other heavenly bodies have intrigued the best minds of every generation. Life holds no greater challenge or joy than this: knowledge of ourselves and the universe we live in. Astrology is one of the keys to this knowledge.

Your Personal Horoscope 2015 gives you the fruits of astrological wisdom. In addition to general guidance on your character and the basic trends of your life, it shows you how to take advantage of planetary influences so you can make the most of the year ahead.

The section on each sign includes a Personality Profile, a look at general trends for 2015, and in-depth month-by-month forecasts. The Glossary (*page 5*) explains some of the astrological terms you may be unfamiliar with.

One of the many helpful features of this book is the 'Best' and 'Most Stressful' days listed at the beginning of each monthly forecast. Read these sections to learn which days in each month will be good overall, good for money, and good for love. Mark them on your calendar – these will be your best days. Similarly, make a note of the days that will be most stressful for you. It is best to avoid booking important meetings or taking major decisions on these days, as well as on those days when important planets in your horoscope are retrograde (moving backwards through the zodiac).

The Major Trends section for your sign lists those days when your vitality is strong or weak, or when relationships with your co-workers or loved ones may need a bit more effort on your part. If you are going through a difficult time, take a look at the colour, metal, gem and scent listed in the 'At a Glance' section of your Personality Profile. Wearing a piece of jewellery that contains your metal and/or gem will strengthen your vitality, just as wearing clothes or decorating your room or office in the colour ruled by your sign, drinking teas made from the herbs ruled by your sign or wearing the scents associated with your sign will sustain you.

Another important virtue of this book is that it will help you to know not only yourself but those around you: your friends, co-workers, partners and/or children. Reading the Personality Profile and forecasts for their signs will provide you with an insight into their behaviour that you won't get anywhere else. You will know when to be more tolerant of them and when they are liable to be difficult or irritable.

In this edition we have included foot reflexology charts as part of the health section. So many health problems could perhaps be avoided or alleviated if we understood which organs were most vulnerable and what we could do to protect them. Though there are many natural and drug-free ways to strengthen vulnerable organs, these charts show a valid way to proceed. The vulnerable organs for the year ahead are clearly marked in the charts. It's very good to massage the whole foot on a regular basis, as the feet contain reflexes to the entire body. Try to pay special attention to the specific areas marked in the charts. If this is done diligently, health problems can be avoided. And even if they can't be completely avoided, their impact can be softened considerably.

I consider you – the reader – my personal client. By studying your Solar Horoscope I gain an awareness of what is going on in your life – what you are feeling and striving for and the challenges you face. I then do my best to address these concerns. Consider this book the next best thing to having your own personal astrologer!

It is my sincere hope that *Your Personal Horoscope 2015* will enhance the quality of your life, make things easier, illuminate the way forward, banish obscurities and make you more aware of your personal connection to the universe. Understood properly and used wisely, astrology is a great guide to knowing yourself, the people around you and the events in your life – but remember that what you do with these insights – the final result – is up to you.

A Note on the 'New Zodiac'

Recently an article was published that postulated two things: the discovery of a new constellation – Ophiuchus – making a thirteenth constellation in the heavens and thus a thirteenth sign, and the statement that because the Earth has shifted relative to the constellations in the past few thousand years, all the signs have shifted backwards by one sign. This has caused much consternation, and I have received a stream of letters, emails and phone calls from people saying things like: 'I don't want to be a Taurus, I'm happy being a Gemini', 'What's my real sign?' or 'Now that I finally understand myself, I'm not who I think I am!'

All of this is 'much ado about nothing'. The article has some partial truth to it. Yes, in two thousand years the planets have shifted relative to the constellations in the heavens. This is old news. We know this and Hindu astrologers take this into account when casting charts. This shift doesn't affect Western astrologers in North America and Europe. We use what is called a 'tropical' zodiac. This zodiac has nothing to do with the constellations in the heavens. They have the same names, but that's about it. The tropical zodiac is based on the Earth's revolution around the Sun. Imagine the circle that this orbit makes, then divide this circle by twelve and you have our zodiac. The Spring Equinox is always 0 degrees (Aries), and the Autumn Equinox is always 0 degrees (Libra). At one time a few thousand years ago, these tropical signs coincided with the actual constellations; they were pretty much interchangeable, and it didn't matter what zodiac you used. But in the course of thousands of years the planets have shifted relative to these constellations. Here in the West it doesn't affect our practice one iota. You are still the sign you always were.

In North America and Europe there is a clear distinction between an astrological sign and a constellation in the heavens. This issue is more of a problem for Hindu astrologers. Their zodiac is based on the actual constellations – this is called the 'sidereal' zodiac. And Hindu astrologers have been accounting for this shift all the time. They keep close tabs on it. In two thousand years there is a shift of 23 degrees, and they subtract this from the Western calculations. So in their system many a Gemini would be a Taurus and this is true for all the signs. This is nothing new – it is all known and accounted for, so there is no bombshell here.

The so-called thirteenth constellation, Ophiuchus, is also not a problem for the Western astrologer. As we mentioned, our zodiac has nothing to do with the constellations. It could be more of a problem for the Hindus, but my feeling is that it's not a problem for them either. What these astronomers are calling a new constellation was probably considered a part of one of the existing constellations. I don't know this as a fact, but I presume it is so intuitively. I'm sure we will soon be getting articles by Hindu astrologers explaining this.

Glossary of Astrological Terms

Ascendant

We experience day and night because the Earth rotates on its axis once every 24 hours. It is because of this rotation that the Sun, Moon and planets seem to rise and set. The zodiac is a fixed belt (imaginary, but very real in spiritual terms) around the Earth. As the Earth rotates, the different signs of the zodiac seem to the observer to rise on the horizon. During a 24-hour period every sign of the zodiac will pass this horizon point at some time or another. The sign that is at the horizon point at any given time is called the Ascendant, or rising sign. The Ascendant is the sign denoting a person's self-image, body and self-concept – the personal ego, as opposed to the spiritual ego indicated by a person's Sun sign.

Aspects

Aspects are the angular relationships between planets, the way in which one planet stimulates or influences another. If a planet makes a harmonious aspect (connection) to another, it tends to stimulate that planet in a positive and helpful way. If, however, it makes a stressful aspect to another planet, this disrupts that planet's normal influence.

Astrological Qualities

There are three astrological qualities: *cardinal*, *fixed* and *mutable*. Each of the 12 signs of the zodiac falls into one of these three categories.

Cardinal Signs

Aries, Cancer, Libra and Capricorn

The cardinal quality is the active, initiating principle. Those born
under these four signs are good at starting new projects.

Fixed Signs

Taurus, Leo, Scorpio and Aquarius

Fixed qualities include stability, persistence, endurance and
perfectionism. People born under these four signs are good at
seeing things through.

Mutable Signs

Gemini, Virgo, Sagittarius and Pisces

Mutable qualities are adaptability, changeability and balance. Those
born under these four signs are creative, if not always practical.

Direct Motion

When the planets move forward through the zodiac – as they normally
do – they are said to be going 'direct'.

Grand Square

A Grand Square differs from a normal Square (usually two planets
separated by 90 degrees) in that four or more planets are involved.
When you look at the pattern in a chart you will see a whole and
complete square. This, though stressful, usually denotes a new manifestation in the life. There is much work and balancing involved in the
manifestation.

Grand Trine

A Grand Trine differs from a normal Trine (where two planets are 120 degrees apart) in that three or more planets are involved. When you look at this pattern in a chart, it takes the form of a complete triangle – a Grand Trine. Usually (but not always) it occurs in one of the four elements: Fire, Earth, Air or Water. Thus the particular element in which it occurs will be highlighted. A Grand Trine in Water is not the same as a Grand Trine in Air or Fire, etc. This is a very fortunate and happy aspect, and quite rare.

Houses

There are 12 signs of the zodiac and 12 houses of experience. The 12 signs are personality types and ways in which a given planet expresses itself; the 12 houses show 'where' in your life this expression takes place. Each house has a different area of interest. A house can become potent and important – a house of power – in different ways: if it contains the Sun, the Moon or the 'ruler' of your chart; if it contains more than one planet; or if the ruler of that house is receiving unusual stimulation from other planets.

1st House
Personal Image and Sensual Delights

2nd House
Money/Finance

3rd House
Communication and Intellectual Interests

4th House
Home and Family

5th House
Children, Fun, Games, Creativity, Speculations and Love Affairs

6th House
Health and Work

7th House
Love, Marriage and Social Activities

8th House
Transformation and Regeneration

9th House
Religion, Foreign Travel, Higher Education and Philosophy

10th House
Career

11th House
Friends, Group Activities and Fondest Wishes

12th House
Spirituality

Karma

Karma is the law of cause and effect which governs all phenomena. We are all where we find ourselves because of karma – because of actions we have performed in the past. The universe is such a balanced instrument that any act immediately sets corrective forces into motion – karma.

Long-term Planets

The planets that take a long time to move through a sign show the long-term trends in a given area of life. They are important for forecasting the prolonged view of things. Because these planets stay in one sign for so long, there are periods in the year when the faster-moving (short-term) planets will join them, further activating and enhancing the importance of a given house.

Jupiter
stays in a sign for about 1 year

Saturn
2½ years

Uranus
7 years

Neptune
14 years

Pluto
15 to 30 years

Lunar

Relating to the Moon. See also 'Phases of the Moon', below.

Natal

Literally means 'birth'. In astrology this term is used to distinguish between planetary positions that occurred at the time of a person's birth (natal) and those that are current (transiting). For example, Natal Sun refers to where the Sun was when you were born; transiting Sun refs to where the Sun's position is currently at any given moment – which usually doesn't coincide with your birth, or Natal, Sun.

Out of Bounds

The planets move through the zodiac at various angles relative to the celestial equator (if you were to draw an imaginary extension of the Earth's equator out into the universe, you would have an illustration of this celestial equator). The Sun – being the most dominant and powerful influence in the Solar system – is the measure astrologers use as a standard. The Sun never goes more than approximately 23 degrees north or south of the celestial equator. At the winter solstice the Sun reaches its maximum southern angle of orbit (declination); at the summer solstice it reaches its maximum northern angle. Any time a planet exceeds this Solar boundary – and occasionally planets do – it is said to be 'out of bounds'. This means that the planet exceeds or tres-passes into strange territory – beyond the limits allowed by the Sun, the ruler of the Solar system. The planet in this condition becomes more emphasized and exceeds its authority, becoming an important influence in the forecast.

Phases of the Moon

After the full Moon, the Moon seems to shrink in size (as perceived from the Earth), gradually growing smaller until it is virtually invisible to the naked eye – at the time of the next new Moon. This is called the waning Moon phase, or the waning Moon.

After the new Moon, the Moon gradually gets bigger in size (as perceived from the Earth) until it reaches its maximum size at the time of the full Moon. This period is called the waxing Moon phase, or waxing Moon.

Retrogrades

The planets move around the Sun at different speeds. Mercury and Venus move much faster than the Earth, while Mars, Jupiter, Saturn, Uranus, Neptune and Pluto move more slowly. Thus there are times when, relative to the Earth, the planets appear to be going backwards. In reality they are always going forward, but relative to our vantage point on Earth they seem to go backwards through the zodiac for a period of time. This is called 'retrograde' motion and tends to weaken the normal influence of a given planet.

Short-term Planets

The fast-moving planets move so quickly through a sign that their effects are generally of a short-term nature. They reflect the immediate, day-to-day trends in a horoscope.

Moon
stays in a sign for only 2½ days

Mercury
20 to 30 days

Sun
30 days

Venus
approximately 1 month

Mars
approximately 2 months

T-square

A T-square differs from a Grand Square (see above) in that it is not a complete square. If you look at the pattern in a chart it appears as 'half a complete square', resembling the T-square tools used by architects and designers. If you cut a complete square in half, diagonally, you have a T-square. Many astrologers consider this more stressful than a Grand Square, as it creates tension that is difficult to resolve. T-squares bring learning experiences.

Transits

This term refers to the movements or motions of the planets at any given time. Astrologers use the word 'transit' to make the distinction between a birth, or Natal, planet (see 'Natal', above) and the planet's current movement in the heavens. For example, if at your birth Saturn was in the sign of Cancer in your 8th house, but is now moving through your 3rd house, it is said to be 'transiting' your 3rd house. Transits are one of the main tools with which astrologers forecast trends.

Aries

THE RAM

Birthdays from
21st March to
20th April

Personality Profile

ARIES AT A GLANCE

Element – Fire

Ruling Planet – Mars
  Career Planet – Saturn
  Love Planet – Venus
  Money Planet – Venus
  Planet of Fun, Entertainment, Creativity and Speculations – Sun
  Planet of Health and Work – Mercury
  Planet of Home and Family Life – Moon
  Planet of Spirituality – Neptune
  Planet of Travel, Education, Religion and Philosophy – Jupiter

Colours – carmine, red, scarlet

Colours that promote love, romance and social harmony – green, jade green

Colour that promotes earning power – green

Gem – amethyst

Metals – iron, steel

Scent – honeysuckle

Quality – cardinal (= activity)

Quality most needed for balance – caution

Strongest virtues – abundant physical energy, courage, honesty, independence, self-reliance

Deepest need – action

Characteristics to avoid – haste, impetuousness, over-aggression, rashness

Signs of greatest overall compatibility – Leo, Sagittarius

Signs of greatest overall incompatibility – Cancer, Libra, Capricorn

Sign most helpful to career – Capricorn

Sign most helpful for emotional support – Cancer

Sign most helpful financially – Taurus

Sign best for marriage and/or partnerships – Libra

Sign most helpful for creative projects – Leo

Best Sign to have fun with – Leo

Signs most helpful in spiritual matters – Sagittarius, Pisces

Best day of the week – Tuesday

Understanding an Aries

Aries is the activist *par excellence* of the zodiac. The Aries need for action is almost an addiction, and those who do not really understand the Aries personality would probably use this hard word to describe it. In reality 'action' is the essence of the Aries psychology – the more direct, blunt and to-the-point the action, the better. When you think about it, this is the ideal psychological makeup for the warrior, the pioneer, the athlete or the manager.

Aries likes to get things done, and in their passion and zeal often lose sight of the consequences for themselves and others. Yes, they often try to be diplomatic and tactful, but it is hard for them. When they do so they feel that they are being dishonest and phoney. It is hard for them even to understand the mindset of the diplomat, the consensus builder, the front office executive. These people are involved in endless meetings, discussions, talks and negotiations – all of which seem a great waste of time when there is so much work to be done, so many real achievements to be gained. An Aries can understand, once it is explained, that talk and negotiations – the social graces – lead ultimately to better, more effective actions. The interesting thing is that an Aries is rarely malicious or spiteful – even when waging war. Aries people fight without hate for their opponents. To them it is all good-natured fun, a grand adventure, a game.

When confronted with a problem many people will say, 'Well, let's think about it, let's analyse the situation.' But not an Aries. An Aries will think, 'Something must be done. Let's get on with it.' Of course neither response is the total answer. Sometimes action is called for, sometimes cool thought. But an Aries tends to err on the side of action.

Action and thought are radically different principles. Physical activity is the use of brute force. Thinking and deliberating require one not to use force – to be still. It is not good for the athlete to be deliberating the next move; this will only slow down his or her reaction time. The athlete must act instinctively and instantly. This is how Aries people tend to behave in life. They are quick, instinctive decision-makers and their decisions tend to be translated into action almost immediately. When their intuition is sharp and well tuned, their actions are powerful and successful. When their intuition is off, their actions can be disastrous.

Do not think this will scare an Aries. Just as a good warrior knows that in the course of combat he or she might acquire a few wounds, so too does an Aries realize – somewhere deep down – that in the course of being true to yourself you might get embroiled in a disaster or two. It is all part of the game. An Aries feels strong enough to weather any storm.

There are many Aries people who are intellectual. They make powerful and creative thinkers. But even in this realm they tend to be pioneers – outspoken and blunt. These types of Aries tend to elevate (or sublimate) their desire for physical combat in favour of intellectual, mental combat. And they are indeed powerful.

In general, Aries people have a faith in themselves that others could learn from. This basic, rock-solid faith carries them through the most tumultuous situations of life. Their courage and self-confidence make them natural leaders. Their leadership is more by way of example than by actually controlling others.

Finance

Aries people often excel as builders or estate agents. Money in and of itself is not as important as are other things – action, adventure, sport, etc. They are motivated by the need to support and be well-thought-of by their partners. Money as a way of attaining pleasure is another important motivation. Aries function best in their own businesses or as managers of their own departments within a large business or corporation. The fewer orders they have to take from higher up, the better. They also function better out in the field rather than behind a desk.

Aries people are hard workers with a lot of endurance; they can earn large sums of money due to the strength of their sheer physical energy.

Venus is their money planet, which means that Aries need to develop more of the social graces in order to realize their full earning potential. Just getting the job done – which is what an Aries excels at – is not enough to create financial success. The co-operation of others needs to be attained. Customers, clients and co-workers need to be made to feel comfortable; many people need to be treated properly in order for success to happen. When Aries people develop these abilities – or hire someone to do this for them – their financial potential is unlimited.

Career and Public Image

One would think that a pioneering type would want to break with the social and political conventions of society. But this is not so with the Aries-born. They are pioneers within conventional limits, in the sense that they like to start their own businesses within an established industry.

Capricorn is on the 10th house of career cusp of Aries' solar horoscope. Saturn is the planet that rules their life's work and professional aspirations. This tells us some interesting things about the Aries character. First off, it shows that, in order for Aries people to reach their full career potential, they need to develop some qualities that are a bit alien to their basic nature: they need to become better administrators and organizers; they need to be able to handle details better and to take a long-range view of their projects and their careers in general. No one can beat an Aries when it comes to achieving short-range objectives, but a career is long term, built over time. You cannot take a 'quickie' approach to it.

Some Aries people find it difficult to stick with a project until the end. Since they get bored quickly and are in constant pursuit of new adventures, they prefer to pass an old project or task on to somebody else in order to start something new. Those Aries who learn how to put off the search for something new until the old is completed will achieve great success in their careers and professional lives.

In general, Aries people like society to judge them on their own merits, on their real and actual achievements. A reputation acquired by 'hype' feels false to them.

Love and Relationships

In marriage and partnerships Aries like those who are more passive, gentle, tactful and diplomatic – people who have the social grace and skills they sometimes lack. Our partners always represent a hidden part of ourselves – a self that we cannot express personally.

An Aries tends to go after what he or she likes aggressively. The tendency is to jump into relationships and marriages. This is especially true if Venus is in Aries as well as the Sun. If an Aries likes you, he or she will have a hard time taking no for an answer; many attempts will be made to sweep you off your feet.

Though Aries can be exasperating in relationships – especially if they are not understood by their partners – they are never consciously or wilfully cruel or malicious. It is just that they are so independent and sure of themselves that they find it almost impossible to see somebody else's viewpoint or position. This is why an Aries needs as a partner someone with lots of social graces.

On the plus side, an Aries is honest, someone you can lean on, someone with whom you will always know where you stand. What he or she lacks in diplomacy is made up for in integrity.

Home and Domestic Life

An Aries is of course the ruler at home – the Boss. The male will tend to delegate domestic matters to the female. The female Aries will want to rule the roost. Both tend to be handy round the house. Both like large families and both believe in the sanctity and importance of the family. An Aries is a good family person, although he or she does not especially like being at home a lot, preferring instead to be roaming about.

Considering that they are by nature so combative and wilful, Aries people can be surprisingly soft, gentle and even vulnerable with their children and partners. The sign of Cancer, ruled by the Moon, is on the cusp of their solar 4th house of home and family. When the Moon is well aspected – under favourable influences – in the birth chart, an Aries will be tender towards the family and will want a family life that is nurturing and supportive. Aries likes to come home after a hard day on the battlefield of life to the understanding arms of their partner and the unconditional love and support of their family. An Aries feels that there is enough 'war' out in the world – and he or she enjoys participating in that. But when Aries comes home, comfort and nurturing are what's needed.

Horoscope for 2015

Major Trends

Uranus has been in your sign since the summer of 2011, and will be there for the year ahead and for some years to come. Thus the theme of your life these days is change. Change, change, change and more change after that – constant and continuous. Change is exciting, but it is also stressful. The cosmos wants you to get comfortable with change, to be comfortable with instability. Expect nothing, be prepared for anything!

Jupiter moved into Leo on July 17, 2014 and started to make beautiful aspects to you. This continues until August 11 of this year. Thus you are in party mode these days, enjoying life, indulging in leisure and fun activities. Most likely there will be foreign travel. Basically, this is a happy period.

On August 11 Jupiter will move into your 6th house of health and work. This is a fabulous aspect for job seekers or for those who employ others. Happy job changes are coming. Many of you will find the 'ideal' job. Those who employ others will expand your workforce and have good fortune from your employees. There's more on this later.

Saturn has been in Scorpio, your 8th house, for the past two years. This year he moves out of there, although he will return for approximately three months as he retrogrades back into Scorpio from June 15 to September 18. But most of the year he will be in your 9th house. With Saturn in Scorpio, the past few years have been about getting the sexual force under control, getting some balance there. Most of you have limited your sexual activity these past few years. The need was to focus on quality and not quantity. Now with Saturn in your 9th house there will be a need to get your religious and philosophical beliefs in right order. These will get tested – a good thing. The ones that are valid and true will remain, but some beliefs will have to be let go.

Your major interests in the year ahead are the body, image and physical appearance; children, fun and creativity (until August 11); health and work (from August 11 onwards); sex, occult studies, personal reinvention and personal transformation (from June 15 to

September 18); religion, philosophy, foreign travel and higher education (from January 1 to June 15 and from September 18 till the end of the year); career; and spirituality. You have many interests this year; try not to spread yourself too thin.

Your paths of greatest fulfilment this year will be love, romance and social activities (until November 13); children, fun, creativity (until August 11); and health and work (from August 11 onwards).

Health

(Please note that this is an astrological perspective on health and not a medical one. In days of yore there was no difference, these perspectives were identical. But now there could be quite a difference. For a medical perspective, please consult your doctor or health practitioner.)

Twenty eleven and 2012 were stressful health years. Things are much improved these days however. You still have two long-term

Important foot reflexology points for the year ahead
Try to massage the whole foot on a regular basis, but pay extra attention to the points highlighted on the chart. When you massage, be aware of 'sore spots', as these need special attention. It is also a good idea to massage the ankles and the tops of the feet.

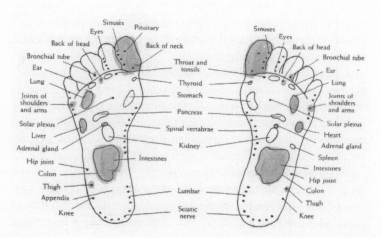

planets stressing you out, but the other long-term planets are either helping you or leaving you alone. Furthermore, when Jupiter enters your 6th house of health and work on August 11 there will be good fortune in health matters. If there has been a health problem you should start hearing good news about it. Health should be good this year.

Good though your health should be, you can make it even better. Give more attention to the following areas (the reflexes are shown in the chart above): the head, face and scalp; the adrenals; the heart; the lungs, small intestine, arms, shoulders and respiratory system; and the liver and thighs – the most vulnerable areas in the year ahead.

The head, face and scalp are always important for you and regular face and scalp massage is always powerful. Craniosacral therapy is good too. When you massage the face and scalp you're not only strengthening those areas (on the energetic level) but it's as if you are giving the entire body an energy boost. The head and face contain reflexes to the entire body.

The adrenals, too, are always important for you. You can see the reflexes in our chart. It is good to avoid anger and fear as these are the two emotions that stress the adrenals. Also avoid worry, the spiritual root cause of heart problems. Heart action can be erratic these days: sometimes too fast, sometimes too slow. The reflexes to the heart are also shown above.

The lungs, small intestine, arms, shoulders and respiratory system are usually important for you and this year is no different. Arms and shoulders should be regularly massaged. Acupuncture or acupressure treatments along the lung and small intestine meridian would be wonderful. The liver and thighs become important from August 11 onwards. Thighs should be regularly massaged. Liver detoxing (there are many natural herbal ways to do this) might be a good idea.

Jupiter in your 6th house indicates that you will benefit from metaphysical kinds of therapies – prayer and such like. It shows the importance of your personal philosophy of health and disease. If health problems arise (God forbid) it would be good to examine your philosophical concepts about health, and maybe revise them in a better way.

In general, your personal philosophy of life is important healthwise. Even if you have good health concepts, if there are other areas in your personal philosophy which are in error, these could manifest as a health problem. Philosophical purity is always a good thing, but this year it is an actual health issue.

Uranus, as we have mentioned, has been in your sign for some years now. This indicates a tendency to experiment with the body – to test its limits. This is basically good. The body is capable of a lot more than any of us think – the yogis affirm that the body is essentially infinite. However, this testing of the body's limits needs to be done safely and mindfully. Disciplines such as yoga, martial arts or tai chi are safe ways to do this. Otherwise there could be a tendency to indulge in daredevil-type stunts and injury could result.

There are many short-term health trends, as Mercury, your health planet, is a fast-moving planet. These short-term trends are best discussed in the monthly reports.

Home and Family

Your 4th house of home and family was strong during the past two years, but not this year. Many of you have moved, renovated or acquired additional homes over the past few years. By now your goals have been achieved and the year ahead seems to be a quiet one. The cosmos is not pushing you one way or another. You have free will to do what you like – but perhaps not the interest. With Uranus in your 1st house you seem more nomadic this year. You will be in different places for long periods of time.

If you're planning to redecorate, in cosmetic kinds of ways, or buying art objects for the home, May 8 to June 5 is a good time. However, if you're planning major renovations or construction projects, June 24 to August 9 would be a good time for this kind of work.

Aries women of childbearing age have been unusually fertile the past few years and the trend continues in the year ahead. But all Aries will be more focused on children or children figures this year. Children or children figures in your life will have a basically good year. They seem successful and optimistic, enjoying the good life. Many are travelling this year. They seem happy-go-lucky and prosperous. If they are of an appropriate age, they too seem unusually fertile. Children could move – and this seems a happy aspect – after August 11.

A parent figure in your life is reinventing him or herself; this has been going on for a while. He or she could have had surgery and/or near-death kinds of experiences in the past few years, and there are still tendencies to this in the year ahead. He or she will benefit greatly from detox regimes.

Siblings or sibling figures in your life are likely to move or renovate the home from August 11 onwards. And parents or parent figures have been moving a lot in recent years and could do so again. Perhaps there have been multiple renovations of the home. They seem restless and nomadic, living in different places for long periods of time. Their moods seem highly unstable. Mood swings are extreme and swift.

Your family planet is the Moon – the fastest-moving of all the planets. Thus there are many short-term trends – depending on where the Moon is and the aspects she receives – that are best dealt with in the monthly reports.

Finance and Career

The year ahead looks prosperous, but your money house is not a house of power. This could be a financial weakness. Perhaps you're not paying enough attention. You will have to force yourself to focus here.

Jupiter's presence in your 5th house until August 11 shows luck in speculations. Some of you might want to invest small sums on the lottery or in some other kind of speculations. Of course you should only do this under intuition and not blindly or automatically. The cosmos has many ways to supply you.

If you are in the creative arts there is good fortune now. Your creativity is marketable and successful.

Jupiter moves into your 6th house of work on August 11, which indicates happy job changes. In some cases it indicates the landing of a dream job; in other cases it shows a happy job change within the present company. Your ability to be productive is greatly increased in the year ahead and this usually translates into more money.

The spouse, partner or current love has had a difficult two years financially – there's been much reorganization going on. This year there is great improvement in this area. Saturn will mostly be out of his or her money house (except for three months); furthermore, Jupiter will start to make beautiful aspects to his or her financial planet from August 11 onwards. This shows a prosperous year ahead, from August onwards. The children or children figures in your life are also prospering greatly.

There is inheritance in this chart. Hopefully no one has to actually die. Perhaps you are named in someone's will or appointed to some administrative position in an estate.

The year ahead also appears good for paying down debt or for taking on loans – depending on your need. Most of you will have increases in your line of credit. You have easier access to outside capital. If you have good ideas, this is a good year (from August 11 onwards) to attract financial backing.

If you are involved in estates or insurance claims, there is good fortune from August 11 onwards.

Favourable financial numbers are 2, 3, 7 and 9.

Saturn, your career planet, shifts back and forth between two signs this year – it zigzags. And this pretty much describes the career. Until June 15 Saturn will be in Sagittarius, your 9th house. This shows success and elevation, and expanded career horizons. It indicates career opportunities in foreign lands or with foreign companies. (There are job opportunities in foreign lands too, after August 11.) It also shows increased business-related travel. In fact, your willingness to travel is important in your career advancement.

With Pluto stuck in your 10th house of career for many years now, there are dramas with bosses and people involved in your career. They could be having surgery, or near-death kinds of experiences. Perhaps you are having career 'near-death' experiences. Always keep in mind that after 'death' comes 'resurrection'. The career will be renewed.

Love and Social Life

Your 7th house of love is not a house of power this year, and this indicates that things will tend to remain the same. Married couples tend to stay married and singles tend to stay single.

With the 7th house basically empty (only the short-terms planets will move through there in the year ahead) there could be a tendency to ignore the love life, to not give it the attention it deserves. This would be a mistake. For as we mentioned this area of life brings great fulfilment in the year ahead. You have to force yourself to pay attention here even when you don't feel like it.

If you are single, working towards your first marriage, you are probably happy staying single. Marriage is not seen here. However, there are hot love affairs happening. You might not marry, but there is no shortage of love. June and July seems especially active in this department.

If you are working towards your second marriage there will be an opportunity in June and July, but I'm not so sure that this will lead to marriage. It would be best not to rush into anything. Let love develop naturally.

If you are working towards your third marriage, romance (and perhaps even marriage) is in the air. It could have happened last year, but if not, the year ahead (especially until August 11) is excellent.

One of the challenges in love is Uranus in your 1st house. We have written about this in previous years but the trend is still very much in effect. Uranus in the 1st house gives a passion for personal freedom. Freedom trumps relationships. A committed relationship is, by definition, a limitation of personal freedom and this is the problem. The ideal lover is someone who will give you lots of space, lots of freedom, within the relationship.

Those involved with an Aries in a romantic way should take note. Give your Aries lover as much freedom as possible so long as it isn't destructive. Try doing unconventional, zany things together. Try being friends with your Aries lover, not just a lover. With Uranus in their 1st house, Aries is into friendship these days. They are comfortable in that role.

In that department – friendships – the year ahead seems very happy and active. Friends seek you out, there is nothing much that you need to do. You seem very involved with groups and group activities – these too seek you out. New and important friendships are happening this year (and this was so last year too).

Parents and parent figures are having a static, stable love year.

Children or children figures of the appropriate age experience serious love this year. If they are single they could get married, or have a relationship that is 'like' a marriage. Grandchildren of an appropriate age also find love this year.

Siblings and sibling figures are having their relationships tested this year. If they are single they are not likely to marry.

Favourable numbers for love are 3, 7 and 11.

Self-improvement

Saturn has been in your 8th house of transformation and regeneration for two years now and spends another few months there in the year ahead. Whatever your age and stage in life, your libido has not been up to its usual standard. From the astrological perspective this is not so much a health issue, more of a cosmic one. The cosmos has been putting the sexual life into right order. If sexual expression has been too low, Saturn increased it. If it has been too much (which is usually the case) Saturn clamped down on it. Sex in many ways is like eating. We need to eat enough – not too much, not too little, just the right amount. Many of you have learned that quality sex is better (and healthier) than mere quantity. Better less sex but good sex than hosts of mediocre experiences.

Saturn will spend most of the coming year in your 9th house of religion, philosophy and higher education. For college students this indicates a need to buckle down and work hard. There are no free rides this year. Focus on your studies. Do the work that is needed. Bear down. Non-students will have their religious and philosophical beliefs tested, as we have mentioned. Your belief system is getting a reality check. Many of us are holding beliefs that are just not correct. Many of us look at the world in a false way and attribute meanings to phenomena that aren't so. This is a year where you learn about this. Generally reality checks are not pleasant, but great good will come of it. As you let go of false, or only partially true, beliefs, new and better ones will come in. And the whole life will improve because of that.

Philosophy, as we have mentioned many times, is much more important than psychology. A person's philosophy will shape and mould the psychology. Philosophy is cause, psychology is effect. So what's going on now (and for the next two years), is very important.

Aries generally have a strong sense of self-esteem. But lately, with the Moon's south node in your 1st house, your self-esteem has not been what it should. There is a feeling of deficiency here. Often when this happens, people over-compensate and become over-bearing and excessively arrogant. Avoid this trap like the plague. There is a correct way to attain healthy self-esteem. This is by recognizing that you are a son or daughter of the Most High – an immortal spiritual being incarnated in a body. You are not your body or personality, but the being that uses these things for its own purposes. A good meditation for this is, 'I AM AN IMMORTAL BEING OF LIGHT, I AM ONE WITH GOD, IN PERFECT UNION AND HARMONY WITH THE UNIVERSE.'

Repeat this a few times a day to yourself, and especially when you feel low. The more time you spend with this meditation, the better.

Month-by-month Forecasts

January

Best Days Overall: 6, 7, 8, 16, 17, 24, 25
Most Stressful Days Overall: 4, 5, 11, 12, 13, 18, 19, 31
Best Days for Love: 1, 11, 12, 13, 21, 22, 31
Best Days for Money: 1, 7, 8, 12, 13, 16, 17, 21, 22, 24, 25, 27, 28, 31
Best Days for Career: 6, 16, 18, 19, 24

Looking out for one's self-interest and looking out for others' interests are really two sides of a single coin. Neither has any intrinsic moral superiority. Your interest is no less nor more important than another's. What we emphasize depends on the cosmic cycle we are in at any given time. You have just come out of a cycle of needing to put others first. Last month, the planets shifted from the Western sector of others to the Eastern sector of self. Now you are more independent (which is very comfortable for Aries). It is right and proper now, and for the next five or so months, to keep a keen eye on your own interests and to pursue them. It will be easier now to make changes in your life, to create conditions as you desire them to be. With 90 per cent of the planets moving forwards this month you should see fast progress towards your goal. Time to have things your way Aries!

Last month you entered one of your yearly career peaks, and this continues until the 20th. Most of the planets are above the horizon of your Horoscope – and this too fosters career activities. Most likely you will not achieve all your career goals in their fullness (these take time and development), but you will see good progress towards them and this counts as success. You will be closer to your goals than you were in the past few months.

You will probably not be travelling as much this year as usual. Necessary travel is OK, but frivolous travel is probably not. Your chart emphasizes travel related to your career. But even so, avoid long journeys between the 1st and the 3rd (if possible).

On the 20th your focus shifts to friends, groups, group activities and organizations. This is not only fun for its own sake but seems to help the bottom line as well. Singles will find romantic opportunities in these venues as well.

Mars, the ruler of your Horoscope, enters your 12th house of spirituality on January 12. Moreover, he travels with Neptune, your planet of spirituality, from the 16th to the 20th. Thus you seem to be meeting a guru or spiritual mentor. This could be someone you already know or someone new. This is indicated as a period for spiritual breakthroughs.

Rest and relax more until the 20th.

February

Best Days Overall: 3, 4, 13, 14, 21, 22
Most Stressful Days Overall: 1, 8, 9, 15, 16, 27, 28
Best Days for Love: 1, 2, 8, 9, 10, 11, 20, 21
Best Days for Money: 1, 2, 3, 4, 10, 11, 13, 14, 20, 21, 22, 23, 24
Best Days for Career: 3, 13, 15, 16, 21

Your love and financial planet, Venus, is travelling with Neptune early in the month. It began late last month on the 30th and continues until the 3rd. This shows good financial intuition. Pay attention to hunches during this period. Take note of dreams. Spiritual people – gurus,

ministers, psychics and astrologers – have important financial information for you. If you have financial doubts or need guidance you can
consult with these kinds of people. Venus will be in your 12th house
until the 20th, so these trends continue.

Love too is very spiritual and idealistic this month. Venus's conjunction with Neptune shows a romantic or social meeting with a spiritual
type of person. The person could also be a musician, poet, dancer or
photographer – a very creative type. Love opportunities happen in
spiritual-type settings during most of the month, at the yoga studio,
the meditation seminar, prayer circle or at a charity event.

This is a very nice period for both love and money. Venus is in her
most exalted position in Pisces. Thus she is more powerful than usual.
Your earning power and social magnetism are much stronger.

Idealism is a wonderful thing in love and finance. We should shoot
for the ideal in life. But keep both feet on the ground in these matters.
Focus on your ideal, but don't neglect the practical issues.

The beloved is more sensitive these days – friends as well. Be very
careful of what you say and how you say it. They can take umbrage over
your tone of voice or your body language. Little things – unintentional
things – can set them off.

Love comes to you this month, especially from the 20th onwards.
There is no need for you to do anything special, it will find you. The
same is true with money. Money and financial opportunity will seek
you out after the 20th. All you have to do is to show up.

Mars and Venus travel together from the 20th to the 24th. Romance
is definitely in the air. This is a classic signal for love.

Your spiritual interests seem to conflict with the career, and perhaps
with people involved in your career. These people don't seem too
receptive. It will take a nice balancing act on your part to handle this.

March

> Best Days Overall: 2, 3, 12, 13, 20, 21, 29, 30, 31
> Most Stressful Days Overall: 1, 7, 8, 14, 15, 27, 28
> Best Days for Love: 2, 3, 7, 8, 12, 13, 22, 23
> Best Days for Money: 2, 3, 12, 13, 20, 21, 22, 23
> Best Days for Career: 2, 12, 14, 15, 20, 29, 30

The planetary power is in its maximum Eastern position this month, and you are in your period of maximum independence and personal power. Make those changes that need to be made. Create your life as you want it to be. Look out for number one. Others will more or less co-operate now. Most of the planets are moving forwards and personal progress and life in general moves swiftly.

There is a very strong solar eclipse on March 20. It occurs just near your Ascendant, on the cusp of your 12th and 1st houses. All of you will feel the effects of this but those of you born early in the sign of Aries – between March 21 and March 23 – will feel them the strongest. Make sure you reduce your schedule during this period and for a few days before and after. Avoid stressful, risk-taking activities and spend some quiet time at home. Read a good book or watch a movie, or even better, meditate.

This solar eclipse indicates a redefinition of your personality. You are changing the way you think of yourself and the way that you want others to see you. Over the next six months you will change your look, your wardrobe, hair style, etc. Generally this is forced on you: if you don't redefine yourself, others will. Sometimes, if a person has not been careful with their diet, it brings a detox of the body. Every solar eclipse impacts on children and children figures in the life and they should be kept out of harm's way during this period. Generally it brings dramas – life-changing kinds of events – to their lives.

Health and energy are basically good this month. The problem can be too much of a good thing – you have too much energy. You are hyper-active and perhaps overly hasty. This can lead to injury. Be especially careful during the eclipse period, and from the 9th to the 12th. Avoid daredevil stunts and activities.

Until the 17th the trends of love and finance are pretty much as we described last month. Love and money come to you. You spend on yourself. Your personal appearance and overall demeanour is a big factor in generating earnings, and you spend freely and impulsively. And perhaps you are prone to jump into relationships impulsively too.

Things calm down after the 17th as Venus moves into stable, conservative Taurus. Your social and financial judgement will be much better in this period. Since Taurus is your money house, you are in a prosperous period. Love opportunities come as you pursue your financial goals and with people who are involved in your finances.

April

Best Days Overall: 8, 9, 17, 18, 25, 26, 27
Most Stressful Days Overall: 3, 4, 5, 10, 11, 12, 23, 24
Best Days for Love: 1, 2, 3, 4, 5, 13, 21, 22
Best Days for Money: 1, 2, 8, 9, 13, 17, 18, 19, 20, 21, 22, 25, 26
Best Days for Career: 8, 10, 11, 12, 17, 25, 26

The love life has been very active and happy of late and things have gone rather easily. Many of you entered into new relationships. Now, a lunar eclipse on the 4th will test these things. A good relationship will weather the storm. However, old laundry – repressed feelings and grievances – will be thrown up and need to be dealt with. The beloved is more temperamental this period, so be more patient. It helps when you understand what is really going on.

This eclipse, like last month's solar eclipse, affects you strongly, so take a nice easy schedule for a few days before and after it. Generally, the cosmos will send a message that the eclipse period has begun. The message will be personal. Perhaps you read of some odd happening in the newspapers or media. Or, some quirky kind of event happens to you.

Friendships will also get tested by this eclipse. Sometimes it is the actual relationship that gets tested, sometimes the eclipse brings life-changing dramas in the lives of friends and this shakes things up.

Every lunar eclipse affects the family and home and this one is no different. If there are flaws in the home, now is when you find out about them so you can correct them. Family members will be more temperamental too – so be more patient.

In spite of all the excitement, many nice things are happening for you. On the 20th the Sun enters your money house and you begin a yearly financial peak. The money house is very powerful this month, so prosperity is good. We mentioned that essential travel is called for this year, but try to schedule these trips before the 20th.

Health is also basically good. You have plenty of energy to achieve whatever you want to do. You are very dynamic and charismatic these days – especially until the 20th.

Children or children figures should be kept out of harm's way from the 4th to the 7th. They should avoid taking risks or doing silly stunts.

The love planet enters Gemini, your 3rd house of communication, on the 11th. Singles will find romantic opportunities in educational-type settings, at lectures and seminars, in the library or as they pursue their intellectual interests. Love is found in the neighbourhood this month.

May

Best Days Overall: 5, 6, 14, 15, 23, 24
Most Stressful Days Overall: 1, 2, 8, 9, 21, 22, 28, 29
Best Days for Love: 1, 2, 12, 13, 21, 22, 28, 29
Best Days for Money: 1, 2, 5, 6, 12, 13, 14, 15, 16, 17, 21, 22, 23, 24, 30, 31
Best Days for Career: 5, 8, 9, 14, 23

On March 20, the planetary power shifted from the upper half of your Horoscope to the lower half. Saturn, your career planet, started a retrograde move on March 14. And this continues through this month. Career issues need time to sort out. You can shift your focus to your home, family and the emotional life. Symbolically speaking this is the night time of your year. A good night's rest is essential for us to perform well and the cosmos supplies this to us. Night does not mean 'inactivity' but a different kind of activity – internal activity that builds up the forces for the next day. So, this is a time for achieving your career goals by 'inner' methods rather than 'outer' action, through visualizing, dreaming and imagining that you have already achieved your goals. When the planets shift again in a few months time, you will be ready to put these dreams into action. It is said that in the winter nature sleeps and dreams and in the spring she wakes up and manifests what she has been dreaming. So it is for us.

You are still in a yearly financial peak until May 21. By then most of your financial goals will have been achieved (or at least good progress towards their achievement will have been made) and the focus will shift to intellectual interests. Your 3rd house is very powerful all month, but especially after the 21st. This is the time to catch up on those emails, letters and phone calls you owe to others. It is a good time too to take courses on subjects that interest you and to attend lectures, workshops and seminars. Time to give the mind the nutrition it needs, for it has needs as much as the physical body does.

Those of you involved in sales and marketing should have a good month.

There is only one fly in the ointment here. Mercury, the planet of communication, goes retrograde on the 14th. This means that more care needs to be taken when you are communicating with others, to avoid misunderstandings. If you're reading a book or attending a lecture, take more time to digest the ideas. The meaning might not be what you think.

Mercury retrograde tends to bring delays in communication – letters don't get delivered or get delivered late. Emails bounce or there is difficulty accessing the email account. Phone services can be erratic. But in spite of these glitches it is still good to focus on communication.

June

Best Days Overall: 2, 3, 10, 11, 20, 21
Most Stressful Days Overall: 4, 5, 17, 18, 19, 24, 25
Best Days for Love: 1, 10, 11, 20, 21, 24, 25, 29, 30
Best Days for Money: 1, 2, 3, 10, 11, 13, 14, 20, 21, 29, 30
Best Days for Career: 1, 4, 5, 10, 19, 28

The planets are now at the nadir (lowest point) in your Horoscope. It is midnight, symbolically speaking, in your year. The body sleeps (or should be sleeping) but mighty internal forces are going on. And so it is with you. Career progress is happening, but it is going on behind the scenes, on the inner levels. Prosperity is happening in this way too. Perhaps you don't see it overtly but prosperity is happening on the invisible levels. This is a time for focusing on the family and for getting the domestic life in order. And it's also a very good time for getting the emotional life in order. Those of you seeing therapists will make much progress this month.

With the 4th house of home and family so powerful this month (60 per cent of the planets are either there or moving through there) there is a tendency towards nostalgia. The past calls to you. You are more interested in history, both personal and general. Old memories come up for review. Venus has been in your 4th house since May 7 and remains there until June 5. Often this indicates a reunion with an old romantic flame. Sometimes it is a literal meeting, sometimes symbolic. You could meet someone with the same looks or personality quirks of the old flame. This may or may not become a serious relationship, but the purpose is to resolve old issues. It is for emotional healing.

Aries of childbearing age have been more fertile since July of 2013. This trend continues this month, and is even more pronounced over the next few months.

Health is more delicate this month. Rest and relax more. If possible spend time in a health spa, or schedule massages or reflexology treatments.

Your career planet changes signs this month. Saturn moves back into Scorpio on the 15th. Again this shows 'behind the scenes' career progress. There are internal changes – and perhaps dramas – in the lives of bosses and authority figures. There are also shake-ups in your industry or profession.

Travel is more favourable this month.

Finances are good. And family support is good. Money and financial opportunities come from the family or through family connections. Your financial intuition is excellent until the 5th. Venus travels with Jupiter towards the end of the month (from the 28th to the 30th), and this indicates a nice payday or windfall. It shows luck in speculations too. For singles, this aspect brings a wonderful romantic meeting.

July

Best Days Overall: 8, 9, 17, 18, 26, 27, 28
Most Stressful Days Overall: 1, 2, 14, 15, 16, 22, 23, 29, 30
Best Days for Love: 8, 9, 17, 18, 22, 23, 26
Best Days for Money: 8, 9, 10, 11, 17, 18, 26, 27, 28
Best Days for Career: 1, 2, 7, 16, 25, 29, 30

Last month on the 21st we had another shift of planetary power, when the planets began to shift to the Western, social sector of your chart. This month the shift becomes even stronger. Though, as we mentioned, there is nothing wrong with self interest, nothing wrong with independence – these are wonderful qualities – now, because you are in a different stage of your yearly cycle, these qualities should be downplayed. Now is the time to be a team player; to achieve your goals through co-operation with others; to focus more on the needs of the other people in your life and let them have their way – so long as it isn't destructive. The cosmos has its ways of pushing you into this. Since the planetary power is moving away from you, rather than towards you, it is harder to take independent action or change conditions to your liking. Hopefully, over the past six months you have made any desired or necessary changes. Now it is time to live with your creation. You have made your bed, as the saying goes, and now you must sleep in it. If you have built properly, conditions will be pleasant. If there have been mistakes you will learn about them over the course of the next six months, and will be able to make corrections when a new period of personal independence comes round – towards the very end of the year.

It is good at times to take a vacation from ourselves and to focus on others. Too much self focus is the root of many problems.

Health is still delicate, until the 23rd. Review our discussion of this last month. After the 23rd, as the Sun enters Leo, your normal energy returns and your health will be greatly improved. You can enhance your health this month by first maintaining high energy levels. Until the 7th give more attention to the lungs, arms, shoulders and respiratory system. Fresh air is good if you feel under the weather. Make sure you're getting enough of it. After the 8th as your health planet moves into Cancer, right diet becomes important. You have a tendency this month to eat too fast. Slow down. Chew your food well. Bless the food. Also give more attention to the stomach. Women should pay more attention to the breasts. Do your best to stay in a positive mood. Emotional disturbances or prolonged negative emotion have a more dramatic impact on the physical body than usual.

Retrograde activity among the planets is greatly increased this month, and by the end of the month half of the planets will be in retrograde motion. The pace of life slows down, and this is as it should be. It is a good time to take your vacation. There is nothing much happening in the world and your 5th house of fun becomes stronger than usual.

August

Best Days Overall: 4, 5, 13, 14, 23, 24, 31
Most Stressful Days Overall: 10, 11, 12, 18, 19, 25, 26
Best Days for Love: 5, 14, 18, 19, 23, 24, 31
Best Days for Money: 5, 6, 7, 14, 15, 23, 24, 25, 31
Best Days for Career: 3, 12, 22, 25, 26, 30

On the 23rd of last month, as the Sun entered your 5th house of fun, you entered one of your yearly personal peaks. This is in effect until the 23rd of this month. It's party time, a time to explore the rapture of life. This personal pleasure peak will be stronger than in most past years as Jupiter is also in the 5th house at the beginning of the month. By the 23rd you will have got some of the high spirits out of your system and will be ready to get more serious in the weeks to come.

Retrograde activity among the planets is still intense, but it is a little less than last month – only 40 per cent of the planets are retrograde. The most important retrograde for you to consider is the rare retrograde of Venus which began late last month (on the 25th). This shows that a review is in order of both the financial and love life. This is not a time for making major purchases, investments or love decisions, but for doing your homework on these matters.

Venus retrograde will not stop earnings or love, but will slow things down a bit. A payment that was promised can be delayed. A cheque you received can bounce – perhaps due to errors at the bank or in the sender's accounting. That great deal on an appliance might turn out to be not such a great deal a few weeks down the road when you find the same item (or a better one) for less in another store. Those shares that you thought were so unbelievably cheap get even cheaper with time. Caution. Caution. Caution.

In spite of the retrograde there are some nice financial and romantic happenings. Venus travels with Jupiter from the 3rd to the 6th. A nice payday and/or romantic meeting is indicated, but it might be delayed because of the retrograde. There is luck in speculations during that period too – only don't lose or misplace your lottery ticket.

There is luck in speculation from the 26th to the 28th too, when the Sun travels with Jupiter. Those of you into the creative arts are especially inspired during this period, and children or children figures of the appropriate age are especially fertile.

Jupiter makes a major move into your 6th house of health and work on the 11th, and will be there well into 2016. This a great aspect for job seekers; there are dream jobs out there for you. The month ahead, in general, is good for job seekers – especially after the 23rd.

Your career planet, Saturn, starts to move forward on August 2. Clarity and direction is happening in your career now, and pretty soon – in the next two months – you can start taking overt actions in this sphere. Right now, however, most of the planets are still below the horizon and the focus is still on home and family.

September

Best Days Overall: 1, 9, 10, 19, 20, 28, 29
Most Stressful Days Overall: 7, 8, 14, 15, 22, 23
Best Days for Love: 1, 9, 10, 14, 15, 19, 20, 28, 29
Best Days for Money: 1, 2, 3, 9, 10, 12, 19, 20, 28, 29, 30
Best Days for Career: 8, 18, 19, 22, 23, 28

There is a hectic and active month ahead, Aries, with lots and lots of changes going on. Venus, your love and financial planet, starts to move forward on the 6th. Your career planet Saturn changes signs and houses on the 18th. And, last but not least, we will have two eclipses this month.

Eclipses tend to be disruptive kinds of events, but there is a cosmic purpose behind them. Sometimes individuals are on the wrong track. Sometimes we make plans that are not in our highest cosmic interest. The eclipse comes and shatters these plans and we have little alternative but to get on the right track. In this sense they are blessings, but they are not so pleasant while they are happening.

The solar eclipse of the 13th occurs in your 6th house of health and work. It indicates job changes, disruptions at work, a change in the conditions of work and dramatic events in the lives of co-workers or employees. If you employ others the eclipse signals employee turnover – instability in the workforce. All of this will turn out well, as benevolent Jupiter is also in your 6th house. The job changes will work out well. You will find a better and higher-paying job – very soon. The same is true with employees. New and better ones are coming into the picture. In many cases this eclipse can show health scares or health problems. Review our discussion of health in the yearly report. There will be important changes in the health regime over the next six months.

Every solar eclipse has an impact on children and children figures, so it is advisable to keep them out of harm's way during this period. They don't need to be involved in risky activities.

The lunar eclipse of the 28th (in the Americas it happens on the 27th) occurs in your own sign and seems to continue the work of the solar eclipse of March 20. You have not yet finished redefining yourself and your image. Whatever has been left undone from the earlier eclipse gets done now. It is good, even healthy, to redefine ourselves periodically. And the eclipse forces the issue. Often we are forced to define and redefine ourselves because people are slandering and bad mouthing us. False impressions get created and it is up to us to create the right one.

Since this eclipse occurs in your own sign, make sure to take it easy during this period. Avoid risk taking or high stress kinds of activities. Every lunar eclipse affects the home and family and this one is no different. There can be a need for repairs to be made in the home. Or perhaps you find unwelcome pests in the attic or basement. Flaws get revealed so that corrective action can happen. Family members will probably have dramas in their lives and life-changing kinds of experiences. As always be patient with them during this period, they are apt to be highly strung.

October

Best Days Overall: 6, 7, 8, 16, 17, 18, 25, 26
Most Stressful Days Overall: 4, 5, 11, 12, 13, 19, 20, 31
Best Days for Love: 8, 9, 11, 12, 13, 19, 20, 27, 28
Best Days for Money: 1, 8, 9, 10, 19, 20, 27, 28
Best Days for Career: 6, 16, 19, 20, 25

The planetary power is now mostly above the horizon in the upper half of your Horoscope. Your career planet is moving forward. It is morning in your yearly cycle. It is time to be up and about and active on the physical plane; time to focus on your outer, external objectives; time to act, physically, on your dreams. You can let home and family issues go for a while and focus on your career.

Your career planet moved back into Sagittarius, your 9th house, last month. Thus it is a good time to take courses, attend workshops and seminars that are related to the career. It is good to educate yourself further in your chosen profession. A willingness to travel is also a career plus these days.

Ever since Jupiter moved into Virgo, your 6th house, on August 11, the aspects have been good for job seekers. This month is exceptionally good (as it was last month). It will be difficult to find an unemployed Aries these days. Your skills are in demand.

Finances have been good, but now that Venus is moving forward again they are even better. Venus spent last month in Leo. This shows happy money, money that is earned in fun kinds of ways. You spent on fun kinds of activities too and enjoyed the wealth that you had. Venus is still in Leo this month until the 8th and then she moves into Virgo. This too is good for finance but in a different way. This aspect gives solid financial judgement. You will get value for your money. You earn your cash the old-fashioned way, through work and service. Your work will create your good luck. Venus will travel with Jupiter from the 24th to the 27th and this shows a very nice payday. There is luck in speculations during that period too.

Health has been more delicate since September 23, and will remain so until the 23rd of this month. Take it easy. Make sure you get enough sleep. Review our discussion of health in the yearly report. Health and energy will improve dramatically after the 23rd.

On September 23, as the Sun entered Libra, you began a yearly love and social peak. You are still in this now until the 23rd. While marriage is not likely right now, you are in the mood for love. Singles will meet people who are potential marriage material, and in general there is more socializing and party going. Venus's conjunction with Jupiter from the 24th to the 27th brings happy romantic opportunity for singles and happy social experiences for those who are married.

November

Best Days Overall: 3, 4, 13, 14, 22, 30
Most Stressful Days Overall: 1, 8, 9, 15, 16, 28, 29
Best Days for Love: 6, 7, 8, 9, 17, 18, 26, 27
Best Days for Money: 5, 6, 7, 15, 16, 17, 18, 24, 25, 26, 27
Best Days for Career: 3, 12, 15, 16, 21, 30

The planetary power is firmly in the Western social sector of the Horoscope this month. Your personal skills and merits don't count for much these days. It is your ability to get on with others, your 'likeability factor', that determines your progress. You are in a stage of the planetary cycle where things get done by consensus and with the co-operation of others. Your social skills will determine your success and failure and so it is good to focus on these. The good news is that you are doing this. Mars, the ruler of the Horoscope, enters your 7th house of love on the 12th. You are focused on others and putting others first. This attitude tends to popularity, and thus the month ahead should be successful.

As you focus on others you find, miraculously, that your personal and financial needs are taken care of. Your financial planet, Venus, will also be in your 7th house from the 8th onwards. Friends seem supportive and provide financial opportunities for you.

When the ruler of your Horoscope is in the 7th house he is most distant from his natural position (the 1st house). He is far, far away from home. You are most distant from yourself and your personal concerns. You are totally immersed with others.

The spouse, partner or significant other is prospering this month. He or she entered a yearly financial peak on October 23 and it continues until the 22nd. He or she seems more generous with you.

Retrograde activity is practically nil this month. By November 18, 90 per cent of the planets will be moving forward. The pace of life quickens. Progress is faster.

Ever since the 23rd of last month you have been in a sexually active kind of period. Your 8th house of regeneration became powerful and remains so until the 22nd of this month. Whatever your age or stage in life, your libido is more active than usual. The 8th house is one of the mystery houses of the zodiac. When it is strong we become interested in the deeper things of life – what is death? Is there life after death? What exactly happens after you die? It is healthy to wrestle with these questions and to study more about it. When we understand death, we understand life.

This is a wonderful period for personal reinvention and personal transformation. Many of you are involved in these kinds of projects (Pluto is very near your Mid-heaven) and they should go well.

December

Best Days Overall: 1, 10, 11, 19, 20, 27, 28, 29
Most Stressful Days Overall: 5, 6, 12, 13, 25, 26
Best Days for Love: 5, 6, 7, 17, 18, 25, 26
Best Days for Money: 2, 3, 4, 7, 12, 13, 17, 18, 21, 22, 25, 26, 30, 31
Best Days for Career: 1, 10, 12, 13, 19, 20, 27, 28

Career has been good of late. On November 24–26 the Sun travelled with your career planet, boosting the career, bringing success and opportunity. But this was only a harbinger of things to come. On December 22 the Sun will cross your Mid-heaven and enter your 10th house and you will enter a yearly career peak. This is when you make real progress. Generally people don't achieve the totality of career goals under good aspects. Career is a long-term project that requires much time. However you will see good progress towards your goals.

Health and energy are good until the 22nd but after that you will have to work to maintain higher energy levels. Health becomes more delicate towards the end of the month. Review our discussion of this in the yearly report. This month, from the 10th onwards, you can enhance the health by giving more attention to the spine, knees, teeth, bones, skin and overall skeletal alignment. A visit to a chiropractor or osteopath might be a good idea. Regular back and knee massage will also be good.

Mars, the ruler of your Horoscope, makes some dynamic aspects with Pluto and Uranus from the 5th to the 12th. Take it nice and easy during this period. Avoid risk taking and confrontations. If you read the newspapers at this time you'll understand why.

Your financial planet moves speedily this month. This shows quick financial progress. Things move swiftly. Until the 5th your social skills and other people are very important financially: attending or hosting parties and gatherings will help the bottom line. From the 5th to the 30th it will be good to use excess cash to pay down debt. However if you need to borrow it will seem easy to do so. There is good fortune indicated with estates and insurance claims. This will also be a good period to clean up the finances, to eliminate waste and redundancies. Get rid of possessions that you no longer need and make room for the new that wants to come in. There will be opportunities to invest in troubled companies or overlooked properties – you have a good sense of the value in these things.

Love is expressed sexually most of the month – from the 5th to the 30th. For singles, the sexual magnetism seems the most important factor. However, most of our readers know that you can't base a real, lasting relationship just on that.

The planetary momentum is overwhelmingly forward this month. In fact, by the 26th *all* the planets will be moving forwards, which is highly unusual. The world and events move quickly these days. Normally this would be a good period for starting new projects – especially after the 21st. But for you it is best to wait until the spring.

Taurus

THE BULL

Birthdays from
21st April to
20th May

Personality Profile

TAURUS AT A GLANCE

Element – Earth

Ruling Planet – Venus
  Career Planet – Uranus
  Love Planet – Pluto
  Money Planet – Mercury
  Planet of Health and Work – Venus
  Planet of Home and Family Life – Sun
  Planet of Spirituality – Mars
  Planet of Travel, Education, Religion and Philosophy – Saturn

Colours – earth tones, green, orange, yellow

Colours that promote love, romance and social harmony – red-violet, violet

Colours that promote earning power – yellow, yellow-orange

Gems – coral, emerald

Metal – copper

Scents – bitter almond, rose, vanilla, violet

Quality – fixed (= stability)

Quality most needed for balance – flexibility

Strongest virtues – endurance, loyalty, patience, stability, a harmonious disposition

Deepest needs – comfort, material ease, wealth

Characteristics to avoid – rigidity, stubbornness, tendency to be overly possessive and materialistic

Signs of greatest overall compatibility – Virgo, Capricorn

Signs of greatest overall incompatibility – Leo, Scorpio, Aquarius

Sign most helpful to career – Aquarius

Sign most helpful for emotional support – Leo

Sign most helpful financially – Gemini

Sign best for marriage and/or partnerships – Scorpio

Sign most helpful for creative projects – Virgo

Best Sign to have fun with – Virgo

Signs most helpful in spiritual matters – Aries, Capricorn

Best day of the week – Friday

Understanding a Taurus

Taurus is the most earthy of all the Earth signs. If you understand that Earth is more than just a physical element, that it is a psychological attitude as well, you will get a better understanding of the Taurus personality.

A Taurus has all the power of action that an Aries has. But Taurus is not satisfied with action for its own sake. Their actions must be productive, practical and wealth-producing. If Taurus cannot see a practical value in an action they will not bother taking it.

Taurus's forte lies in their power to make real their own or other people's ideas. They are generally not very inventive but they can take another's invention and perfect it, making it more practical and useful. The same is true for all projects. Taurus is not especially keen on starting new projects, but once they get involved they bring things to completion. Taurus carries everything through. They are finishers and will go the distance, so long as no unavoidable calamity intervenes.

Many people find Taurus too stubborn, conservative, fixed and immovable. This is understandable, because Taurus dislikes change – in the environment or in their routine. They even dislike changing their minds! On the other hand, this is their virtue. It is not good for a wheel's axle to waver. The axle must be fixed, stable and unmovable. Taurus is the axle of society and the heavens. Without their stability and so-called stubbornness, the wheels of the world (and especially the wheels of commerce) would not turn.

Taurus loves routine. A routine, if it is good, has many virtues. It is a fixed – and, ideally, perfect – way of taking care of things. Mistakes can happen when spontaneity comes into the equation, and mistakes cause discomfort and uneasiness – something almost unacceptable to a Taurus. Meddling with Taurus's comfort and security is a sure way to irritate and anger them.

While an Aries loves speed, a Taurus likes things slow. They are slow thinkers – but do not make the mistake of assuming they lack intelligence. On the contrary, Taurus people are very intelligent. It is just that they like to chew on ideas, to deliberate and weigh them up.

Only after due deliberation is an idea accepted or a decision taken. Taurus is slow to anger – but once aroused, take care!

Finance

Taurus is very money-conscious. Wealth is more important to them than to many other signs. Wealth to a Taurus means comfort and security. Wealth means stability. Where some zodiac signs feel that they are spiritually rich if they have ideas, talents or skills, Taurus only feels wealth when they can see and touch it. Taurus's way of thinking is, 'What good is a talent if it has not been translated into a home, furniture, car and holidays?'

These are all reasons why Taurus excels in estate agency and agricultural industries. Usually a Taurus will end up owning land. They love to feel their connection to the Earth. Material wealth began with agriculture, the tilling of the soil. Owning a piece of land was humanity's earliest form of wealth: Taurus still feels that primeval connection.

It is in the pursuit of wealth that Taurus develops intellectual and communication ability. Also, in this pursuit Taurus is forced to develop some flexibility. It is in the quest for wealth that they learn the practical value of the intellect and come to admire it. If it were not for the search for wealth and material things, Taurus people might not try to reach a higher intellect.

Some Taurus people are 'born lucky' – the type who win any gamble or speculation. This luck is due to other factors in their horoscope; it is not part of their essential nature. By nature they are not gamblers. They are hard workers and like to earn what they get. Taurus's innate conservatism makes them abhor unnecessary risks in finance and in other areas of their lives.

Career and Public Image

Being essentially down-to-earth people, simple and uncomplicated, Taurus tends to look up to those who are original, unconventional and inventive. Taurus people like their bosses to be creative and original – since they themselves are content to perfect their superiors' brainwaves. They admire people who have a wider social or political consciousness and they feel that someday (when they have all the comfort and security they need) they too would like to be involved in these big issues.

In business affairs Taurus can be very shrewd – and that makes them valuable to their employers. They are never lazy; they enjoy working and getting good results. Taurus does not like taking unnecessary risks and they do well in positions of authority, which makes them good managers and supervisors. Their managerial skills are reinforced by their natural talents for organization and handling details, their patience and thoroughness. As mentioned, through their connection with the earth, Taurus people also do well in farming and agriculture.

In general a Taurus will choose money and earning power over public esteem and prestige. A position that pays more – though it has less prestige – is preferred to a position with a lot of prestige but lower earnings. Many other signs do not feel this way, but a Taurus does, especially if there is nothing in his or her personal birth chart that modifies this. Taurus will pursue glory and prestige only if it can be shown that these things have a direct and immediate impact on their wallet.

Love and Relationships

In love, the Taurus-born likes to have and to hold. They are the marrying kind. They like commitment and they like the terms of a relationship to be clearly defined. More importantly, Taurus likes to be faithful to one lover, and they expect that lover to reciprocate this fidelity. When this doesn't happen, their whole world comes crashing down. When they are in love Taurus people are loyal, but they are also very possessive. They are capable of great fits of jealousy if they are hurt in love.

Taurus is satisfied with the simple things in a relationship. If you are involved romantically with a Taurus there is no need for lavish entertainments and constant courtship. Give them enough love, food and comfortable shelter and they will be quite content to stay home and enjoy your company. They will be loyal to you for life. Make a Taurus feel comfortable and – above all – secure in the relationship, and you will rarely have a problem.

In love, Taurus can sometimes make the mistake of trying to control their partners, which can cause great pain on both sides. The reasoning behind their actions is basically simple: Taurus people feel a sense of ownership over their partners and will want to make changes that will increase their own general comfort and security. This attitude is OK when it comes to inanimate, material things – but is dangerous when applied to people. Taurus needs to be careful and attentive to this possible trait within themselves.

Home and Domestic Life

Home and family are vitally important to Taurus. They like children. They also like a comfortable and perhaps glamorous home – something they can show off. They tend to buy heavy, ponderous furniture – usually of the best quality. This is because Taurus likes a feeling of substance in their environment. Their house is not only their home but their place of creativity and entertainment. The Taurus' home tends to be truly their castle. If they could choose, Taurus people would prefer living in the countryside to being city-dwellers. If they cannot do so during their working lives, many Taurus individuals like to holiday in or even retire to the country, away from the city and closer to the land.

At home a Taurus is like a country squire – lord (or lady) of the manor. They love to entertain lavishly, to make others feel secure in their home and to encourage others to derive the same sense of satisfaction as they do from it. If you are invited for dinner at the home of a Taurus you can expect the best food and best entertainment. Be prepared for a tour of the house and expect to see your Taurus friend exhibit a lot of pride and satisfaction in his or her possessions.

Taurus people like children but they are usually strict with them. The reason for this is they tend to treat their children – as they do most things in life – as their possessions. The positive side to this is that their children will be well cared for and well supervised. They will get every material thing they need to grow up properly. On the down side, Taurus can get too repressive with their children. If a child dares to upset the daily routine – which Taurus loves to follow – he or she will have a problem with a Taurus parent.

Horoscope for 2015

Major Trends

Uranus has been in your 12th house of spirituality for some years now and will be there for a few more years yet. This indicates dramatic spiritual change – interior change. It might not be visible to others as yet, but in due course it will be. You are in a period of great spiritual experimentation and discovery.

Saturn has been in your 7th house of love for the past two years. This has been a challenging period for the love life. Those who are married have had their relationships tested, while those who are singles most likely stayed single. There have been disappointments with friends and love relationships have broken up. Happily things are improving in this department as Saturn moves out of your 7th house for most of the year (he will retrograde back in for only three months and then leave permanently). There's more on this later.

Saturn will spend most of 2015 in your 8th house of transformation and regeneration. This shows that the spouse, partner or current love is having financial challenges and needs to consolidate and re-order their finances. It also shows a need to bring the libido under more control and not to overdo things.

Jupiter entered your 4th house in July last year, and will be there until August 11 this year. This shows happiness in home and family affairs, with good family support and happy moves or renovations. You are in a period of great psychological growth and progress. More details later.

Jupiter enters your 5th house of creativity and fun on August 11. This heralds an enjoyable, happy kind period for the rest of the year. You will have the wherewithal and the opportunity to explore the rapturous side of life. It shows fertility for Taurus people of childbearing age and prosperity and success for the children or children figures in your life.

Your important areas of interest in the year ahead will be home and family (until August 11); children, fun and personal creativity (from August 11 onwards); love and romance (from June 15 to September 18); sex, other people's money, debt and personal transformation (January 1 to June 15 and September 18 to the end of the year); religion, philosophy, metaphysics and higher education; friends, groups and group activities; and spirituality.

Your paths of greatest fulfilment in the year ahead will be home and family (until August 11); children, fun and personal creativity (from August 11 onwards); and health and work (until November 13).

Health

(Please note that this is an astrological perspective on health and not a medical one. In days of yore there was no difference, these perspectives were identical. But these days there could be quite a difference. For a medical perspective, please consult your doctor or health practitioner.)

If health has been good over the past two years it should get even better this year. Only one long-term planet – Saturn – has been stressing you out, and Saturn now (for the most part) is away from his stressful aspect. If there have been health problems you should hear good news this year.

The north node of the Moon spends most of the year in your 6th house of health. This shows good fortune in this area. However, sometimes it indicates an 'excessive' focus on health – even where it isn't warranted. The problem here could be hypochondria, magnifying little minor things, into big things. Sometimes this aspect leads to 'health fanaticism'. This focus should be directed properly towards healthy lifestyles and regimes.

Venus is both your personal planet and your health planet. This in itself shows that health is important to you and that you tend to focus attention here. It shows that your state of health immediately affects on your personal appearance. For you, good health is the best cosmetic there is. With this kind of aspect, if you feel under the weather you should do something that enhances your appearance: buy a new outfit, have your hair styled, or buy some nice accessory. You'll start to feel better.

Good though your health is, you can make it even better. Give more attention to the neck and throat, and to the kidneys and hips (the reflexes to these areas are shown on the chart above). The neck and throat are always important for Taurus. Regular neck massage is always powerful for you and craniosacral therapy is also good. Hips should be regularly massaged, and kidney detoxing is generally a good idea for you too.

Since Taurus rules the throat and the vocal chords, they respond very well to sound-oriented therapies – chanting mantras, singing and humming in the different keys. Chanting the five vowel sounds – A E I O U – will also be beneficial if you feel under the weather. (Try chanting them up and down the tones of the musical scales.)

Venus, as our regular readers know, is a fast-moving planet. During the year she will move through all the signs and houses of your Horoscope. Thus there are many short-term trends in your health depending on where Venus is and the aspects she receives. These are best covered in the monthly reports.

Siblings and sibling figures need to take on a strict health regime this year. They need to give more attention to the spine, knees, teeth and skin. Parents or parent figures could have had surgical procedures over the past few years and this trend continues in the year ahead.

Important foot reflexology points for the year ahead

Try to massage the whole foot on a regular basis, but pay extra attention to the points highlighted on the chart. When you massage, be aware of 'sore spots', as these need special attention. It is also a good idea to massage the ankles and the tops of the feet.

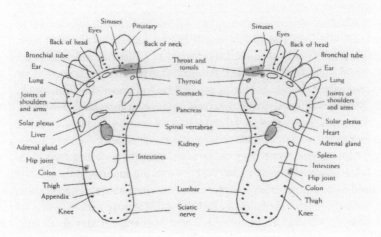

Detox regimes are good for them too. The spouse, partner or current love seems very experimental in health matters these days. They will benefit from alternative therapies.

Home and Family

Your 4th house of home and family has been powerful since July of last year as we have mentioned. Thus this area is a major (and happy) focus this year. Moves or renovations could have happened last year but are still likely in the year ahead. Sometimes people don't actually move but acquire an additional home. These are happy things. There is good fortune in the purchase or sale of a home and in the residential real estate field in general.

The family circle gets enlarged this year (and it could have happened last year too). Generally this is through marriage or births. But often one meets people who are like family – people who play this kind of role in the life.

As we have mentioned, Taurus women of childbearing age are much more fertile than usual. The whole year ahead is like this.

Parents and parent figures in your life are prospering this year and seem more generous with you. Family support, in general, is good. The children or children figures in your life become prosperous this year too – especially after August 11. If they are very young they receive expensive, big ticket items. If they are older they travel more and live the high life.

Siblings and sibling figures are having a status quo kind of year. They seem basically content where they are. A lunar eclipse on April 4 could shake things up a bit, but this need not result in a move. Parents and parent figures are staying put this year – children too. Children in your life might feel cramped in their home but a move is not advisable. There are delays, delays, delays.

Moves for you, Taurus, have good aspects until August 11. Renovations – especially major ones – are good until September 25, while redecorating or beautifying the home is good from June 5 to July 19.

In the year ahead there will be two solar eclipses – one on March 20 and the other on September 13. These will tend to cause short-term disturbance in the home and family. Family members will be more temperamental during those periods and it is good to have more patience with them.

Finance and Career

Money is always important to a Taurus, but this year less so than usual. Your 2nd money house is not strong. On the positive side you have more freedom to shape this area as you will. The cosmos is not obstructing you. On the other hand, reduced interest tends towards the status quo. You seem basically content with finance and have no need to make major dramatic changes.

Taurus people have a naturally good feel for real estate. The basic instincts are sound and this year this feeling is better than usual – especially in the residential real estate area. There is good fortune here – especially until August 11. I also like industries that cater to children – toy makers, games developers and the entertainment industry. You have a good feeling for this from August 11 onwards.

As we have mentioned earlier, family support seems unusually strong this year.

Your financial planet, Mercury, is very fast moving. Only the Moon moves faster than him. Thus earnings and earning opportunities come to you in a variety of ways and through a variety of people and situations. It all depends on where Mercury is at any given time and the kind of aspects he receives. These short-term trends are best covered in the monthly reports.

Jupiter's move into Leo last July was very good for the career. September 2014 was exceptionally good. There were promotions and pay rises, either with the present company or a new one, and there was more recognition for your professional achievements and perhaps even honours or awards. There is more of this in the year ahead. March and June 2015 look especially strong for career.

Generally career elevation translates into higher earnings. But earnings don't seem the main consideration for you. Rather, they are just a side effect.

There have been many career changes over the past few years, and perhaps a few 'near death' experiences in the career. But things look more stable for the year ahead. Jupiter's beautiful aspects to your career planet Uranus also indicate happy career opportunities that come to you.

Uranus has been in your spiritual 12th house for some years now. Thus (as we have written in past years) you are more idealistic about your career. Just making money and being successful is not enough for you. You want to do something that is meaningful, something that benefits the world as a whole. You want to feel 'divine approval' for your career path. This indicates that getting involved in charities and altruistic causes (causes that you believe in) will further your career. You make important connections through those activities. And in many cases, Taurus, you will actually opt for a spiritual career.

The career of a parent or parent figure will improve greatly this year. The past two years have been very challenging for this person. Sibling and sibling figures have experienced great career instability for some years now. Things will settle down a bit in the year ahead. Children and children figures have a static, stable kind of career year – though they seem prosperous.

The spouse, partner or current love needs to reorganize the finances this year. He or she needs to work harder for earnings than usual, to go the extra mile. He or she seems to be carrying additional financial burdens – things that can't be escaped.

Favourable numbers for finance are 1, 3, 6, 8 and 11.

Love and Social Life

As we have mentioned, the past two years have been difficult in the love department. Saturn has been camped out in your 7th house of love; marriages have been tested and many have broken up. However, those that survived are probably better than ever. By now the problems have been ironed out.

In general social activity has been less than it is usually. This is not punishment, but a reordering of the social life. The cosmos wants you to focus on quality relationships – even though they are fewer in number – rather than many relationships of a lukewarm nature.

Saturn will spend most of the year in your 8th house of regeneration. Thus the sex life and sexual expression is getting reordered. This means your libido might not be up to its usual standards. Here too the tendency will be to focus on the quality of sex rather than the quantity. If you are involved romantically with a Taurus allow more warm-up time – more foreplay – when having sex.

Singles have been dating less, but this will improve in the year ahead. There could be a social 'dry spell' though from June 15 to September 18.

With Saturn in your 7th house of love for the past two years, you could have been perceived as cold, aloof and unfeeling. You are not like this but this could have been the perception. So, it was necessary (and will still be necessary from June 15 to September 18 when Saturn retrogrades back into your 7th house) to make special efforts to project warmth and love to others.

While marriage doesn't seem in the cards this year, there will be plenty of romantic opportunities of the 'less serious' kind: love affairs and amusement.

The love life will really come into its own after September 18. Saturn will be out of your 7th house and Jupiter will be making nice aspects to your love planet, Pluto. Serious romance can happen after September 18. Social activity will increase then too. The two-and-a-half-year dry spell will have made you better able to deal with real love when it comes. But there's no need to rush into anything.

Your love planet has been in the sign of Capricorn for many years. Thus you are slow to fall in love. Love needs time to develop, and this is not a time for elopements or things of that nature. For singles, marriage is more likely in 2016 than this year.

In the year ahead you are emerging from a dark tunnel. You are not yet completely through it – this will happen after September 18. But even before this you can see light at the end of the tunnel.

Your love planet in the 9th house shows that you are attracted to refined, highly educated people. You are attracted to people you can learn from, and those from other lands. Romantic opportunities happen at religious or academic functions and perhaps in foreign lands. You have (and have had) the kind of aspects of someone who falls in love with a minister or professor.

Self-improvement

Your spiritual life is one of the most exciting areas of life this year. Indeed, this has been so for some years now and will continue for a few more. You like to experiment here, as we have mentioned, and this is basically good. We learn what works for us through trial, error and experiment. There is no right or wrong spiritual path. Each person, ultimately, is their own path and this is discovered through experiment. This is so even in the mainstream religions. Each person practises their religion in a unique kind of way. (This is why there are so many sects within any given religion.)

One of the problems with Uranus being in your 12th house is that one can overdo a good thing. One can become a spiritual faddist, jumping from one teaching to the next, depending on the fashionable trends of the time. Thus, one never gets a chance to work a path and see the results. Experiment by all means, but allow time to see how it works out.

Neptune, the most spiritual of all the planets, has been in your 11th house of friends for some years now. This reinforces what we've been saying above. But it also shows that you are attracting spiritual-type friends and are involved in spiritual groups and organizations. Perhaps you think that there is some 'mass' way to salvation and enlightenment. This would be the tendency now. But in truth enlightenment and spiritual breakthroughs (and there will be many in the year ahead) are always solitary experiences. Even if you are in a group, sitting in a lecture with hundreds in attendance, your personal experience will be unique. No one else will have the same experience as you.

Spiritual compatibility seems the criteria for friendship this year. Those who are not on your spiritual path are not your friends. Someone who is on your path will become a friend even if you just meet him or her for a brief time. These relationships tend to endure.

Saturn, as we mentioned, will spend most of the year in your 8th house of sexuality. Thus the cosmos is putting this department of life in 'right order'. If you have been irresponsible in this area, the bills come due in the next few years. But if you have been responsible, Saturn will show you how to enhance this area in healthy ways.

The sexual force is perhaps the most powerful in the universe. It can create or destroy. There is a right and wrong way to use this force and these are some of the lessons that are going to be learned in the coming years.

Month-by-month Forecasts

January

Best Days Overall: 9, 10, 18, 19, 27, 28
Most Stressful Days Overall: 6, 7, 8, 14, 15, 20, 21
Best Days for Love: 1, 9, 10, 12, 13, 14, 15, 18, 19, 21, 22, 27, 28, 31
Best Days for Money: 1, 2, 3, 7, 8, 11, 12, 16, 17, 20, 21, 24, 25, 29, 30
Best Days for Career: 6, 7, 16, 17, 20, 21, 24, 25

You begin your year with at least 80 per cent (and sometimes 90 per cent) of the planets above the horizon – An overwhelming percentage. Your 10th house of career is chock-full of planets (half of the planets are either there or moving through there this month). On the 20th, as the Sun crosses the Mid-heaven and enters your 10th house, you begin a yearly career peak. The message is very clear. Home and family are important, but you can downplay these issues and focus on your career. You are in the noon time of your year. You need to be achieving your outer goals in the world. And, you will. You might not achieve all your career goals this month, but you will certainly see much progress towards them. The good news here is that the family seem to encourage the career. Family members are also more ambitious these days.

The planetary momentum is overwhelmingly forward this month. Until the 21st almost all of them are in forward motion. Normally this would be a great time to start new projects or to launch new products into the world. But for you it might be better to wait until your birthday. In a pinch, if you're pressed for time, the current period is acceptable.

Career is really the main headline for the month ahead. Even the financial life seems to happen there. Mercury, your financial planet, moves into your career house on the 5th. This shows pay rises. You have the financial favour of elders, bosses and authority figures. The government and government bureaucracies also seem favourably disposed towards you. Parents and parent figures too. It should be a prosperous month.

The only challenge that we see right now is health and energy. Overwork is the main danger. When energy levels get too low a person becomes vulnerable to opportunistic infections. So by all means follow your ambitions, but do so in a steady way. Delegate important tasks where possible, and make sure you get enough sleep. Schedule in some massages or time at a health spa. Don't burn the candle at both ends.

For the past six or so months the planetary power was in the social, Western sector of the Horoscope. This month a shift happens and by the 20th most of the planets will be in the independent, Eastern sector. You are less dependent on others now. The planetary power moves towards you rather than away from you. It is time to stand on your own two feet and create what you want in your life. If conditions are unpleasant make the necessary changes. You have the energy to do this.

February

Best Days Overall: 5, 6, 7, 15, 16, 23, 24
Most Stressful Days Overall: 3, 4, 10, 11, 17, 18
Best Days for Love: 1, 2, 5, 6, 7, 10, 11, 15, 16, 20, 21, 23, 24
Best Days for Money: 3, 4, 8, 9, 13, 14, 17, 18, 21, 22, 25, 26
Best Days for Career: 3, 4, 13, 14, 17, 18, 21, 22

Like last month the focus is on career – especially until the 20th. You are still in a yearly career peak until then. Home and family issues can safely be downplayed and, like last month, the family seems supportive of your career.

Mercury, your financial planet, went into retrograde motion on January 21 and will be retrograde until the 11th. This will not stop earnings from happening, but it does slow things down a bit. There are more glitches and delays involved in finance. Payments can arrive late. Deals can be delayed. Customers can change their minds. The bank or credit card companies can make errors and take time to resolve things. The important thing now is to make sure your financial dealings and transactions are as perfect as you can make them. Make sure your account number is on your payment slip and is written accurately. Make sure the customer understands the details of his or her purchase. Avoid making major purchases or investments or important financial decisions during this period. This is a time for financial review, a time for attaining mental clarity on your financial position or pending purchases. A time for seeing where improvements can be made here. After the 11th you can act on these plans.

Mercury retrograde doesn't mean that you make *no* purchases. Sure, you shop for groceries and the minor things in life. It is the major purchases – the expensive items – that should be avoided. However (and it has happened to me), sometimes there is no choice – a major purchase *must* be made under a Mercury retrograde. In those cases do your best to protect yourself. Make sure the store has a good returns policy.

By the 18th most career goals should have been achieved (or satisfactory progress made) and the focus will shift to spirituality and friendship. The Sun enters Pisces, your 11th house, and starts to travel with Neptune (the Sun will be most closely conjunct to Neptune from the 23rd to the 27th, but you will feel it even before). The family becomes more idealistic. You and family members will have spiritual breakthroughs and an active dream life. You will have all kinds of synchronistic and supernatural experiences. You will meet up with spiritual-type friends and perhaps be involved in spiritual or charitable organizations. Your challenge will be to integrate your religious beliefs with your spiritual experiences. Religious and academic figures in your life might challenge these things.

Health is much improved after the 18th.

March

Best Days Overall: 4, 5, 6, 14, 15, 22, 23
Most Stressful Days Overall: 2, 3, 9, 10, 16, 17, 29, 30, 31
Best Days for Love: 2, 3, 4, 5, 6, 9, 10, 12, 13, 14, 15, 22, 23
Best Days for Money: 2, 3, 7, 8, 12, 13, 18, 19, 20, 21, 24, 25, 26, 29, 30, 31
Best Days for Career: 2, 3, 12, 13, 16, 17, 20, 21, 29, 30

You are entering your period of maximum independence and personal power now. This will go on for another two months. It is time to focus on number one. Some people might consider this as 'selfishness', but self-interest (so long as others are not harmed) is a good thing – especially given the cycle you are in right now. As the old saying goes, 'If I am not for me who will be for me?' Your interest is no less important than another's. You have the power to create conditions as you desire them to be; why not use it? In a few months it will be more difficult to make these changes, so don't squander the opportunity. Your happiness is in your own hands right now.

Health and energy are excellent right now. You can enhance it even further by giving more attention to the head, face and adrenal glands until the 17th, and to the neck and throat afterwards. Head and face massage and craniosacral therapy are powerful until the 17th. Neck massage is powerful afterwards. Those of you on the spiritual path will benefit from mantra chanting this month. Spiritual healing in general is powerful until the 17th.

Finances look good this month. Your financial planet Mercury is moving forward, so you have good financial clarity and judgement. Until March 13 you still have the financial favour and support of bosses, elders, parents and the authority figures in your life. If pay rises haven't happened yet, they can still occur until that date. Your good professional reputation is a major factor in your earning power until the 13th (as it has been for the past few months). Guard that reputation. After the 13th Mercury enters Pisces, your 11th house. This indicates an excellent financial intuition, but you must trust it and follow it. Don't ignore your dreams or messages from psychics, astrologers and spiritual channels. They have important financial guidance for you.

There is a solar eclipse on the 20th that happens right on the cusp of your 11th and 12th houses. It is basically benign to you and will tend to impact more on friends and family. It won't hurt to reduce your schedule during this period though, and family members should do so too. If there are flaws in the home, an eclipse period is when you find out about them and can make the necessary corrections. Family members will be more temperamental at this time, so be more patient with them. There are shake-ups in a spiritual organization that you are involved with. There are changes in your spiritual practice and attitudes too – generally these are brought about through some kind of crisis or disturbance.

April

Best Days Overall: 1, 2, 10, 11, 12, 19, 20, 28, 29
Most Stressful Days Overall: 6, 7, 13, 14, 25, 26, 27
Best Days for Love: 1, 2, 6, 7, 10, 11, 12, 13, 19, 20, 21, 22, 28, 29
Best Days for Money: 8, 9, 17, 18, 19, 20, 21, 22, 25, 26, 28, 29
Best Days for Career: 8, 9, 13, 14, 17, 18, 26, 27

Though a lunar eclipse on the 4th creates some excitement and disturbance, the month ahead looks happy and successful. The eclipse will just add a little drama to the mix. It will keep things from getting too dull. Venus, the ruler of your Horoscope, has been in your sign since March 17. Mars will be in your sign all month. You look good. You have a good sense of style. There is plenty of energy and charisma this month.

The month ahead looks very prosperous – always important for a Taurus. Mercury, your financial planet, crosses the Ascendant and moves into your 1st house on the 14th. This brings windfalls and financial opportunities to you. Money pursues you rather than vice versa. The money people in your life seem friendly and co-operative.

The lunar eclipse of the 4th occurs in your 6th house of health and work. Health is good this month, but perhaps there is some sort of scare or disturbance. Most likely it will be nothing more than a scare. This aspect also tends to show job changes. Such a change can be within your present company or with another one. With Venus in your sign until the 11th job opportunities are seeking you out (as has been the case since March 17). This could be the reason for the job changes. If you employ others, this eclipse brings employee turnover and instability with the workforce. Often there are dramas in the lives of your employees that cause these things.

This eclipse impacts on Pluto and Uranus. Thus there are career changes happening – and they look happy. There could be dramas – life-changing events – in the lives of bosses or with the leaders of your profession or industry. The square to Pluto shows the testing of love and partnerships. Be more patient with the beloved this period as he or she will tend to be more irritable and highly strung.

In spite of the eclipse the love life is wonderful these days. Venus has been making nice aspects to your love planet Pluto since March 17. And Venus and Mars in your own sign make you attractive to the opposite sex. Love challenges should be resolved in a good way.

On the 20th the Sun moves into your sign and you enter one of your yearly personal pleasure peaks. This is when the body gets pampered. New clothing or some nice personal accessories come to you this month. It's a very good period for getting your body and image in shape, the way you want it to be. What's more, the love life will improve even further after the 20th.

May

Best Days Overall: 8, 9, 16, 17, 25, 26, 27
Most Stressful Days Overall: 3, 4, 10, 11, 23, 24, 30, 31
Best Days for Love: 1, 2, 3, 4, 8, 9, 13, 16, 17, 21, 22, 25, 26, 30, 31
Best Days for Money: 1, 2, 5, 6, 10, 11, 14, 15, 18, 19, 23, 24, 28, 29
Best Days for Career: 5, 6, 7, 10, 11, 14, 15, 23, 24

Last month there was a planetary shift. The planetary power moved to the lower half of the Horoscope. The lower half, the subjective half of the Horoscope will be strong for the next five months or so. This represents a psychological shift for you. It is now time to de-emphasize your career and focus more on the home, family and your emotional well-being. It is time to regroup and get ready for the next career push in five months time.

Career is still important in this period, but when the planets are the way they are it is best to pursue your career goals by interior methods – through controlled visualization, meditation and prayer. Feel where you want to be in your career. Imagine this state vividly. And then let go and let your inner consciousness get to work on it. Repeat as necessary. When you work this way you imitate nature, which does the exact same things. In the winter she imagines what she will manifest in the spring. When spring comes, she leaps into overt action.

The planetary momentum is still mostly forward this month. This was the case last month too. Since many of you are having your birthday this month you are in an excellent time to start new projects or launch new products into the world. Both the universal and personal solar cycles are waxing now. Early in the month is best to start things – until the 4th. The Moon will also be waxing during that period. After the 14th retrograde activity increases – Mercury starts to retrograde – and thus it is a less favourable time for these things.

When the Sun and Mercury entered your sign last month you entered a multi-month cycle of prosperity. This month prosperity is even stronger than last month. On the 21st you begin a yearly financial peak. Your money house is very powerful this month – half the planets (and they are mostly benevolent ones) are either in your money house or moving through there. This is a lot of financial power. Earnings should soar now.

There is only one financial weakness seen here, and this will begin on the 14th when your financial planet, Mercury, starts its retrograde motion. You are still going to prosper, but perhaps more slowly than expected. There will tend to be glitches and delays. As we mentioned when we discussed the last Mercury retrograde, it is important that your financial transactions be as perfect as possible. This will prevent some delays. It probably won't stop all of them but it will minimize them. You probably won't be able to avoid important financial decisions or major purchases either – there is too much going on here – but you can do more homework on these things.

June

Best Days Overall: 4, 5, 13, 14, 22, 23
Most Stressful Days Overall: 6, 7, 20, 21, 27, 28
Best Days for Love: 1, 4, 5, 10, 11, 13, 14, 20, 21, 22, 23, 27, 28, 29, 30
Best Days for Money: 2, 3, 6, 7, 10, 11, 15, 16, 20, 21, 24, 25, 29, 30
Best Days for Career: 2, 3, 6, 7, 10, 11, 20, 21, 29, 30

Saturn retrogrades back into Scorpio on the 15th – a stressful aspect for you. Most of you won't feel it too much, but those of you born late in the sign of Taurus – from May 19 to May 21 – will feel it strongly. By itself Saturn is not enough to cause health problems, but later on in the month (and especially after the 24th) some short-term planets move into a stressful aspect and you will need to be more careful. You can enhance the health in the ways mentioned in the yearly report. But there is more you can do in the coming period too. You need to be more diet conscious. Eat foods that are easy to digest. Give more attention to the stomach, and women should give more attention to the breasts. After June 5 give more attention to the heart. Those of you of an appropriate age need to watch the blood pressure. Good emotional health is important all month. Keep in harmony with the family and family members and avoid depression like the plague. Keep your mood positive and constructive. Meditation is a big help here.

The yearly financial peak continues this month and will last for longer than usual. Your financial planet will be in your money house all month. Mercury will also start moving forward on the 11th which is another positive for finance. Your financial judgement will be much better. Confidence improves too. Good sales, marketing and PR is always important for you financially, but this month more so than usual. People need to know about your product or service. Family support was good last month and is good this month too – especially until the 21st.

Your 3rd house of communication and intellectual interests is powerful this month – especially after the 21st. This is a great time to catch up on your reading and to attend lectures and seminars, and to catch up on those letters and emails that you owe. If you have a good knowledge base or expertise in a given field, this is a good time to disseminate that knowledge.

This is not one of your best love periods. The beloved seems stressed out and probably needs to rest and relax more. You haven't been in sync with the beloved that much lately. You seem distant. However, important love decisions shouldn't be made now. Your love planet, Pluto, has been retrograde since April 17, and Saturn in your 7th house (from June 15 onwards) is not helping matters. Singles are probably doing less dating. This is not a trend for the year or for your life, so don't panic. Love will improve in the coming months.

July

Best Days Overall: 1, 2, 10, 11, 19, 20, 29, 30
Most Stressful Days Overall: 3, 4, 5, 17, 18, 24, 25, 31
Best Days for Love: 1, 2, 8, 9, 10, 11, 17, 18, 19, 20, 24, 25, 26, 29, 30
Best Days for Money: 7, 8, 9, 12, 13, 17, 18, 27, 28, 29, 30
Best Days for Career: 3, 4, 5, 8, 9, 17, 18, 26, 27, 31

Retrograde activity spikes this month. By the end of the month half the planets will be in retrograde motion – the maximum for the year. So, it is a slow month in many areas of life. Slow doesn't mean 'bad', just a slower pace of life. It is, however, a great period to review your image, your career, love life and health regime. See where improvements can be made, and when the planets start moving forwards again you can set your plans in motion. It is a time for resolving doubts and gaining mental clarity. This is the most important thing now. If this 'cosmic pause' is used properly your future actions will be more successful.

Though there are many retrograde movements this month, Mercury, your financial planet, is moving forward speedily. Financial progress is rapid. Financial confidence is good. It should be a prosperous kind of month. Sales, marketing and PR are still important until the 22nd. From the 8th onwards there is good family support. Family connections seem important financially. Many of you will be earning money from home – and these kinds of opportunities will come to you.

The love life has been in the doldrums for the past month or so, but you should see improvement towards the end of the month.

The planetary power reaches its nadir (its lowest point) in your chart this month. Your 4th house of home and family is powerful all month but especially after the 23rd. Your career planet, Uranus, goes retrograde on the 26th. So, there are no quick answers on any career issues. Only time will solve things. Give your attention to your home, family and emotional life. Work on your career by the internal methods of night (you are approaching the midnight point of your year): visualize, dream and imagine you are where you want to be. This builds the psychological foundations for future career success – and we could argue that the foundation of a building is just as important as the building itself.

Venus, the ruler of your chart and your health planet, makes one of her rare retrogrades this month on the 25th. So you might feel that you lack direction and confidence. Self-esteem and self-confidence could be lacking. This is why it is good to review why you feel as you do and to make the internal corrections needed.

Health is more delicate this month, and especially from the 23rd onwards. Saturn and Jupiter are in stressful aspect to you and the short-term planets are joining in the party. So rest and relax more and make sure you get plenty of sleep. Review our discussion of health in the yearly report.

August

Best Days Overall: 6, 7, 15, 16, 17, 25, 26
Most Stressful Days Overall: 1, 13, 14, 20, 21, 22, 27, 28
Best Days for Love: 5, 6, 7, 14, 15, 16, 20, 21, 22, 23, 24, 25, 26, 31
Best Days for Money: 5, 8, 9, 15, 16, 25, 26, 27
Best Days for Career: 1, 4, 5, 13, 14, 23, 24, 27, 28, 31

Last month the planets began to make an important shift from the Eastern, independent sector to the Western, social sector. This month, from the 9th onwards, this shift is completed. The Western sector will dominate for the rest of the year ahead. This means that the planetary power is moving away from you rather than towards you. The focus is now on other people, rather than on your own personal interests and desires. Your good comes through others and not from your personal merit or personal actions. The cosmos impels you to develop your social skills, to attain your ends by consensus and through the co-operation of others. As we have mentioned, there is nothing wrong with self-interest, but you are now in a different stage of your cycle. It is more difficult now to have things your way, and if the truth be told, your way is probably not the best way these days. Hopefully you have used your creative power to create pleasant circumstances for yourself over the previous months. Now is the time for living with your creation. If it is good, you will enjoy the good. If there have been mistakes, you will experience the unpleasantness. When your next cycle of independence comes – early next year – you will be able to make the appropriate changes again.

Love, as we mentioned, has not been particularly good the past few months. However, this is about to change. Jupiter enters your 5th house of fun and love affairs on the 11th and starts to make beautiful aspects to Pluto, your love planet. Romance is starting to happen. Saturn, though, is still in your 7th house and you will still need to go slowly. But Saturn will be gone next month and the social life starts to bloom.

Jupiter's move into your 5th house brings opportunities for love affairs, rather than necessarily serious romance. Serious romance will happen later on, but at least the frozen love life is starting to melt.

Health still needs watching until the 23rd. Review our discussion of this in last month's forecast. After the 23rd you will feel huge improvement. Next month will be healthier than this one.

Your 4th house of home and family became very powerful on July 23 and is powerful until the 23rd of this month. This is a month for making psychological progress. Many psychological breakthroughs and insights will come to you. It is very natural under these transits to become nostalgic, to relive the past, to look at memories of the past. Old memories will arise spontaneously and if you examine them from your present perspective of things, healing will happen. Things that were traumatic as a youngster seem like trifles from the present perspective. We can smile at them. And this makes them lose whatever power they had over us.

September

Best Days Overall: 2, 3, 12, 13, 22, 23, 30
Most Stressful Days Overall: 9, 10, 17, 18, 24, 25
Best Days for Love: 1, 2, 3, 9, 10, 12, 13, 17, 18, 19, 20, 22, 23, 28, 29, 30
Best Days for Money: 2, 4, 5, 6, 12, 14, 15, 24, 25, 30
Best Days for Career: 1, 9, 10, 19, 20, 24, 25, 28, 29

The stage is being set for greater happiness this month. Venus, the ruler of your Horoscope, starts moving forward on the 6th bringing more self-confidence and self-esteem. Saturn finally leaves your 7th house of love, and Jupiter moves closer to an exact trine with Pluto. Love is starting to blossom now. Health and energy are much improved over the past few months.

Even the two eclipses this month will serve to break down barriers to your good. The effects are not generally pleasant while they happen, but the end result is good. Sometimes the cosmos has to employ dramatic methods to bring you your good.

The solar eclipse of September 13 occurs in your 5th house. It is basically benign to you but it won't hurt to take things easy over this period. This eclipse affects children, children figures and family members. They should stay out of harm's way at this time and avoid risky kinds of activities. Avoid activities where you need 100 per cent concentration – reschedule them for another time. Those of you in the creative arts will see a shift in your creativity. Speculations are not favourable during this eclipse period either. A parent or parent figure will be forced to make dramatic financial changes.

The lunar eclipse of the 28th (in the Americas it falls on the 27th) occurs in your 12th house of spirituality. This will bring changes in your spiritual practice and attitudes. Sometimes there will be changes in the teachings you follow. There are dramas in the lives of gurus or spiritual mentors in your life and there are shake-ups in charitable organizations you are involved with. This eclipse will also test your car and communication equipment. It will be a good idea to drive more defensively during this period. Siblings and sibling figures in your life are affected by this eclipse and they should reduce their schedules. They will tend to experience life-changing kinds of dramas.

In spite of the eclipses, this is a fun kind of month and you should take advantage of it. On August 23 you entered one of your yearly personal pleasure peaks and it continues until the 23rd of the month ahead. With Jupiter also in your 5th house, the pleasure and joy should be stronger than in previous years. There is renewed luck in speculations these days.

Your financial planet Mercury starts to retrograde on the 17th. So it is again time to review the finances and see where improvements can be made. Try not to make important financial investments, decisions or major purchases until you have attained some mental clarity on the issues involved and your doubts are dissolved.

October

Best Days Overall: 1, 9, 10, 19, 20, 27, 28
Most Stressful Days Overall: 6, 7, 8, 14, 15, 21, 22
Best Days for Love: 1, 8, 9, 10, 14, 15, 19, 20, 27, 28
Best Days for Money: 1, 2, 3, 9, 10, 11, 12, 13, 19, 20, 22, 23, 27, 28, 29, 30
Best Days for Career: 6, 7, 16, 17, 21, 22, 25, 26

When the Sun entered your 6th house of health and work on September 23, job seekers had good aspects. And these good aspects continue until the 23rd of this month. Job opportunities come through family members or family connections. If you hire others, the family or family connections provide useful contacts.

You are in a more serious kind of period – a work-oriented period. You are in the mood for work and are enjoying it. Thus it is a good time to deal with those mundane, boring kinds of tasks such as doing your accounts, bookkeeping, cleaning up computer files and hard drive, etc. You are still having fun, but work becomes just as important.

The main headline this month is the love life. It is a kind of 'rags to riches' story – from a dearth of romantic prospects to plenty. Those of you whose marriages survived the past two years of testing are having a much easier time. The testing is over and there is harmony with the beloved. Those of you who are single might not be single too much longer. Jupiter's aspect to Pluto, the love planet, becomes exact this month, and on the 23rd the Sun enters your 7th house and you begin a yearly love and romantic peak. This will continue well into next month too.

Venus conjuncts Jupiter from the 24th to the 27th, signalling a more sexually active kind of period. You project more sex appeal than usual. This is also a wonderful financial aspect and brings luck in speculations. Job seekers can have wonderful dream job offers. Money can come from insurance claims or estates. It is easier to borrow or pay down debt. The spouse, partner or current love has a good financial period and is more generous with you.

Finances are improving in other ways too. On the 9th Mercury starts moving forward again. Mercury presence in your 6th house all month shows that money is earned the old-fashioned way through hard work. Perhaps you take on an extra job and this increases your income.

On the 23rd your health becomes more delicate again, but it will be nowhere near as bad as during July and August. It will be a breeze compared to that. Still, this is not one of your best health periods and you should rest and relax more. Enhance the health in the ways mentioned in the yearly report and by paying more attention to the small intestine.

November

Best Days Overall: 5, 6, 15, 16, 24, 25
Most Stressful Days Overall: 3, 4, 10, 11, 17, 18, 30
Best Days for Love: 5, 6, 7, 10, 11, 15, 16, 17, 18, 24, 25, 26, 27
Best Days for Money: 5, 6, 10, 11, 15, 16, 21, 24, 25, 26, 27, 30
Best Days for Career: 3, 4, 13, 14, 17, 18, 21, 22, 30

The planetary power shifts this month from the lower half of the Horoscope to the upper half. This represents a psychological shift for you. Dawn is breaking in your yearly cycle. It is time to be up and about and taking physical actions to achieve your outer goals. Hopefully by now you have found your point of emotional harmony, and the domestic life should be in reasonable order. It's time to focus on the career and make those dreams and visions happen. Happily, in your case, your family goes along with this. They too are more ambitious these days.

Health still needs watching until the 22nd, but overall health is basically good. You might feel more fatigued but this is not sickness. If you have any pre-existing health conditions they could be more troublesome until the 22nd but not seriously so. It will be a good idea to rest and relax more though. The good news here is that your 6th house is strong this month and you are focused on health matters. Aside from the ways mentioned in the yearly report, health can be enhanced with vigorous physical exercise (according to your personal capacity) and by giving more attention to the head, face and adrenal glands. Head and face massages are more powerful than usual this month.

The pace of life and of events quickens this month. The planetary momentum is overwhelming forward. By the 18th almost all of the planets will be in forward motion, with only Uranus, your career planet, still retrograde. But he will move forward next month.

Finances also look good this month. Your financial planet is moving speedily now. You make fast progress and cover a lot of territory. Social connections play a huge role in your financial affairs from the 2nd to the 20th. Perhaps a business partnership or joint venture is happening. You seem very involved with the finances of the spouse or current love. He or she is prospering now too. The month ahead is excellent for paying down debt, for borrowing (if you need to), for refinancing mortgages, dealing with estates and insurance issues, and for earning through creative financing.

Taurus people by nature like to collect things. They like to amass possessions. There's nothing wrong with this but sometimes they do overdo it. The period after the 20th is a good time to get rid of the things that you don't use or need. Clear the decks so that the new and better can come in.

A yearly love and social peak still operates until the 23rd.

December

Best Days Overall: 2, 3, 4, 12, 13, 21, 22, 30, 31
Most Stressful Days Overall: 1, 7, 8, 9, 14, 15, 16, 27, 28, 29
Best Days for Love: 2, 3, 7, 8, 9, 12, 13, 17, 18, 21, 22, 25, 26, 30, 31
Best Days for Money: 1, 2, 3, 4, 12, 13, 21, 22, 23, 24, 30, 31
Best Days for Career: 1, 10, 11, 14, 15, 16, 19, 20, 27, 28, 29

Health and energy are much improved now. Optimism is high. You are catching the lucky breaks in life. A happy and successful month ahead.

The shift of planetary power to the upper half of the Horoscope becomes even stronger this month as Venus moves over the horizon on the 5th. At least 70 per cent of the planets are above the horizon this month. As a bonus, your career planet Uranus will start moving forward on the 26th. Mental clarity is happening in the career. Much progress will be made in coming months.

Though technically your yearly love and social peak is over with, there is still good news in the love department. Venus, the ruler of the Horoscope, spends most of the month in your 7th house. You are looking out for others very much these days (which is as it should be). You are putting others first and you are more popular in general. You are not sitting around waiting for the phone to ring but are proactive in love. If you like someone, they know it. You go after what you want. Pluto, your love planet, receives very nice aspects from the 22nd onwards. Romance is happening or developing as it should.

Your 8th house of transformation and regeneration has been powerful since November 22. This indicates the prosperity of the spouse, partner or current love. He or she is in a yearly financial peak and is more generous with you. They are in need of financial reorganization and have been feeling squeezed moneywise, but this is one of their better financial periods.

There are things in our lives in need of resurrection – perhaps a project, a friendship, an area of the body. This is the time to work on these things. Nature is engaged in resurrection continuously. It is not something alien to us. An old year dies and a new one is born. An old month dies and a new one is born. An old day dies and a new one is born. Death is never the end, only a new birth deeply disguised.

Many of you are involved in projects involving personal transformation and reinvention. These projects go well too.

Mars makes dynamic aspects with Pluto and Uranus from the 5th to the 12th. This impacts more on the spouse or partner than on you. Let him or her take it easy during this period. They should drive more defensively and avoid confrontations and stressful activities.

Gemini

Ⅱ

THE TWINS

Birthdays from
21st May to
20th June

Personality Profile

GEMINI AT A GLANCE

Element – Air

Ruling Planet – Mercury
  Career Planet – Neptune
  Love Planet – Jupiter
  Money Planet – Moon
  Planet of Health and Work – Pluto
  Planet of Home and Family Life – Mercury

Colours – blue, yellow, yellow-orange

Colour that promotes love, romance and social harmony – sky blue

Colours that promote earning power – grey, silver

Gems – agate, aquamarine

Metal – quicksilver

Scents – lavender, lilac, lily of the valley, storax

Quality – mutable (= flexibility)

Quality most needed for balance – thought that is deep rather than superficial

Strongest virtues – great communication skills, quickness and agility of thought, ability to learn quickly

Deepest need – communication

Characteristics to avoid – gossiping, hurting others with harsh speech, superficiality, using words to mislead or misinform

Signs of greatest overall compatibility – Libra, Aquarius

Signs of greatest overall incompatibility – Virgo, Sagittarius, Pisces

Sign most helpful to career – Pisces

Sign most helpful for emotional support – Virgo

Sign most helpful financially – Cancer

Sign best for marriage and/or partnerships – Sagittarius

Sign most helpful for creative projects – Libra

Best Sign to have fun with – Libra

Signs most helpful in spiritual matters – Taurus, Aquarius

Best day of the week – Wednesday

Understanding a Gemini

Gemini is to society what the nervous system is to the body. It does not introduce any new information but is a vital transmitter of impulses from the senses to the brain and vice versa. The nervous system does not judge or weigh these impulses – it only conveys information. And it does so perfectly.

This analogy should give you an indication of a Gemini's role in society. Geminis are the communicators and conveyors of information. To Geminis the truth or falsehood of information is irrelevant, they only transmit what they see, hear or read about. Thus they are capable of spreading the most outrageous rumours as well as conveying truth and light. Geminis sometimes tend to be unscrupulous in their communications and can do both great good or great evil with their power. This is why the sign of Gemini is symbolized by twins: Geminis have a dual nature.

Their ability to convey a message – to communicate with such ease – makes Geminis ideal teachers, writers and media and marketing people. This is helped by the fact that Mercury, the ruling planet of Gemini, also rules these activities.

Geminis have the gift of the gab. And what a gift this is! They can make conversation about anything, anywhere, at any time. There is almost nothing that is more fun to Geminis than a good conversation – especially if they can learn something new as well. They love to learn and they love to teach. To deprive a Gemini of conversation, or of books and magazines, is cruel and unusual punishment.

Geminis are almost always excellent students and take well to education. Their minds are generally stocked with all kinds of information, trivia, anecdotes, stories, news items, rarities, facts and statistics. Thus they can support any intellectual position that they care to take. They are awesome debaters and, if involved in politics, make good orators. Geminis are so verbally smooth that even if they do not know what they are talking about, they can make you think that they do. They will always dazzle you with their brilliance.

Finance

Geminis tend to be more concerned with the wealth of learning and ideas than with actual material wealth. As mentioned, they excel in professions that involve writing, teaching, sales and journalism – and not all of these professions pay very well. But to sacrifice intellectual needs merely for money is unthinkable to a Gemini. Geminis strive to combine the two. Cancer is on Gemini's solar 2nd house of money cusp, which indicates that Geminis can earn extra income (in a harmonious and natural way) from investments in residential property, restaurants and hotels. Given their verbal skills, Geminis love to bargain and negotiate in any situation, and especially when it has to do with money.

The Moon rules Gemini's 2nd solar house. The Moon is not only the fastest-moving planet in the zodiac but actually moves through every sign and house every 28 days. No other heavenly body matches the Moon for swiftness or the ability to change quickly. An analysis of the Moon – and lunar phenomena in general – describes Gemini's financial attitudes very well. Geminis are financially versatile and flexible; they can earn money in many different ways. Their financial attitudes and needs seem to change daily. Their feelings about money change also: sometimes they are very enthusiastic about it, at other times they could not care less.

For a Gemini, financial goals and money are often seen only as means of supporting a family; these things have little meaning otherwise.

The Moon, as Gemini's money planet, has another important message for Gemini financially: in order for Geminis to realize their financial potential they need to develop more of an understanding of the emotional side of life. They need to combine their awesome powers of logic with an understanding of human psychology. Feelings have their own logic; Geminis need to learn this and apply it to financial matters.

Career and Public Image

Geminis know that they have been given the gift of communication for a reason, that it is a power that can achieve great good or cause unthinkable distress. They long to put this power at the service of the highest and most transcendental truths. This is their primary goal, to communicate the eternal verities and prove them logically. They look up to people who can transcend the intellect – to poets, artists, musicians and mystics. They may be awed by stories of religious saints and martyrs. A Gemini's highest achievement is to teach the truth, whether it is scientific, inspirational or historical. Those who can transcend the intellect are Gemini's natural superiors – and a Gemini realizes this.

The sign of Pisces is in Gemini's solar 10th house of career. Neptune, the planet of spirituality and altruism, is Gemini's career planet. If Geminis are to realize their highest career potential they need to develop their transcendental – their spiritual and altruistic – side. They need to understand the larger cosmic picture, the vast flow of human evolution – where it came from and where it is heading. Only then can a Gemini's intellectual powers take their true position and he or she can become the 'messenger of the gods'. Geminis need to cultivate a facility for 'inspiration', which is something that does not originate in the intellect but which comes through the intellect. This will further enrich and empower a Gemini's mind.

Love and Relationships

Geminis bring their natural garrulousness and brilliance into their love life and social life as well. A good talk or a verbal joust is an interesting prelude to romance. Their only problem in love is that their intellect is too cool and passionless to incite ardour in others. Emotions sometimes disturb them, and their partners tend to complain about this. If you are in love with a Gemini you must understand why this is so. Geminis avoid deep passions because these would interfere with their ability to think and communicate. If they are cool towards you, understand that this is their nature.

Nevertheless, Geminis must understand that it is one thing to talk about love and another actually to love – to feel it and radiate it. Talking about love glibly will get them nowhere. They need to feel it and act on it. Love is not of the intellect but of the heart. If you want to know how a Gemini feels about love you should not listen to what he or she says, but rather, observe what he or she does. Geminis can be quite generous to those they love.

Geminis like their partners to be refined, well educated and well travelled. If their partners are more wealthy than they, that is all the better. If you are in love with a Gemini you had better be a good listener as well.

The ideal relationship for the Gemini is a relationship of the mind. They enjoy the physical and emotional aspects, of course, but if the intellectual communion is not there they will suffer.

Home and Domestic Life

At home the Gemini can be uncharacteristically neat and meticulous. They tend to want their children and partner to live up to their idealistic standards. When these standards are not met they moan and criticize. However, Geminis are good family people and like to serve their families in practical and useful ways.

The Gemini home is comfortable and pleasant. They like to invite people over and they make great hosts. Geminis are also good at repairs and improvements around the house – all fuelled by their need to stay active and occupied with something they like to do. Geminis have many hobbies and interests that keep them busy when they are home alone.

Geminis understand and get along well with their children, mainly because they are very youthful people themselves. As great communicators, Geminis know how to explain things to children; in this way they gain their children's love and respect. Geminis also encourage children to be creative and talkative, just like they are.

Horoscope for 2015

Major Trends

You have just come out of a strong prosperity cycle. The years 2012 to 2014 have been happy and prosperous. Money is less of a focus these days however. Most of you have more or less attained to your financial goals and now it's time to follow your greatest loves of reading, studying, communicating and expanding your knowledge base. Jupiter entered your 3rd house of communication in July 2014 and is there until August 11 this year. Those of you with a lot of knowledge and expertise should start disseminating this knowledge through the written or spoken word. There's more on this later.

The love life has been good over the past few years. Love and social opportunities sought you out. Many of you married or entered into serious relationships during this time. Now, your relationships get tested. The honeymoon period is over. Now the cosmos will show you if love is real or not. More details later.

Jupiter will move into your 4th house of home and family on August 11 and stay there well into next year. This often shows moves, renovations, or the acquisition of additional homes. Home and family will be a happy area in the year ahead.

Neptune has been in your 10th house of career for some years now and will be there for many more years. Thus you are more idealistic about your career. You long for a career that is meaningful, that benefits the whole planet and all people. You are being shown how to do this. More on this later.

Friendships have been unstable for some years now and this trend continues. Basically you are learning how to handle social instability.

Your most important areas of interest in 2015 are communication and intellectual interests (especially until August 11); home and family (from August 11 onwards); health and work (from June 15 to September 18); love, romance and social activities (January 1 to June 15 and September 18 onwards); sex, personal transformation and re-invention, occult studies, debt and repayment of debt; career; and friends, groups and group activities. You have so many interests this year, be careful not to spread yourself too thin.

Your areas of greatest fulfilment this year are communication and intellectual interests (until August 11); home and family (from August 11 onwards); and children, fun and personal creativity (until November 13).

Health

(Please note that this is an astrological perspective on health and not a medical one. In days of yore there was no difference, these perspectives were identical. But now there could be quite a difference. For a medical perspective, please consult your doctor or health practitioner.)

Health has basically been good over the past few years. Certainly there have been periods where your health was less easy than usual, but these periods came from the short-term planetary transits – they were temporary blips rather than trends.

In the year ahead health should be good too, but more delicate than in the past few years. In December last year, Saturn moved into Sagittarius, in stressful aspect to you, while Neptune has also been in stressful aspect for some years now. And on August 11, Jupiter makes stressful aspects too. Thus health needs more attention this year, especially from September 18 onwards.

The most important thing is to watch your energy levels. Do your best to maintain high levels of energy. If you are tired, rest, and in general try to get more sleep. Try to arrange your activities so that more gets done with less effort, and delegate tasks wherever possible.

Give more attention to the following areas this year – these are the most vulnerable areas this year: the lungs, arms, shoulders and respiratory system; the colon, bladder and sexual organs; and the spine, knees, teeth, bones, skin and overall skeletal alignment. The lungs, arms, shoulders and respiratory system are always important for Gemini and the reflexes to these areas are shown in the chart above. Arms and shoulders should be regularly massaged. Don't allow excess tension to build up in the shoulders. Air purity is always important for you and you might want to invest in an air purifier.

The reflexes for the colon, bladder and sexual organs are also shown in our chart. The colon needs to be kept clean and regular colonics might be a good idea. Safe sex and sexual moderation are important too.

Regular back and knee massages will be useful (the chart above shows the specific reflexes), as will regular visits to a chiropractor or osteopath. The vertebrae need to be kept in the right alignment. Yoga, Pilates, the Alexander Technique and Feldenkrais are excellent therapies for the spine and posture. Give the knees more support when you exercise. If you're out in the sun remember to use a good sun screen. Regular visits to the dentist might also be a good idea.

Pluto, the planet that rules surgery, is your health planet so you have a natural tendency to surgery; you tend to see it as a quick fix. In the past two years (and for part of this year) Saturn has been in your 6th house of health, which reinforces this tendency. Keep in mind though that this also indicates that detox regimes are good for you.

When I look at your Horoscope on an overall level, I see a lack of the air element in the chart. There will be periods in the year where there

Important foot reflexology points for the year ahead

Try to massage the whole foot on a regular basis, but pay extra attention to the points highlighted on the chart. When you massage, be aware of 'sore spots', as these need special attention. It is also a good idea to massage the ankles and the tops of the feet.

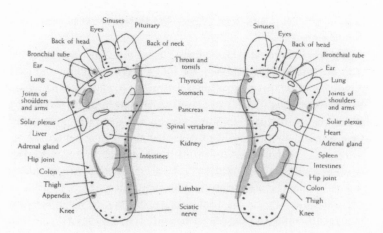

is more air than usual (January 20 to February 18, May 21 to June 20 and September 23 to October 23) but this element is weak on an overall level. Make sure you are getting enough air. Watch your breathing and try to breathe deeply as often as possible. Regular breathing exercises will be beneficial.

Home and Family

Your 4th house of home and family becomes powerful – in a happy way – from August 11 onwards when Jupiter moves there. It will be strong next year as well. If you've been planning a move – and many of you have – this is the year (and early next year too) to do it. If you've been planning to buy a second or third home, or to buy that timeshare, the year ahead looks very good.

Jupiter in the 4th house doesn't always bring 'literal' moves. Sometimes people renovate or enlarge the existing home, or install expensive items in the home. The whole effect is 'as if' a move had happened. The current home is larger and happier than before.

The family unit also expands under this transit. Generally this happens through births or marriages (and Gemini women of childbearing age become much more fertile from August 11 onwards), but I have seen where it happens through meeting people who are 'like' family to you – people who play this kind of role in your life. Family support will be good this year. A parent or parent figure is prospering and is more generous towards you. The net worth of the family as a whole is increased.

The 4th house rules other things besides home and family. It rules the subconscious mind and our 'habitual' moods, feelings and emotional reactions – the subjects that psychologists study. So this is a year for making important psychological breakthroughs, for understanding the origins of these things. Once the origins of emotional reactions are understood they can be changed to more positive ones.

Jupiter is your love planet. His transit through your 4th house gives us other messages too. There will be a lot more entertaining from home and much more socializing with family members this year. This transit also shows that you are beautifying the home, buying *objet d'art* and redecorating. You might not necessarily buy the trinkets – they can come to you as gifts – But by the end of the year your home will be more beautiful. This all looks happy. Redecoration projects will go well from August 11 onwards, but especially between October 8 and November 8. Construction projects or major repairs go well from September 25 to November 8.

A parent or parent figure is prospering, as we have mentioned, but he or she also seems to be travelling more this year. They will need to watch their weight, especially from August 11 onwards. However, a move is not advisable this year.

Siblings and sibling figures are also prospering. Marriage is seen in the chart (this could have happened last year too.) A move this year is not advisable for them either. Children and children figures are having a spiritual kind of year – a year of interior growth. Looks like renovations are going on in their homes or rooms.

Finance and Career

As we have mentioned, you have just come through a two-year cycle of prosperity. Financial goals should have been attained – and if they have not been completely attained, much progress has been made towards reaching them. Money is not a big issue this year. The money house is basically empty; only short-term planets will move through there – briefly – in the year ahead.

However, in spite of the empty money house, I'm still seeing prosperity. Jupiter is in your 3rd house of communication until August 11. Many Geminis (a disproportionate percentage) are involved in communication fields – journalism, teaching, writing, sales, marketing and PR – and this is a great year for these activities. There is success and good fortune here.

The Horoscope is also signalling a new car and new, high-end communication equipment. This could have materialized last year, but if not, this will happen in the year ahead.

Jupiter moving into your 4th house in August shows good family support, as we have mentioned, but also good fortune in the purchase or sale of a home.

One of the problems with an empty money house is lack of attention. In most cases, this is a good sign – you don't pay too much attention because there's no need to. Your finances are OK and there's no need to make dramatic changes or concentrate too hard on them. However, if you are facing financial challenges, not enough attention being paid could be the root cause of them. In this case you will have to force yourself to pay more attention – even when you don't feel like it.

The past two years have not only been good financially but career-wise as well. Many of you have had promotions, or have received honours and recognition. Your professional achievements have been appreciated. This year we don't see anything special careerwise, but nor do we see any disasters.

Ever since Neptune moved into your career house in 2012 you've been idealistic in career matters. This is a long-term trend which will continue for many more years. If you're following a worldly, mundane kind of career, you can enhance it by getting involved in charities and altruistic causes – causes that you believe in. These things are good in their own right, but in your case they will lead to connections that will enhance your career and public standing. In fact, in most cases, you are better known for your charitable and spiritual achievements than for your professional ones.

The other message we get from this position is the importance of intuition in career decisions. The intuition is basically excellent and needs to be trusted. In the short term intuition can lead to moves that seem strange and illogical. With hindsight, however, they are seen as highly logical and rational. There is really no conflict between logic and intuition. Intuition merely sees data not seen by the material, prosaic mind.

Our regular readers undoubtedly know that your financial planet is the Moon, Gemini, the fastest of all the planets. In any given month the Moon will move through all the signs and houses of your Horoscope. Thus money can come to you in a variety of ways and through a variety of people. It all depends on where the Moon is on any given day (and the aspects she receives). These show the short-term financial trends which are best dealt with in the monthly reports.

Love and Social Life

The social life has been active and happy for the past few years. You've made many new friends and have entered serious love relationships. Now it is time to consolidate, to separate the wheat from the chaff, the fruit from the peel.

Saturn is mostly in your 7th house this year (he will be absent for only three months, approximately, from June 15 to September 18), and will remain there for two more years. This means your love relationships and friendships will get tested. These testings are usually not pleasant but they serve a good purpose. Good relationships will survive and get even better. So-so relationships will most likely dissolve. And it is good that they do not last. The cosmos wants the best for you, anything less gets swept away.

In the good times, when the sun is shining and the birds are singing and everything is honeymoonish, we don't really know if love is real. In such conditions social harmony is natural. It is only in the tough times that we learn the depth (or lack thereof) of love. This is what is happening these days.

Singles are not likely to marry this year – nor does it seem advisable. In general there is less dating, less partying and less going out. This is a year (and this holds for the next two years) where the focus should be on quality not quantity. Fewer friends, but good ones, are preferable to hordes of lukewarm ones. Fewer dates, but quality ones, are preferable to loads of so-so dates.

Saturn in your 7th house can create a perception of coldness and aloofness to others. You are not like this, but others could perceive you that way. They respond to this Saturn energy going through you. Thus it is good to project warmth and love to others. This will take conscious effort on your part.

Your love planet Jupiter will move through two signs and houses of your Horoscope this year. Until August 11, he will be in your 3rd house. This indicates that mental compatibility is important for you in love. Love is shown through communication. You need someone you can talk to and share ideas with – someone on the same page intellectually. Ease of communication is an important turn-on in love. Also this transit shows that romantic opportunities occur close to home (perhaps with neighbours). There will be no need to travel far and wide in search for love. Romantic opportunities will also happen in intellectual settings – at school, the library or at a lecture. You find love as you pursue your intellectual interests.

On August 11 the love planet will move into your 4th house of home and family. This signals a shift in your love attitudes and needs. From now on you crave emotional support and intimacy as much as physical or intellectual intimacy. The person who can share feelings with you is the one that attracts you. Romantic opportunities still occur close to home and can happen through family connections or through the intervention of family members. You like people with strong family values.

Often with this kind of transit an old flame from the past makes an appearance. Sometimes this happens literally – the actual person comes back into your life. Sometimes the appearance is more allegorical. You meet someone with the same personality patterns or appearance as the old flame. On the emotional level it is 'as if' you are with the old flame. The cosmic purpose of these things is to resolve old issues so that you can progress further in your love life.

Self-improvement

Saturn in your 7th house of love for most of the year shows a need, as we have mentioned, to project love and warmth to others. This can be hard work at times. You have to project warmth even when you don't really feel it, psychologically speaking. A good meditation for this is 'DIVINE LOVE FLOWS THROUGH MY CONSCIOUSNESS NOW'. This meditation takes the intention out of your hands. Regardless of what you personally feel, the love from a Higher Power is flowing through you. If this meditation is practised regularly the love life will improve dramatically.

Saturn in the 7th house tends to bring disappointments with the current love and with friends. With this kind of transit it is important to master the art of forgiveness. Real forgiveness doesn't whitewash the wrong that was done. The action was wrong and we acknowledge that, but we forgive the person. We understand that the other who has hurt us had their own issues and problems to deal with, and had we been in their shoes, we might have acted the same way. Don't allow grudges to fester in the consciousness. In fact the previous meditation will work well in these kinds of situations. 'You did what you did, but Divine Love flows through my consciousness now.'

Ever since Neptune moved into your 10th career house in 2012 you have been subjected to very intense spiritual energy. For a logical, rational Gemini this can be hard to handle. Spiritual energy has its own logic and its own laws and often violates Gemini's vaunted logic. Neptune is still very near the Mid-heaven of your Horoscope, which shows that your spiritual life is perhaps the most important thing these days. If you are not on a spiritual path, this is the time to find one. If you are already on a path, this is a period to explore it more deeply.

In many cases, Gemini, you will actually opt for a spiritual career in ministry, spiritual counselling, spiritual teaching or writing. The fine arts – which require inspiration from above – would also be appealing these days. The business side of these callings would also be appealing.

Pluto has been in your 8th house of transformation for many years now. Thus you are dealing with death and death issues these days. Perhaps you have had a few encounters with death of late. Perhaps people you know have departed or have had near-death kinds of experiences. None of this is punitive, only educational. You are confronting these things so that you will have a deeper understanding of them. The fear of death – the primal fear in the psyche – is what keeps people from their dreams and from their true potential. When this is dealt with (and it's happening now) you will start to soar.

I'm generally not a fan of past-life regression, but this year – and especially after August 11 – it might be a good idea. You are in a period where you need to come to terms with your past. You need to assimilate its wisdom and move on from there.

Month-by-month Forecasts

January

Best Days Overall: 2, 3, 11, 12, 13, 20, 21, 29, 30
Most Stressful Days Overall: 9, 10, 16, 17, 22, 23
Best Days for Love: 1, 7, 8, 12, 13, 16, 17, 21, 22, 24, 25, 31
Best Days for Money: 1, 4, 5, 7, 8, 16, 17, 20, 21, 29, 30, 31
Best Days for Career: 4, 14, 22, 23, 31

You begin your year with an overwhelming percentage of power in the upper half of the Horoscope. Until the 17th, 80 per cent of the planets are above the horizon, and from the 17th to the 28th the percentage increases to 90 per cent. Your career house is strong: almost half of the planets are there or moving through there. Your house of home and family, by contrast, is empty. Only the Moon will pay a brief visit here on the 9th and 10th. So we have a very clear message. Focus on the career and your outer objectives. Home and family issues can safely be downplayed. You can best serve your family by achieving your career goals, and the family seem supportive of this.

The planetary power is mostly in the Western, social sector this month, as it has been for the past five or so months. It will change next month, but for now you are still focused on others and downplaying your own personal interests. You still need to achieve your aims through consensus rather than personal will, but it will be useful now to make a note of those conditions in your life that displease you. Though it is not yet the time to make any changes, you can at least plan them. These changes will be easier to make in the coming months. There is nothing wrong with self-interest (so long as it isn't destructive) but you are not yet in that cycle. Focus on the needs of others for the moment.

Love relationships are being tested all year, but the month ahead seems particularly trying. Much of what's happening is not your fault. The beloved is under much stress and it impacts on you. He or she should rest and relax more this month.

Earning power will be strongest from the 1st to the 5th and from the 20th onwards, as the Moon waxes. The 9th, 10th, 18th, 19th, 24th and 25th are stressful financial days. Extra or unexpected expenses could happen then, but you will get through it. You might be forced to make some dramatic financial changes then, but the changes will be good.

Health and energy are basically good this month, especially from the 20th onwards. You can enhance your health further in the ways mentioned in the yearly report.

Until the 20th your 8th house of transformation is very powerful. This favours physical, emotional, mental and financial detoxifications. It is good periodically to get rid of old material in the body and possessions that you no longer use or need: clear the decks for the new and better that wants to come in.

February

    Best Days Overall: 8, 9, 17, 18, 25, 26
    Most Stressful Days Overall: 5, 6, 7, 13, 14, 19, 20
    Best Days for Love: 1, 2, 3, 4, 10, 11, 13, 14, 20, 21, 22
    Best Days for Money: 1, 3, 4, 13, 14, 17, 18, 27, 28
    Best Days for Career: 1, 10, 19, 20

On February 18 the planetary power makes an important shift from the West, where it has been for six or so months, into the Eastern, independent sector. Your days of needing to 'people please' are about over. Now your personal power will start to increase and you can have your way in things. This shift will become even stronger next month. You are entering a period of independence now; your happiness is in your own hands. Start to make the necessary corrective changes now to life's conditions that displease you. It will be easier to do and others will go along with you. It is wonderful to think of others and put them first, but it is also wonderful to pursue your own interests – and this is the stage you are entering this month.

Other things happen on the 18th too. The Sun crosses the Mid-heaven and enters your 10th house of career. You begin a yearly career peak and will see much forward progress in your career – for we get what we focus on. There are career challenges ahead to be sure. There are obstacles to be dealt with, but you will have all the energy you need to overcome them. You can diminish your attention on the home and focus on the career.

A parent, boss or parent figure could be having a surgical procedure this month, and your own health and energy needs watching more from the 18th onwards. Review our discussion of this in the yearly report. It is good to be ambitious, but do it calmly. Make sure to get enough rest.

Earning power is strongest from the 1st to the 3rd and from the 18th to the 28th. Finances become more stressful on the 8th, 9th, 15th, 16th, 21st and 22nd. Stressful financial days do not mean lack or failure necessarily. It only means that you need to work harder to achieve your goals. If you put in the work, earnings will happen.

Love is improved over last month, but it is not yet what it should be. You need to work harder to project love and warmth to others. Your love planet Jupiter has been retrograde since the beginning of the year, so the love life is under review. If you are single, give some thought to the kind of person you want to be involved with, the qualities that would please you, the activities that you'd indulge in. See what can be done to improve the present love life. The same goes for those of you who are married. What can be done to improve things? There's no need to make any major decisions yet, just review the options.

March

Best Days Overall: 7, 8, 16, 17, 24, 25, 26
Most Stressful Days Overall: 4, 5, 6, 12, 13, 18, 19
Best Days for Love: 2, 3, 12, 13, 20, 21, 22, 23
Best Days for Money: 1, 2, 3, 10, 11, 12, 13, 18, 19, 20, 21, 27, 28, 29, 30
Best Days for Career: 1, 9, 10, 18, 19, 27

Health and energy still need watching this month, especially until the 20th. Review our discussion of this last month and in the yearly report. From the 9th to the 12th your health seems especially delicate, as Mars makes stressful aspects to Pluto, your health planet. This could indicate a surgical procedure – either actual or recommended. Watch the temper during that period, and avoid confrontations or risk-taking activities. This is a very dynamic aspect. Health and energy greatly improve after the 20th.

You are still in the midst of a yearly career peak and, like last month, the upper hemisphere of your chart is dominant. Keep your focus on the career, but make sure you get enough rest too.

A solar eclipse on the 20th will affect all of you, but mostly those born later in the sign of Gemini – from June 19 to 21. If you are part of this group take it nice and easy that period. Spend more quiet time at home. Read a book, watch a movie, invite friends over or meditate. This eclipse affects you strongly. It will be a good idea to drive more defensively during this period. Cars and communication equipment will get tested, and often they will need to be replaced. This eclipse impacts on two solar houses – the 10th and the 11th. Thus it can bring dramas to the lives of friends, bosses, elders and authority figures. The government can change rules and policies that affect your industry or career. Your high-tech equipment gets tested and it will be a good idea to have all your files backed up.

Aside from the excellent career progress happening, there is more good news this month. The love life starts to improve after the 20th. Your love planet starts receiving very nice aspects. The current love should be in a better state of mind than last month, and things should go better between you. If you are unattached or not in a serious relationship, romantic meetings are likely. It is doubtful that these will lead to marriage, not this year anyway, but at least these people are potential marriage material. There is no rush in love right now, though you might feel this. Allow love to develop as it will. Saturn is still in your 7th house and your love planet is still retrograde. Enjoy these romantic meetings for what they are without projecting too much on them.

Your personal power and independence are stronger than last month. You are not at the peak yet – this will happen in a few months – but every day your independence grows. Create conditions as you desire them to be. Take charge and responsibility for your own happiness.

April

Best Days Overall: 3, 4, 5, 13, 14, 21, 22
Most Stressful Days Overall: 1, 2, 8, 9, 15, 16, 28, 29
Best Days for Love: 1, 2, 8, 9, 13, 17, 18, 21, 22, 25, 26
Best Days for Money: 8, 9, 17, 18, 19, 23, 24, 25, 26, 28
Best Days for Career: 6, 7, 15, 16, 23, 24

The main headline this month is the lunar eclipse on the 4th. This lunar eclipse is more powerful than most in that it affects Uranus and Pluto as well. Every lunar eclipse affects your finances as the Moon, the eclipsed planet, is your financial ruler. In a way this is a blessing. Finance is a dynamic thing, always changing. Twice a year, thanks to the lunar eclipses, you get the opportunity to revise your thinking and strategy on these matters – whether you like it or not. Scenarios caused by the eclipse force you.

The eclipse occurs in your 5th house so children and children figures in your life are affected here. They should reduce their schedule around this period if they can, and do their best to stay out of harm's way. This is not a good period for speculative investments or travel. Sometimes we must travel, however; if this is your case, try to schedule your trip around the eclipse period – a few days before or after it. Children and children figures in your life are redefining themselves, changing their self-concept and changing the image that they present to the world. This will be a six-month process.

The impact the eclipse has on Pluto indicates health scares and important changes in your health regime. Health and energy are good this month, so hopefully any scares will be just that – a scare and nothing more. The eclipse also shows job changes and changes in the conditions of work. There are dramas in the lives of co-workers and employees (if you have them). There is instability in the workplace and employee turnover now. (This could happen over the next six months as well.)

Your 12th house of spirituality is very powerful this month – especially after the 20th. Half of the planets are either there or moving through there. This is a month for spiritual growth, interior growth. Geminis are rational people, but during this period you will learn that there is more to life than what the intellect can explain. As usual when the 12th house is strong the dream life will become hyperactive and prophetic. Dreams will tend to happen in Technicolor – not black and white. You will have hunches and intuitions and they will turn out to be right. You will arrive at correct conclusions without the laborious process of thinking things through logically. You will be more idealistic about life. You will enjoy being involved with charities and good causes. Spiritual studies – and inspired literature – will be more appealing. Those on a spiritual path will have breakthroughs this month.

The love life – a difficult area this year – improves until the 20th. Jupiter, your love planet, moves forward on the 8th after many months of retrograde motion. He receives good aspects too. But after the 20th things become challenging again.

May

Best Days Overall: 1, 2, 10, 11, 18, 19, 28, 29
Most Stressful Days Overall: 5, 6, 7, 12, 13, 25, 26, 27
Best Days for Love: 1, 2, 5, 6, 7, 14, 15, 21, 22, 23, 24, 30, 31
Best Days for Money: 5, 6, 8, 9, 14, 15, 17, 18, 21, 22, 23, 24, 28, 29
Best Days for Career: 3, 4, 12, 13, 21, 22, 30, 31

Your house of spirituality remains strong until the 21st of this month. Review our discussion of this last month. Many of you are having birthdays in May, although with some of you it will be next month. Until the 21st it is a very good time to review your past year. Your birthday (in astrology we refer to it as your Solar Return) is your personal new year. You begin a new cycle. The past year is dead. A new year begins. So, it is good to see what has and has not been achieved, to atone for past mistakes and vow never to repeat them, and to formulate targets for the year ahead. How much money would you like to make? How would you go about doing this? What kind of love life do you want? What kind of lifestyle? This will be a road map for the coming year. Write your goals down and look at them every night before going to sleep. Imagine that they have been attained.

The planetary power is now in the maximum Eastern position this month. You are at the height of your personal power and independence this month and the next. Other people are always important and should be respected, but you can have things your way – and indeed you should (so long as it isn't destructive). Your way might not be the best way in ultimate terms, but it is best for you. Create happiness in your life. Design your life according to your personal specifications. Later on it will be harder to do.

If you're having a birthday this month, you are in an excellent period for starting new projects or launching new products into the world. From your birthday to the end of the month is the best for this. The only drawback is the retrograde of Mercury, the ruler of your Horoscope. However, if you've done sufficient homework and allow more time for the project, it could work well. Next month might even be an even better time though, from the 25th onwards: Mercury will be moving forward then.

The month ahead is basically happy. On the 21st you enter one of your yearly personal pleasure peaks. Mars is in your sign from the 12th onwards, so you have plenty of energy and charisma. Health should be good. Self-confidence and self-esteem are much improved after the 21st. And the troubled love life also improves at that time.

On May 7 Venus enters your money house. This is a happy transit and brings good financial intuition and 'happy' money. You earn money in enjoyable ways. Speculations are favourable. You enjoy the wealth that you have. You spend on fun activities. Earning power will be strongest from the 1st to the 4th and from the 18th onwards, as the Moon waxes. You have some good financial days after the 4th, but the ones after the 18th will be better.

June

Best Days Overall: 6, 7, 15, 16, 24, 25
Most Stressful Days Overall: 2, 3, 8, 9, 22, 23, 29, 30
Best Days for Love: 1, 2, 3, 10, 11, 20, 21, 29, 30
Best Days for Money: 2, 3, 6, 7, 10, 11, 15, 16, 17, 18, 19, 20, 21, 27, 29, 30
Best Days for Career: 8, 9, 17, 18, 27, 28

You are still in a yearly personal pleasure peak until June 21. This is when the body gets indulged and seems happy. It is a very good period to get it (and your overall image) in right shape and order. The new Moon of the 25th seems particularly fortuitous, as it occurs in your own sign. It brings money and personal pleasure.

On the 21st you enter a yearly financial peak. The focus is on finance and this tends to prosperity. We get what we focus on.

The love life continues to improve this month. Saturn moves out of your 7th house on the 15th and Venus travels with your love planet Jupiter towards the end of the month. Singles have excellent romantic opportunities then (especially from the 28th to the 30th). The love life is far from perfect but it's improved in the short term. Keep in mind that any relationship you enter into these days will get tested a few months from now. Continue to focus on quality rather than quantity.

This month the challenges are mostly at the job. This seems a troubled area. Your work planet, Pluto, receives stressful aspects this month and Saturn moves into your 6th house of work on the 15th. The workplace is more restrictive. Rules are tightened; co-workers are more temperamental and more difficult to get along with. Patience, patience, patience.

Though your general health and energy are good this month, there are problems with the overall health regime. Perhaps the people involved in your health are stressed out these days. Surgery or a surgical procedure could be recommended, but get a second opinion.

Last month the planetary power began to shift from the upper to the lower half of your Horoscope. It is now time to de-emphasize career and outer goals. Your career planet, Neptune, goes retrograde on the 12th, which reinforces what we say here. Career issues will only be solved by time. There are no quick answers now. This is a time for a wait-and-see attitude – a time to gain mental clarity about the career situation. Things are not as they appear to be. Thus it is good to focus on the home, family and your emotional well-being at this time. Without a good psychological foundation, career success won't happen – at least not lasting success anyway.

July

Best Days Overall: 3, 4, 5, 12, 13, 22, 23, 31
Most Stressful Days Overall: 6, 7, 19, 20, 26, 27, 28
Best Days for Love: 8, 9, 17, 18, 26, 27, 28
Best Days for Money: 6, 7, 9, 14, 15, 16, 18, 26, 27, 28
Best Days for Career: 6, 7, 14, 15, 24, 25

Many of the trends we wrote of last month are still very much in effect. You are still in a yearly financial peak (until July 23). Not surprisingly, your communication skills play a huge role here. Friends also seem helpful and supportive. When the money house is strong it seems as if the whole universe conspires to bring you wealth. Mercury will be in your money house from the 8th to the 23rd, and this is another good sign for finance. The ruler of your Horoscope always brings benefit. This aspect indicates that you spend on yourself, that you project an image of wealth, dress expensively, etc. Personal appearance and overall demeanour is a big factor in earning power.

The problems we saw in the workplace are still happening, but they should ease up a bit after the 23rd. The 14th to the 17th seems especially stressful. Avoid confrontations or arguments with co-workers during that period. People could overreact.

That same period – the 14th to the 17th – could bring surgery or a recommendation for surgery. Like last month, it is advisable to get a second opinion. Computer and high-tech equipment seems more temperamental at this time too.

Mars will make a stressful aspect with Uranus from the 24th to the 27th. This is a very dynamic kind of aspect. Again, computer and high-tech equipment get tested. It will be a good idea to have all your files backed up and in good order. This will not be an especially good time for foreign travel either.

Overall, health and energy are good this month. The short-term planets are either helping you or leaving you alone, and Saturn has moved away from his stressful aspect (temporarily). Detox regimes will be useful this month.

On July 23 you enter Gemini heaven. Your 3rd house of communication and intellectual interests becomes very powerful. It has been strong since July of last year, but now it gets even stronger. Your always keen mind becomes keener and sharper. Your communication skills, always good, become even better. You absorb information like a sponge. The facts are always at your command. You are naturally and unconsciously eloquent in your speech and writing. The Muses are with you.

The only danger for you is that all this could become too much of a good thing. Your always active mind can become hyperactive. The tendency will be to think too much or talk too much. This can cause insomnia or other nervous problems, and it may drain energy that the body needs for other things.

August

Best Days Overall: 1, 8, 9, 18, 19, 27, 28
Most Stressful Days Overall: 2, 3, 15, 16, 17, 23, 24, 29, 30
Best Days for Love: 5, 14, 15, 23, 24, 25, 31
Best Days for Money: 4, 5, 10, 11, 12, 13, 14, 15, 25
Best Days for Career: 2, 3, 10, 11, 20, 21, 29, 30

Last month (and continuing into this month) retrograde activity among the planets reached its peak for the year. Even after the 2nd, as Saturn starts moving forwards again, we are near the peak of retrograde activity. Things move slower in the world at large. Interestingly, you don't seem too much affected by all this, not in a personal way. Mercury, the ruler of your Horoscope, has been moving speedily – faster than usual. This shows that you are covering a lot of ground and making much personal progress. For you things haven't slowed down that much.

Mercury's speedy motion indicates good levels of self-confidence and self-esteem. You are never in one place for too long. You are achieving and doing.

The other major headline this month is Jupiter's move into Virgo on the 11th. The last time he was here was twelve years ago. This is an important transit; Jupiter is your love planet, so this move shows important changes here. Your needs in love are changing. Communication is always important for you in love, but now you want emotional intimacy – emotional sharing – too. You show love by giving emotional support and this is how you feel loved. Never mind the wise-cracks and witticisms now; give emotional support.

The love planet in the sign of Virgo produces other challenges. You and the beloved (and the people you meet) can be too perfectionist in love. This can lead to destructive criticism, which is always a killer for romance. Criticism will not get you closer to perfection. It will be a challenge to keep the criticism constructive, and to withhold it when the timing is not right.

In the month ahead love is improved. The 3rd to the 8th brings happy romantic opportunities: Venus conjuncts Jupiter from the 3rd to the 6th and Mercury conjuncts the love planet from the 6th to the 8th. Marriage is not likely – not this year anyway – but the trysts are happy.

Your 4th house of home and family becomes very powerful after the 23rd. Moves or opportunities to move are likely. There will be more entertaining from home and more socializing with family members. Pursue your career by the methods of night. Visualize, dream and affirm. Enter, as best you can, the feeling-state of being where you want to be careerwise. Later, when the planetary power shifts, you will be able to take outward, overt actions towards these things.

September

Best Days Overall: 4, 5, 6, 14, 15, 24, 25
Most Stressful Days Overall: 12, 13, 19, 20, 26, 27
Best Days for Love: 1, 2, 9, 10, 12, 19, 20, 28, 29, 30
Best Days for Money: 2, 3, 7, 8, 12, 13, 24, 30
Best Days for Career: 7, 17, 26, 27

An eventful month ahead. Saturn moves back into your 7th house and we have two eclipses this month. There are many shake-ups and changes happening now. It is understandable that you feel direction-less this month, especially after the 17th. But you should let the dust settle from the eclipses and gain mental clarity before making any major decisions.

The solar eclipse of the 13th occurs in your 4th house of home and family. This, combined with Jupiter's entry here last month, suggests a move. Moves are very disruptive and it would fit the symbolism of the eclipse. Happy things can be just as disruptive as unpleasant things. But there are other scenarios indicated too. The eclipse could signal the birth of a child – either your own if you are of the appropriate age, or of someone else in the family. This too is happy, but tends to make for big changes. Family members can be more temperamental now, so be more patient with them. Perhaps some flaw is found in the home and you are forced to renovate and enlarge the home. The disruption becomes an opportunity for improvement.

Every solar eclipse tests communications equipment and cars and this one is no different. Drive more defensively this period. Siblings and sibling figures tend to be affected by solar eclipses too. They bring drama into their lives and they are forced to redefine themselves, change their self-concept and image.

Often solar eclipses bring radical changes to your neighbourhood. Often we see major construction happening, roads are closed or blocked, etc.

The lunar eclipse of 28th (the 27th in the Americas) occurs in your 11th house of friends. This will test friendships. Good ones will survive and get better. Flawed ones could end. There are dramas in your friends' lives as well. Often it is these life-changing dramas that test the relationship. Computers and high-tech equipment get tested as well, so it is a good idea to make sure your anti-virus software is functioning and up to date, and to keep your files backed up.

Every lunar eclipse affects your finances and this one is no different. Important financial changes are happening. They will be good ultimately, but usually not pleasant while they're happening.

Health and energy are more delicate until the 23rd. Make sure you get enough rest and review our discussion of this in the yearly report.

October

Best Days Overall: 2, 3, 11, 12, 13, 21, 22, 29, 30
Most Stressful Days Overall: 9, 10, 16, 17, 18, 23, 24
Best Days for Love: 1, 8, 9, 10, 16, 17, 18, 19, 20, 27, 28
Best Days for Money: 1, 2, 3, 4, 5, 9, 10, 12, 13, 19, 20, 22, 23, 27, 28, 29, 31
Best Days for Career: 4, 5, 14, 15, 23, 24, 31

Health and energy improved greatly after the 23rd of last month. Saturn is still in stressful aspect with you, but the short-term planets are making favourable aspects. Health should be good this month. Your health planet Pluto went forward on the 25th of last month as well. There is more clarity in these matters now, and it is safer to make the changes in the health regime that need to be made.

On the 23rd of last month, as the Sun entered your 5th house, you began another of your yearly personal pleasure peaks, and this remains in effect until the 23rd of this month. The job situation doesn't seem that happy, so you might as well have some fun. A bit of recreation will enable you to be better focused on work later on.

The planetary power began to shift two months ago and this shift is felt even more strongly now. The power is in the Western, social sector. Personal merit, personal attainments are always important, but these days less so. It is the 'likeability factor' that is important now, your ability to get on with others, your social skills. It is more difficult these days to have life on your terms or to change conditions to suit you. Now you are better off adapting to things as best you can. Make a note of what displeases you and when your next cycle of independence comes – next year – you will be in a position to make the necessary changes. Adapting to things is also a useful skill. With Saturn in your 7th house of love you need to project warmth and love to others. You have to make a special effort. It is not happening naturally.

Love is not where it should be these days. The testing of love and romantic relationships continues. From a long-term perspective these things are very good, but it is not so pleasant in the short term. A friend is coming into the romantic picture from the 15th to the 18th. He or she is a friend but seems to want to be more than that. Another happy romantic period occurs between the 24th and the 27th, but this looks more like a fun kind of relationship, rather than anything serious.

The month ahead looks prosperous. Your financial planet, the Moon, spends four days (twice the normal time) in your own sign, and three days (also longer than usual) in the money house. In your own sign it brings actual physical cash to you and financial opportunity. There's nothing special that you need to do here. In the money house this aspect shows stronger earning power. In general your earning power is strongest from the 1st to the 13th and from the 27th onwards – the periods when the Moon is waxing.

November

Best Days Overall: 8, 9, 17, 18, 26, 27
Most Stressful Days Overall: 5, 6, 13, 14, 19, 20
Best Days for Love: 5, 6, 7, 13, 14, 15, 16, 17, 18, 24, 25, 26, 27
Best Days for Money: 1, 5, 6, 10, 11, 21, 22, 24, 25, 28, 29, 30
Best Days for Career: 10, 19, 20, 28

You are still having fun this month but work is also a priority. Job seekers have better aspects now than in the past few months. You are in the mood for work and employers pick up on the vibration. The situation seems easier for those of you in an existing job too.

With your 6th house of work strong until the 23rd it is a good time to do all those detailed, boring kinds of jobs that need to be done. Get your files in order. Update the bookkeeping and accounts. Organize your receipts. These tasks will be done better and more easily now.

The planetary power makes another important shift this month. On the 22nd the power shifts from the lower half to the upper half of the Horoscope. It is dawn in your yearly cycle. It is time to be up and about and active, time to pursue your worldly goals in a physical kind of way, time to make all those dreams and visions physical reality. With Jupiter in your 4th house well into next year you're not going to ignore home and family, but you will serve them by being successful in the world. Success here is as much a form of service to your family as attending the soccer match or school play. Career is going to be a major focus for the rest of the year ahead and well into next year. Just emphasizing this is the forward motion of Neptune, the career planet, which has been retrograde for many months. On November 18 it finally moves forward again. By now career issues are clarified and you can step on the gas.

Love is far from perfect and needs time and development; nevertheless, in the short term it is more active this month. On the 23rd you enter a yearly love and social peak. Singles will date more, and those of you who are married will attend more parties and gatherings. Romantic meetings will happen for singles, but they are very complicated. It will not be a smooth ride. Again take it nice and slow. Focus more on quality than quantity. Continue to project love and warmth to others – this is a long-term project. Otherwise people will perceive you as cold and aloof.

Avoid risk taking and confrontations from the 24th to the 26th.

Your finances look good this month. Your financial planet will spend three days in the money house – more time than usual. Earning power is strongest from the 11th to the 25th as the Moon waxes. There can be short-term financial challenges on the 8th, 9th, 15th and 16th, but these will pass. Earnings look good on the 21st and 22nd, but you have to work harder for them.

December

Best Days Overall: 5, 6, 14, 15, 16, 23, 24
Most Stressful Days Overall: 2, 3, 4, 10, 11, 17, 18, 30, 31
Best Days for Love: 2, 3, 4, 7, 10, 11, 12, 13, 17, 18, 21, 22, 25, 26, 30, 31
Best Days for Money: 1, 2, 3, 4, 10, 11, 12, 13, 20, 21, 22, 25, 26, 30, 31
Best Days for Career: 7, 8, 17, 18, 25, 26

Health and energy become more delicate on November 22, and it still needs attention until the 22nd of this month. Review our discussion of this in the yearly report. When energy is low things that normally can be done easily become major labours. And if the activity involves danger – such as climbing ladders or handling knives or sharp objects – injury can result. As always, do your best to maintain high energy levels. Your health will improve after the 22nd. Those of you involved in athletics will probably not perform up to your usual standards. It's no reflection on your inherent skills, just a lack of your normal energy.

Mars makes dynamic aspects with Uranus and Pluto from the 5th to the 12th, so avoid risky kinds of activities, arguments or confrontations during this period. People can overreact under these aspects. Surgery or a surgical procedure can be recommended at this time, but, as always, get a second opinion.

These aspects of Mars affect computers and high-tech equipment. Make sure your files are backed up and your anti-virus software is up to date. Friends can have dramatic kinds of experiences – near-death kinds of encounters.

You are still in the midst of a yearly love and social peak until the 22nd but, like last month, it is not a smooth ride. There are challenges and glitches in love. Love should improve after the 10th as Mercury starts to make better aspects to your love planet. There is a happy romantic meeting or experience between the 24th and the 26th. There is more harmony with the beloved that period too.

Home and family life still seems happy. Family support is good and you are socializing more with family members. But your focus still needs to be on the career. Career progress will be good all month, but especially after the 10th.

Your 8th house of transformation and renewal is powerful from the 22nd onwards. This is wonderful for detox and weight-loss regimes, and also for dealing with tax, insurance and estate issues. The spouse, partner or current love is prospering this month. If you have good ideas, this is a good period to attract outside investors to your projects.

It will be beneficial to do serious house cleaning after the 22nd. The house cleaning should be physical, but also mental and emotional. Get rid of possessions that you don't use or need. Get rid of ideas, thoughts and emotions that don't serve your interests. These just clog up the works and prevent further progress.

Cancer

THE CRAB

Birthdays from
21st June to
20th July

Personality Profile

CANCER AT A GLANCE

Element – Water

Ruling Planet – Moon
   Career Planet – Mars
   Love Planet – Saturn
   Money Planet – Sun
   Planet of Fun and Games – Pluto
   Planet of Good Fortune – Neptune
   Planet of Health and Work – Jupiter
   Planet of Home and Family Life – Venus
   Planet of Spirituality – Mercury

Colours – blue, puce, silver

Colours that promote love, romance and social harmony – black, indigo

Colours that promote earning power – gold, orange

Gems – moonstone, pearl

Metal – silver

Scents – jasmine, sandalwood

Quality – cardinal (= activity)

Quality most needed for balance – mood control

Strongest virtues – emotional sensitivity, tenacity, the urge to nurture

Deepest need – a harmonious home and family life

Characteristics to avoid – over-sensitivity, negative moods

Signs of greatest overall compatibility – Scorpio, Pisces

Signs of greatest overall incompatibility – Aries, Libra, Capricorn

Sign most helpful to career – Aries

Sign most helpful for emotional support – Libra

Sign most helpful financially – Leo

Sign best for marriage and/or partnerships – Capricorn

Sign most helpful for creative projects – Scorpio

Best Sign to have fun with – Scorpio

Signs most helpful in spiritual matters – Gemini, Pisces

Best day of the week – Monday

Understanding a Cancer

In the sign of Cancer the heavens are developing the feeling side of things. This is what a true Cancerian is all about – feelings. Where Aries will tend to err on the side of action, Taurus on the side of inaction and Gemini on the side of thought, Cancer will tend to err on the side of feeling.

Cancerians tend to mistrust logic. Perhaps rightfully so. For them it is not enough for an argument or a project to be logical – it must feel right as well. If it does not feel right a Cancerian will reject it or chafe against it. The phrase 'follow your heart' could have been coined by a Cancerian, because it describes exactly the Cancerian attitude to life.

The power to feel is a more direct – more immediate – method of knowing than thinking is. Thinking is indirect. Thinking about a thing never touches the thing itself. Feeling is a faculty that touches directly the thing or issue in question. We actually experience it. Emotional feeling is almost like another sense which humans possess – a psychic sense. Since the realities that we come in contact with during our lifetime are often painful and even destructive, it is not surprising that the Cancerian chooses to erect barriers – a shell – to protect his or her vulnerable, sensitive nature. To a Cancerian this is only common sense.

If Cancerians are in the presence of people they do not know, or find themselves in a hostile environment, up goes the shell and they feel protected. Other people often complain about this, but one must question these people's motives. Why does this shell disturb them? Is it perhaps because they would like to sting, and feel frustrated that they cannot? If your intentions are honourable and you are patient, have no fear. The shell will open up and you will be accepted as part of the Cancerian's circle of family and friends.

Thought-processes are generally analytic and dissociating. In order to think clearly we must make distinctions, comparisons and the like. But feeling is unifying and integrative.

To think clearly about something you have to distance yourself from it. To feel something you must get close to it. Once a Cancerian has accepted you as a friend he or she will hang on to you. You have to be really bad to lose the friendship of a Cancerian. If you are related to Cancerians they will never let you go no matter what you do. They will always try to maintain some kind of connection even in the most extreme circumstances.

Finance

The Cancer-born has a deep sense of what other people feel about things and why they feel as they do. This faculty is a great asset in the workplace and in the business world. Of course it is also indispensable in raising a family and building a home, but it has its uses in business. Cancerians often attain great wealth in a family business. Even if the business is not a family operation, they will treat it as one. If the Cancerian works for somebody else, then the boss is the parental figure and the co-workers are brothers and sisters. If a Cancerian is the boss, then all the workers are his or her children. Cancerians like the feeling of being providers for others. They enjoy knowing that others derive their sustenance because of what they do. It is another form of nurturing.

With Leo on their solar 2nd money house cusp, Cancerians are often lucky speculators, especially with residential property or hotels and restaurants. Resort hotels and nightclubs are also profitable for the Cancerian. Waterside properties attract them. Though they are basically conventional people, they sometimes like to earn their livelihood in glamorous ways.

The Sun, Cancer's money planet, represents an important financial message: in financial matters Cancerians need to be less moody, more stable and fixed. They cannot allow their moods – which are here today and gone tomorrow – to get in the way of their business lives. They need to develop their self-esteem and feelings of self-worth if they are to realize their greatest financial potential.

Career and Public Image

Aries rules the 10th solar career house cusp of Cancer, which indicates that Cancerians long to start their own business, to be more active publicly and politically and to be more independent. Family responsibilities and a fear of hurting other people's feelings – or getting hurt themselves – often inhibit them from attaining these goals. However, this is what they want and long to do.

Cancerians like their bosses and leaders to act freely and to be a bit self-willed. They can deal with that in a superior. They expect their leaders to be fierce on their behalf. When the Cancerian is in the position of boss or superior he or she behaves very much like a 'warlord'. Of course the wars they wage are not egocentric but in defence of those under their care. If they lack some of this fighting instinct – independence and pioneering spirit – Cancerians will have extreme difficulty in attaining their highest career goals. They will be hampered in their attempts to lead others.

Since they are so parental, Cancerians like to work with children and make great educators and teachers.

Love and Relationships

Like Taurus, Cancer likes committed relationships. Cancerians function best when the relationship is clearly defined and everyone knows his or her role. When they marry it is usually for life. They are extremely loyal to their beloved. But there is a deep little secret that most Cancerians will never admit to: commitment or partnership is really a chore and a duty to them. They enter into it because they know of no other way to create the family that they desire. Union is just a way – a means to an end – rather than an end in itself. The family is the ultimate end for them.

If you are in love with a Cancerian you must tread lightly on his or her feelings. It will take you a good deal of time to realize how deep and sensitive Cancerians can be. The smallest negativity upsets them. Your tone of voice, your irritation, a look in your eye or an expression on your face can cause great distress for the Cancerian. Your slightest gesture is registered by them and reacted to. This can be hard to get used to, but stick by your love – Cancerians make great partners once you learn how to deal with them. Your Cancerian lover will react not so much to what you say but to the way you are actually feeling at the moment.

Home and Domestic Life

This is where Cancerians really excel. The home environment and the family are their personal works of art. They strive to make things of beauty that will outlast them. Very often they succeed.

Cancerians feel very close to their family, their relatives and especially their mothers. These bonds last throughout their lives and mature as they grow older. They are very fond of those members of their family who become successful, and they are also quite attached to family heirlooms and mementos. Cancerians also love children and like to provide them with all the things they need and want. With their nurturing, feeling nature, Cancerians make very good parents – especially the Cancerian woman, who is the mother *par excellence* of the zodiac.

As a parent the Cancerian's attitude is 'my children right or wrong'. Unconditional devotion is the order of the day. No matter what a family member does, the Cancerian will eventually forgive him or her, because 'you are, after all, family'. The preservation of the institution – the tradition – of the family is one of the Cancerian's main reasons for living. They have many lessons to teach others about this.

Being so family-orientated, the Cancerian's home is always clean, orderly and comfortable. They like old-fashioned furnishings but they also like to have all the modern comforts. Cancerians love to have family and friends over, to organize parties and to entertain at home – they make great hosts.

Horoscope for 2015

Major Trends

In 2013, as Jupiter entered your sign, you began a cycle of prosperity. This cycle is still in effect for much of the year ahead. Jupiter, the planet of wealth and abundance, is in your 2nd money house until August 11. On August 11 Jupiter will leave your money house and enter your 3rd house of communication and intellectual interests. Thus learning and teaching (depending on your stage in life) becomes a major focus. More on this later.

Saturn will spend most of the year ahead in your 6th house of health and work. From a health perspective it shows a need to pursue a healthy lifestyle and a daily disciplined health regime. Since Saturn is your love planet, his move from your 5th house (where he's been for the past two years) to the 6th shows important changes in the love life and in your attitudes to love. There's more on this later.

Uranus has been in your 10th house of career for some years now and is still there in 2015. This shows many career changes happening. There is instability in the career, but also excitement. You seem ready to change careers at the drop of a hat. More details below.

Neptune, the most spiritual of all the planets, has been in your 9th house since 2012. This aspect is bringing a refinement of your religious and philosophical beliefs – they are being spiritualized. A spiritual perspective is being brought to bear on these things. Also this aspect shows sea travel – cruising – in the year ahead and in future years.

Your most important interests in the year ahead will be finance (until August 11); communication and intellectual interests (from August 11 onwards); children, fun and personal creativity (from June 15 to September 18); health and work (from January 1 to June 15 and from September 18 onwards); love, romance and social activities; religion, philosophy, higher learning and foreign travel; and career.

Your paths of greatest fulfilment in coming year will be finance (until August 11); communication and intellectual interests (from August 11 onwards); and home and family (until November 13).

Health

(Please note that this is an astrological perspective on health and not a medical one. In days of yore there was no difference, these perspectives were identical. But now there could be quite a difference. For a medical perspective, please consult your doctor or health practitioner.)

Health is much improved over 2011 and 2012 (things were actually dangerous then) but it still needs watching in the year ahead. You still have two long-term, powerful planets stressing you here – Uranus and Pluto. Furthermore, Saturn, which was in harmonious aspect with you for the past two years, now moves away from this aspect. Happily, your 6th house of health is strong for most of the year and you will be paying attention here. Neglecting your health would be the main danger.

There is more good news. There is much that you can do to improve the health and overall energy. Give more attention to the following areas – the vulnerable areas in your Horoscope: the stomach and breasts; the heart; the liver and thighs; the small intestine; and the spine, knees, teeth, bones, skin and overall skeletal alignment. Reflex points to these are shown on the chart above.

The stomach and breasts are always important for you. Diet, as always, is important in health matters. Try to eat slowly and calmly. Chew your food well. Have nice soothing music playing as you eat. Bless your food (in your own words) and give thanks for it. This will not only change the energy vibrations of the food but the vibrations of the whole digestive system.

The liver and thighs are another important area for you. Regular thigh massage will be beneficial, as will natural, herbal liver

Important foot reflexology points for the year ahead

Try to massage the whole foot on a regular basis, but pay extra attention to the points highlighted on the chart. When you massage, be aware of 'sore spots', as these need special attention. It is also a good idea to massage the ankles and the tops of the feet.

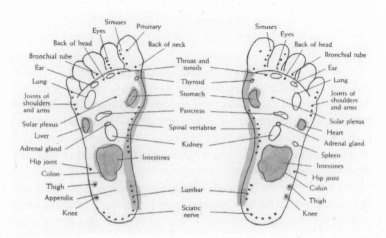

detoxifications. Try to avoid worry and anxiety too, as they are the spiritual root causes of heart problems.

Regular back and knee massage will be good, together with regular visits to a chiropractor or osteopath. Yoga, Pilates, the Alexander Technique and Feldenkrais are excellent therapies for the spine and general skeletal alignment. Regular dental check-ups and cleanings are beneficial too, and if you're out in the sun use a good sun screen. Give the knees more support when exercising.

Saturn is your love planet. His position in your 6th house of health gives us all kinds of messages. First, it shows that you are very involved in the health of your friends, spouse or current love. For you, in the years ahead (remember, this trend goes on for another two years), good health means good social health – a healthy love and romantic life. If there are problems here, the actual physical health can be affected. If problems, God forbid, arise check this area out and restore harmony as quickly as possible.

Good mental health is always a good thing, but this year – especially until August 11 – it is a health issue. Good health also means good mental health. Moods should be positive, uplifting and constructive. Depression should be avoided like the plague and should be considered the first symptom of disease. Meditation will be a big help here. Very often health problems have their origins in the cellular memory. Old traumas get re-stimulated and they produce the symptoms of disease. If health problems arise this should be checked out and cleansed. Meditation is helpful for this as well.

Home and Family

Though home and family is always important to a Cancerian, this year they are less so than usual. Your 4th house is not strong this year. However, the north node of the Moon spends most of the year in this house. Often this indicates excessive focus, more than is needed. You might be overdoing things this year, creating dramas where none really exist or making changes that don't need to be made.

There will be a few legitimate dramas in the home and family this year. We have two lunar eclipses, which will create family crises or upheavals. The first one, on April 4, seems the strongest because it also occurs in your 4th house. The second, on September 28, occurs in your 10th house and could affect the career and people involved in your career as much as the family. We will discuss this in more detail in the monthly reports.

Venus, your family planet, is a fast-moving planet. So there will be many short-term trends in the home and family that are best dealt with in the monthly reports. However, Venus does make one of her rare retrogrades this year – from July 25 to September 6. This will be a period for reviewing home and family issues. When Venus is retrograde the home and family conditions revealed might not be as you imagine them to be – neither as bad nor as good.

If you're planning to do any redecorating, major repairs or renovation around the home, November 8 to the end of the year has good aspects. Decorating is better done before December 5.

Parents or parent figures in the life seem to be doing major repairs in the home. A move could have happened in the previous two years. Siblings and sibling figures are in a cycle of prosperity from August 11 onwards. They are travelling and living the good life. Moves are not advisable this year, or for the next few years.

Children and children figures in the life are facing some financial challenges this year. They need to consolidate and reorganize their financial life. Moves could have happened last year, but can still happen in the year ahead. Grandchildren are having a stable year family-wise. If they are of appropriate age they have wonderful job opportunities in the year ahead. Also after August 11 they have a very strong social year. If they are of the appropriate age, marriage or serious relationships are likely.

Finance and Career

On June 26, 2013 you entered a cycle of prosperity, and it is very much still in effect in the year ahead. Jupiter, the planet of abundance, has been occupying your money house since July 17 last year and will be there until August 11. This is a classic signal of prosperity.

This aspect shows a person who is catching the lucky financial breaks. Speculations were favourable last year and are still favourable until August 11. So, it might be wise to invest harmless sums on a lottery or in some other kind of speculation. As always this should be done under intuitive guidance, not automatically. The cosmos has many ways to prosper you.

With Jupiter in your money house assets you own increase in value. Something that you thought was worthless could be worth rather more than you think. Jupiter also brings happy financial opportunities – new and perhaps undreamed of ways to make money. Your financial horizons are greatly expanded.

Since Jupiter is your planet of health and work, his position in the money house shows that happy job opportunities come (this could have happened last year too.) Co-workers seem supportive of your financial goals. You are spending more on health but can earn from this field too.

Industries that cater to children – such as entertainment and music – are always interesting investments for you, but this year more so than usual. This year investments in the health field – and there are many public companies involved with this – also look good. The travel business, for-profit higher education, and investments in foreign countries or foreign companies are good. Job opportunities can come to you in foreign lands or with foreign companies. And while the new job involves a lot of work, it seems lucrative.

Jupiter moving through your 3rd house shows a new car and communication equipment coming.

Favourable financial numbers are 5, 6, 8 and 19.

Career, as we have mentioned, is exciting but unstable. Dramatic changes have been happening both personally and in the lives of people involved with your career. There have been major changes in your industry too. Every time you think you have the ideal career or ideal set up, a new idea, a new ideal, is revealed, and so you make new changes. It is a constant process of upgrading the career, the career goals and the career path. You upgrade much in the same way as you upgrade your software or mobile apps.

Your technology skills and expertise are very important in the career. Some of you will actually enter this kind of career, but whatever the actual career it is very important to stay up to date with the latest gadgetry and technology. It is also important to be involved in groups and professional organizations. They enhance the career too.

Love and Social Life

Pluto has been in your 7th house of love for many years now. Thus a cosmic detox is happening in your love and social life. This will continue for many more years. Impure elements – people, attitudes, relationships – get expunged and the love and social life becomes 'renewed' – resurrected on a better and healthier level.

Many a marriage or friendship has broken up in recent years. Good marriages, good relationships, have had 'near death' experiences and have emerged renewed.

Pluto in the 7th house also indicates that friends and partners have had surgical procedures over the past few years, and there are likely to be more to come.

Your love planet, Saturn, made a major move in December 2014 from your 5th house to your 6th. He will spend most of the year ahead in this house. This shows an important shift in your love attitudes. For the past two years love was about fun and entertainment. It was supposed to be honeymoonish all the time. It was difficult for you or your partner to handle the tough times. But things are different now. Love is about service to the beloved. Love is shown through practical service. If you love someone you will serve him or her. And this is what you expect in return. It is a more serious, sober perspective on things.

For singles there are love and social opportunities at the workplace and with co-workers. In fact, part of the allure of any job is the social opportunities it provides. There are interesting job opportunities happening this year, but you will probably pick the one that offers the best social opportunities.

There are also love and social opportunities as you pursue your health goals and with people involved in your health. Health professionals are especially attractive to you this year. Romantic and social opportunities could also occur in your place of worship, at religious functions, or in a university setting.

Saturn in the sign of Sagittarius shows that foreigners and foreign places are conducive to love. If there are problems in a marriage or current relationship, a foreign trip could bring back some harmony. There is nothing against marriage this year, but nothing that especially favours it either. There's a lot of free will in this department.

Those working towards their second marriage had great opportunities to achieve this in 2013 and 2014. This year the aspects are lacklustre. However, there are opportunities in spiritual settings – at charity events or spiritual seminars or lectures.

Those working towards their third marriage have a stable year romance-wise.

Parents and parent figures are having their marriages tested. This has been going on for some time. Children or children figures of marriageable age are making lots of friends and are socially active, but marriage is not in the cards.

Self-improvement

Jupiter, as we mentioned before, moves into your 3rd house of communication and intellectual interests on August 11. This is therefore a great time to take courses in subjects that interest you, to read more and build up the knowledge base. The mind is much expanded this year. Its capacity is greater than you think. Those of you who have expertise in a given field should start to disseminate this knowledge now. Teach, write, give seminars and workshops.

Neptune in your 9th house is refining and elevating your personal philosophy, religious beliefs and world view. This is a most interesting development. Religion is a very important thing. Everyone has a personal religion, conscious or unconscious. Religious practices have many good and valid points. Unfortunately there is much out there that is little more than superstition. This transit will enable you to see what is and isn't valid. This will happen through personal spiritual experiences and interior revelation.

Pluto has been in your 7th house of love for many years now. The love pangs and disappointments you feel are really birth pangs. You are giving birth to the love life of your dreams – to your ideal love life. But birth doesn't come easily and generally there is a lot of blood and gore involved. But the end result is good, and most people go through it willingly for that reason. So it is with your love life. Keep your mind on the end result and not the temporary challenges that are happening.

All the changes going on in your career have a cosmic agenda behind them. There is a liberation happening. By the time Uranus is finished with you (in the next few years) you will be free to follow the career of your dreams. Many old attachments and obstructions are being blasted away these days.

Sudden change – though often exciting – tends to bring insecurity. Learning to deal with career insecurity and instability is the major lesson these days. You need to become comfortable with it. Change should be seen as friendly.

Month-by-month Forecasts

January

Best Days Overall: 4, 5, 14, 15, 22, 23, 31
Most Stressful Days Overall: 11, 12, 13, 18, 19, 24, 25
Best Days for Love: 1, 6, 12, 13, 16, 18, 19, 21, 22, 24, 31
Best Days for Money: 1, 6, 7, 8, 9, 10, 16, 17, 20, 21, 24, 25, 29, 30
Best Days for Career: 2, 3, 14, 22, 23, 24, 25, 31

You begin your year with the planetary power mostly in the Western, social sector of your chart. This means that the planetary power is distant from you, moving away from you. Thus power is in your life. Personal interests and personal desires are de-emphasized and personal independence and power is less. The cosmos is focused on others and their needs, and so should you be. There's nothing wrong with self-interest, but you are in a different stage of your yearly cycle right now. It is through others that you learn about yourself and through others that you attain your personal desires. Thus it is a time to cultivate your social skills and to attain your ends through consensus and co-operation. If conditions irk you, make note and in a few months, when you enter a cycle of personal independence, any changes will be more easily made. Right now, adapt yourself as best you can.

Last month the planetary power shifted from the lower half to the upper half of your chart. Family is always important to you, but there are many ways to serve your family. Now you serve them by being successful in the outer world. The focus now is on career and your outer worldly objectives.

Towards the end of last month you entered a yearly love and social peak and this continues until the 20th. Your 7th house of love is very strong during this period. Half of the planets are either there or moving through there this month, which is a lot of power. For singles this shows too many love opportunities, rather than too few. There are too many choices! For those of you who are married it indicates many, many parties and gatherings – perhaps more than can be handled.

This is a prosperous year ahead generally, but earnings come with more work and effort from the 20th onwards (they come much more easily before the 20th). If you put in the necessary work, however, prosperity will happen.

There is some financial drama, some upheaval, from the 2nd to the 4th as your financial planet, the Sun, makes stressful aspects with Uranus and Pluto. Avoid speculations during this period. There are changes that need to be made and this is the time to make them.

Until January 20 earnings come via your social contacts. The spouse, partner or current love seems supportive (and you are also supportive of him or her). It will be a good idea to attend parties and gatherings at this time as they have bottom-line benefits. After the 20th the beloved enters a yearly financial peak and will be more generous with you.

February

Best Days Overall: 1, 10, 11, 19, 20, 27, 28
Most Stressful Days Overall: 8, 9, 15, 16, 21, 22
Best Days for Love: 1, 2, 3, 10, 11, 13, 15, 16, 20, 21
Best Days for Money: 3, 4, 8, 9, 13, 14, 17, 18, 21, 22, 27, 28
Best Days for Career: 1, 2, 10, 11, 20, 21, 22

The financial challenges you face this month are just temporary bumps on the road. Your overall prosperity is not affected in the least. Go the extra mile and put in the necessary work and earnings will come much more easily after the 18th. The spouse, partner or current love is still in a yearly financial peak and you seem very involved with this.

Ever since your financial planet entered your 8th house of transformation on the 20th of last month you have been in a monetary detox phase. This is a good period to cut out waste and redundancy. Go through your possessions. Take stock and get rid of what you don't need or use. If your possessions are still good, you can sell them or give them to charity. If they are worn out throw them away. The cosmos wants to give you more, but there's no room. The cosmos is very rich and is always re-supplying us. There's no need to hoard things. The criterion for keeping something should be usefulness.

Those of you of the appropriate age will benefit from estate and tax planning now. This is a good month to channel any spare cash into the repayment of debt. But if you need to borrow, there is good fortune too. If you have good business ideas, this is good month to approach outside investors. Be alert for opportunities to invest in troubled companies or properties – there are profits to be made here. Of course, do your homework first.

On the 18th the Sun enters Pisces, your 9th house. This is another favourable financial transit. According to the Hindu astrologers, the 9th house is the most beneficent of all the houses. So this is a prosperous period. Moreover, Pisces is the most spiritual of all the signs. Thus your financial intuition is superb this month (especially from the 23rd to the 27th). Pay attention to your dreams and hunches during this period. If there are questions or doubts about finance, see a good psychic, astrologer, minister, spiritual medium or tarot reader. These people have important financial guidance for you.

This is a period for 'miracle money' rather than 'natural' money, and especially for those of you on a spiritual path. It is a period where you go deeper into the spiritual sources of supply. February will be a very good month for attending investment or financial seminars to enlarge your knowledge about finance.

With your 9th house prominent after the 18th you will probably be travelling too. However, there could be delays and glitches here. Don't schedule connecting flights too tightly. Allow enough time to get to your destination.

Health and energy are excellent from the 18th onwards.

March

Best Days Overall: 1, 9, 10, 18, 19, 27, 28
Most Stressful Days Overall: 7, 8, 14, 15, 20, 21
Best Days for Love: 2, 3, 12, 13, 14, 15, 20, 22, 23, 29, 30
Best Days for Money: 1, 2, 3, 10, 11, 12, 13, 18, 19, 20, 21, 29, 30, 31
Best Days for Career: 2, 3, 12, 13, 20, 21, 30, 31

There are two main headlines this month. The first is the power in your 10th house of career from the 20th onwards. The second is the solar eclipse of the 20th.

Career has been prominent since the beginning of the year. But now, on the 20th, you enter a yearly career peak. The 10th house is by far the strongest house this month, with half of the planets either there or moving through there. The 4th house of home and family, by contrast, is empty (only the Moon will move through there on the 7th and 8th). So keep the focus on career and downplay family issues. A lot of progress will be made this month. A yearly career peak doesn't mean that every career objective is attained however. Career is a long-term project and in many cases it is never ending. So we never achieve all our goals in one month or one year. But if good progress is made, this is success. You will be closer to your ultimate goals by the end of the month than you were at the month's beginning.

It is interesting that your yearly career peak coincides with a solar eclipse. This indicates career changes for many of you. Those of you born early in the sign of Cancer (June 21–23) are most affected by this eclipse, and if you fall into this category take it nice and easy during this. If stressful activities or appointments can be re-scheduled it might be a good idea to do so. Those of you born later in the sign of Cancer will feel the effects of the eclipse, but less violently.

The eclipse occurs right on the border or cusp of your 9th and 10th houses. Thus the affairs of both houses are affected. For students this can mean a change of school or upheavals in the present school or college. There are disturbances in your place of worship too. There can be dramas in your industry or company and in the lives of bosses, parents, parent figures or authority figures in your life.

As Uranus has been in your 10th house for many years now, you are getting used to career change and instability. This eclipse will therefore be easier to handle.

Every solar eclipse affects your financial life, as the Sun is your financial planet. This eclipse is no different. It brings financial changes – changes in thinking and strategy. Generally this happens through some disturbance or crisis. We don't normally change our ways unless we are forced to. The changes will be good, but they are not particularly pleasant while they're happening.

Health and energy needs attention from the 20th onwards. Review our discussion of this in the yearly report.

April

Best Days Overall: 6, 7, 15, 16, 23, 24
Most Stressful Days Overall: 3, 4, 5, 10, 11, 12, 17, 18
Best Days for Love: 1, 2, 8, 10, 11, 12, 13, 17, 21, 22, 25, 26
Best Days for Money: 8, 9, 17, 18, 19, 25, 26, 27, 28
Best Days for Career: 1, 2, 10, 11, 12, 17, 18, 19, 20, 28, 29

A lunar eclipse on the 4th affects you strongly, so reduce your commitments and schedule for a few days before and after it. Many of you, the sensitive types, will feel the effects of this eclipse a week to ten days before it happens. You will get the cosmic message, perhaps by some weird event that happens to you or by something you read in the papers or hear from friends. This will alert you that the eclipse period is in effect and that you should start taking it easy. This eclipse affects you strongly for many reasons. It occurs in Libra, which is a stressful aspect for you, and the eclipsed planet is the Moon, the ruler of your Horoscope. Also, it impacts on two powerful planets, Uranus and Pluto. Don't play around now; avoid stressful, risky activities.

Every lunar eclipse forces you to redefine yourself. If you don't, others will and that might not be pleasant. It's how *you* think of yourself that matters ultimately. It is wonderful that, twice a year, you get the opportunity to do this. Generally this redefinition brings wardrobe and image changes. You are presenting a new look to the world. You want others to see you in a new way. This will go on for the next six months.

Every lunar eclipse affects the home and family – the Moon is the natural ruler of this area. But this one has an even greater effect. It occurs in the 4th house. So there are dramas in the lives of family members and/or parent figures – with people who are 'like' family to you. Often it reveals flaws or problems in the physical home so that you can correct them. Often repairs are needed. This is not pleasant to be sure, but the end result is good.

Also, since you are still in a yearly career peak and need to stay focused here, this eclipse becomes a distraction for you. Children and children figures should be kept out of harm's way, as much as possible. This is easier with young children. Older children might not listen, but you can make discreet suggestions. Don't scare them: just suggest that they take it easy for a few days.

Financial drama and change continue this month. The Sun travels with Uranus and squares Pluto from the 4th to the 7th. (The eclipse is a factor here too.) There can be sudden expenses or obligations arising, but sudden and unexpected money can also come. Your overall prosperity is not really affected. The changes will only enhance it.

The period from the 4th to the 7th can bring a financial 'near death' kind of experience. Keep in mind that after death or near death comes resurrection.

Continue to pay more attention to your health until the 20th.

May

Best Days Overall: 3, 4, 12, 13, 21, 22, 30, 31
Most Stressful Days Overall: 1, 2, 8, 9, 14, 15, 28, 29
Best Days for Love: 1, 2, 5, 8, 9, 12, 13, 14, 21, 22, 23, 30, 31
Best Days for Money: 5, 6, 8, 9, 14, 15, 17, 18, 23, 24, 28, 29
Best Days for Career: 9, 14, 15, 18, 19, 28, 29

Health and energy are much improved since the Sun entered Taurus on April 20. You can enhance the health even further in the ways mentioned in the yearly report.

Last month, other changes happened besides the eclipse. The planetary power began to shift from the West (where it has been all year) to the independent East. This means that the cosmic energy, the planetary power, is moving towards you rather than away from you. Day by day it gets closer to you. Thus you are entering a cycle of personal independence and power. You are in less need of other people. The cosmos is supporting your personal interests and desires. Unselfishness is very nice, but now it is time to give attention to your own interests. It is time to have things your way, time to change conditions to your liking and to design your life according to your personal specifications. Take advantage of this opportunity. Later on in the year it will again be more difficult to do.

Last month on the 20th your 11th house of friends became powerful, and it remains so until the 21st. Thus you are in a social period; not necessarily romantic, but social. The focus is on friends, groups and group activities. This is a period for gaining more knowledge about technology, science, astronomy and astrology. These studies will go much better this month. I have found that people who have never had their horoscopes done will often do it when their 11th house is strong (or when the ruler of their 11th house is powerful).

This focus on friends is fun in its own right, but also has bottom-line consequences. There is financial opportunity here. Friends seem financially supportive. Technology becomes important on the financial level too. You are probably spending on new high-tech equipment, but you can earn from it too during this time.

Friends seem successful and are helping you careerwise.

The 11th house is often referred to as the 'house of fondest hopes and wishes'. Thus many of your hopes and wishes are fulfilled now (especially in finance and your career). But 'fondest hopes and wishes' are not static things. When some are attained, new ones are formed. Like career goals, they are rarely fully attained, but progress is made.

It is always nice for you to accessorize with silver – both the colour and the metal. This month, with Venus moving into your sign on the 7th, green is also a good colour for you. Emeralds are nice gems to wear.

June

Best Days Overall: 8, 9, 17, 18, 19, 27, 28
Most Stressful Days Overall: 4, 5, 10, 11, 24, 25
Best Days for Love: 1, 4, 5, 10, 11, 19, 20, 21, 28, 29, 30
Best Days for Money: 2, 3, 6, 7, 10, 11, 15, 16, 20, 21, 27, 29, 30
Best Days for Career: 8, 9, 10, 11, 17, 18, 19, 27, 28

Last month on the 21st you entered one of the most spiritual periods of your year. Half of the planets were in or moving through your 12th house. The 12th house is still strong this month – until the 21st – but less so, and this is a month for spiritual, interior growth. It will be a very good time for meditation, prayer and the expansion of your inner life. Very good too to involve yourself in charities and causes that you believe in. With the financial planet also in the 12th house at this time you are giving more to charities and good causes. And, curiously, as you do this, you have more to give. Your finances are not diminished. In February and March your financial intuition was excellent and you learned the value of it. The same is true this month.

You are in a period of 'inner' experiences. The inner life is more interesting than the outer, material life. Cancerians always have a vivid dream life, but now even more than normal. You start to experience supernatural, inexplicable kinds of things. You think of someone and they call. You want some information from a book or phone book and it falls open at the exact page you want. Your hunches tend to be accurate. You drive to a crowded store and a parking space appears just as you get there. The invisible world is letting you know it is around.

We are all much more than our bodies and personal identities. This is a mere fraction of who we are. We are a unit of the cosmos – the all – in a particular expression. And this is a great period to get in touch with this. Things that happen are not necessarily about us, as individuals, but about the ALL moving and shaping things according to its plan.

This period, from the 21st of last month to the 21st of this, is a very good one for reviewing your past year, evaluating your progress (or lack thereof), correcting past mistakes and setting goals for the year ahead. Astrologically speaking your birthday (your Solar Return) is your personal new year and one should take that approach. A new cycle is being born and you want to be ready for it. If you are having your birthday next month, it is good to do this review until your birthday.

Health and energy are wonderful this month – especially from the 21st onwards. You have plenty of energy and can achieve anything you set your mind to. Personal power and independence is now at its maximum extent for the year (as it is next month too). Use this power to create what you want in your life.

The month ahead is very prosperous too. On the 21st the financial planet crosses the Ascendant and enters your 1st house. This always brings money and financial opportunity. Best of all, it comes rather effortlessly. There's nothing special that you need to do. You are entering a multi-month cycle of prosperity, beginning on the 21st.

July

Best Days Overall: 6, 7, 14, 15, 16, 24, 25
Most Stressful Days Overall: 1, 2, 8, 9, 22, 23, 29, 30
Best Days for Love: 1, 2, 7, 8, 9, 16, 17, 18, 25, 26, 29, 30
Best Days for Money: 6, 7, 9, 14, 15, 16, 17, 18, 26, 27, 28
Best Days for Career: 6, 7, 8, 9, 14, 15, 16, 24, 25

A happy and healthy month ahead – Enjoy!

Last month on the 21st you entered a yearly personal pleasure peak. You are experiencing all the pleasures of the body – good food, wine, clothing, accessories, massages, etc. A physical kind of nirvana. You look good too. You have plenty of energy, grace and charisma. This is all very good for the love life, as the opposite sex takes notice. Mars in your own sign all month signals that you look successful – people see you as successful. It also indicates the favour of bosses, elders, parents and parent figures. Career opportunities are seeking you out: nothing much you need to do.

This month, on the 8th, the planetary power begins to shift once more. This time it is energizing the bottom half of your chart. Career becomes less important now. The focus is going to be on the home, family and emotional well-being for the next six months or so. Career opportunities happen, but you can examine them more closely. No matter how lucrative they seem, they should not violate your emotional or family harmony. This is a period where you serve your family by being there for them, in a physical kind of way. Rather than negotiating the next deal or angling for the next promotion, it is better to attend the soccer match or school play.

Most of your career goals have been attained by now, and even if they've not been fully realized, much progress towards them has been made. Now it is time to step back and gather strength for your next career push in about six months time.

Finances are unusually good this month. Benevolent Jupiter is still in your money house, and your money house is very powerful – 50 per cent of the planets (and they are all beneficent) are either there or moving through there. There is a cosmic conspiracy to enrich you now. On the 23rd you enter a yearly financial peak. This is a multi-year financial peak. For some of you it is a lifetime peak.

Love is good but more complicated these days. Your love planet, Saturn, has been retrograde since March. This doesn't stop love from happening, but it slows things down a bit. Singles are still dating, but the social confidence – and perhaps choices – are not what they should be. It would be a good idea to review the love life and see where improvements can be made. Don't rush a current relationship, let things develop. Enjoy the relationship for what it is without projecting too much on to it. Clarity will come next month.

August

Best Days Overall: 2, 3, 10, 11, 12, 20, 21, 22, 29, 30
Most Stressful Days Overall: 4, 5, 18, 19, 25, 26, 31
Best Days for Love: 3, 5, 12, 14, 22, 23, 24, 25, 26, 30, 31
Best Days for Money: 4, 5, 13, 14, 15, 25
Best Days for Career: 3, 4, 13, 23, 24, 31

Your money house gets even stronger in the month ahead. In August 60 per cent of the planets are either in or moving through your 2nd house. Wow! That's a lot of earning power. This is the main headline this month.

On the 9th Mars, your career planet (and also the planet that rules bosses, parents and parent figures) moves into your money house and will be there for the month ahead. This shows that you have the financial favour of these people. Money can come from the government too. Pay rises can also happen.

By the 23rd most of your financial goals have either been attained or good progress has been made towards them. You seem satiated and are ready to move on to other interests. Though the interest in finance is waning there is a very nice payday period from the 26th to the 28th. This could also be a higher-paying job opportunity.

On August 11, Jupiter, which has been in your money house since July 2014, moves into your 3rd house of communication. The Sun will follow on the 23rd. This gives us many messages. First, you are probably getting a new car (and a good one too) and new communication equipment in the year ahead. You spend on communication and can earn from that too. Those of you in sales, marketing, advertising or PR – and those of you who are teachers and writers – will have a banner financial month. Whatever business you're involved with, good sales and marketing, good PR, good use of the media are very important.

Siblings and sibling figures start to prosper now and they seem financially supportive. Money is earned close to home in the neighbourhood, and perhaps through neighbours. Siblings and neighbours seem open to your financial ideas and financial thinking.

You are in an intellectual stage in your life now. Intellectual wealth is just as much wealth as financial wealth, and this is what is happening for you now. You are building your intellectual property portfolio these days.

This power in the 3rd house is wonderful for students at both school and college level. There is success in studies now. College applicants should hear good news.

As we mentioned, clarity is starting to happen in love. Saturn moves forward on the 2nd after many months of retrograde motion. You are ready to move forward too. Social confidence is much stronger these days – and the judgement will be better too. Love happens more easily after the 23rd than before.

Health and energy are still excellent. They are not perfect, but they are good. You can enhance your health even further in the ways mentioned in the yearly report.

September

Best Days Overall: 7, 8, 17, 18, 26, 27
Most Stressful Days Overall: 1, 14, 15, 22, 23, 28, 29
Best Days for Love: 1, 8, 9, 10, 18, 19, 20, 22, 23, 28, 29
Best Days for Money: 2, 3, 9, 10, 12, 13, 24, 30
Best Days for Career: 1, 9, 10, 20, 28, 29, 30

The main headline this month is the two eclipses that occur. This ensures a dramatic, eventful kind of month.

Eclipses always bring disruption, turmoil and change. They bring events that can't be ignored. There's no way to sweep these things under the rug. They must be dealt with and they tend to take up much of our time and energy.

The solar eclipse of the 13th occurs in your 3rd house of communication. As solar eclipses go, for you it is a mild one. Still, it won't hurt to reduce your schedule and avoid stressful activities. It might not be so mild for the people around you. For students this eclipse can indicate a change of schools, a change of courses, or shake-ups in the administration of their school. There are dramas, probably good ones, in the lives of siblings, sibling figures and neighbours. Cars and communication equipment get tested and often need replacement. It will be a good idea to drive more carefully during this period. It might also be a good idea to make sure you have a service contract or insurance for your smart phone.

Every solar eclipse brings financial drama and change and this one is no different. As we have mentioned, finance is a dynamic kind of thing, always changing, and it is good to go along with the changes. These changes probably needed to be made long ago, but now the eclipse forces the issue.

The lunar eclipse of the 28th (in the Americas it occurs on the 27th) affects you much more, so take it nice and easy and do your best to stay out of harm's way. This eclipse occurs in your 10th house of career, signalling career changes. This doesn't necessarily mean that you will literally change careers (though this can happen). But changes in your industry or profession can be dramatic, changing the rules of the game. Often there are shake-ups in the hierarchies of your company and industry. (This has been going on for some years now.) Sometimes the government agency which regulates your industry or profession changes the rules. There are life-changing events too in the lives of bosses, parents, parent figures and authority figures in your life.

Every lunar eclipse forces a redefinition of your personality and self-concept, as we have mentioned. Once again you redefine yourself and change your wardrobe and 'look'.

Health becomes more delicate after the 23rd. Be sure to get enough sleep and rest. Review our discussion of this in the yearly report.

October

Best Days Overall: 4, 5, 14, 15, 23, 24, 31
Most Stressful Days Overall: 11, 12, 13, 19, 20, 25, 26
Best Days for Love: 6, 8, 9, 16, 19, 20, 25, 27, 28
Best Days for Money: 1, 2, 3, 6, 7, 8, 9, 10, 12, 13, 19, 20, 22, 23, 27, 28, 29
Best Days for Career: 1, 9, 10, 19, 20, 25, 26, 27, 28

Your love planet Saturn changed signs last month. It moved out of Scorpio, where it has been for the past three months and into Sagittarius, where it will be for the next two years. You are always practical when it comes to matters of the heart, but now even more so. You appreciate the person who 'does' for you, who serves your interests. For you, service is love in action these days. Love opportunities occur at the workplace or as you pursue your health goals. The good news now is that there is clarity in love. Saturn is finally moving forward and will be moving forward for months to come. Relationships are going forward.

On the 23rd of last month you entered Cancer heaven. Your 4th house of home and family became very powerful and remains so until the 23rd of the current month. The cosmos impels you to do what you most love – be involved with the family and the domestic routine.

The planetary power is now at its nadir (lowest point) of your chart. It is midnight in your year. The midnight hour is when all kinds of magical and miraculous things happen. Outer activity is more or less in abeyance, but inner activity is strong. The inner life is the focus now.

You are having happy career opportunities this month – especially from the 15th to the 18th – but this will be a 'side effect' of your inner work. Continue to pursue your career goals by the methods of night: dream and visualize what you want to happen and where you want to be. Get into the feeling of what it would be like to have attained some career goal. If the feeling happens, the outer event is very close.

Cancerians are always interested in the past. They are the most nostalgic of all the signs, and this is particularly apparent this month. There is a cosmic logic to this. As we grow, the past gets redefined according to our present state of consciousness. Thus the past memories that are surfacing are being resolved, redefined and healed.

Health is more delicate these days (and has been since September 23), so make sure you get enough rest. Review our discussion of health in the yearly report. Health and energy will improve towards the end of the month.

Finance is good this month but there are a few bumps in the road. From the 5th to the 7th the Sun squares Pluto – avoid speculations then. Expenses involving the children (or children figures) can be stressful. And between the 11th and 12th the Sun opposes Uranus, creating a financial disturbance – something sudden and unexpected. This will lead to change, which will be good.

November

Best Days Overall: 1, 10, 11, 19, 20, 28, 29
Most Stressful Days Overall: 8, 9, 15, 16, 22
Best Days for Love: 3, 6, 7, 12, 15, 16, 17, 18, 21, 26, 27, 30
Best Days for Money: 1, 3, 4, 5, 6, 10, 11, 15, 16, 21, 22, 24, 25, 30
Best Days for Career: 6, 7, 8, 17, 18, 21, 22, 26, 27

Back in September the planetary power began to make another important shift, from the independent East to the social West. This month, as Venus and Mars move westwards, the shift becomes much stronger. The planetary power is moving away from you and towards other people, and you should (and most likely will) follow suit. Self-interest is a great thing but now you are in a different stage of your cycle. Your interest is important but so are the interests of others. It is time to take a vacation from yourself and to focus on others. Now it is best to adapt to situations as best you can, rather than try to change them. Now is the time to cultivate your social skills. Your good comes through the good graces of others.

On the 23rd of last month the Sun entered your 5th house of fun and enjoyment and you entered a yearly personal pleasure peak. This continues until the 22nd. This is the time to have some fun and to explore the rapture side of life. Those of you in the creative arts will be especially creative now. Children are the focus now. No one knows how to enjoy life more than the child. There is much we can learn from them.

Finances are strong this month. Speculations are favourable until the 22nd. Money is earned in happy ways and you spend on happy, fun things. Children and children figures motivate your earnings. If they are of an appropriate age, the children figures in your life seem supportive. You spend on children but can earn from them as well. It is a time for enjoying your wealth. A business partnership or joint venture can happen towards the end of the month – the 29th–30th. The spouse, partner or current love seems financially supportive. You might spend on a party or gathering.

On the 6th, as Mars, your career planet, moves into your 4th house, you will probably be working more from home. But this also reinforces what we have been saying earlier – home and family is the career these days, high on your priorities.

Love is good this month. Saturn, the love planet, gets positive stimulation after the 20th. Social activity will increase.

Health is good all month but especially until the 22nd. You can enhance it further in the ways mentioned in the yearly report. After the 20th pay more attention to the lungs, small intestine, arms, shoulders and respiratory system. Arm and shoulder massage will be especially powerful.

December

Best Days Overall: 7, 8, 9, 17, 18, 25, 26
Most Stressful Days Overall: 5, 6, 12, 13, 19, 20
Best Days for Love: 1, 7, 10, 12, 13, 17, 18, 19, 25, 26, 27, 28
Best Days for Money: 1, 2, 3, 4, 10, 11, 12, 13, 20, 21, 22, 27, 28, 29, 30, 31
Best Days for Career: 5, 6, 14, 15, 16, 19, 20, 23, 24

Your 6th house of health and work became very powerful on the 22nd of last month and becomes even stronger in December. This is a very nice aspect for job seekers and for those who employ others. Job opportunities (and job applicants) seem plentiful. It will also be very beneficial to focus on your health, health regime and health knowledge at this time.

Romance is good this month, and the workplace is the venue for romance. Saturn is getting much positive stimulation. The best days for love shown above are when romantic meetings and opportunities are most likely. On the 22nd the Sun enters your 7th house and you begin a yearly love and social peak.

Finances also look good. Until the 22nd, the financial planet is in Sagittarius, which generates an expansive energy – earnings should increase. There is a financial optimism and faith abroad. You spend freely (especially from the 13th to the 15th) but you earn more too. Money seems to come the old-fashioned way – from work. Many of you will take second jobs or jobs on the side – these seem plentiful. After the 22nd, as the Sun enters Capricorn, you become more conservative about money. You are less the free-spender. You want value for your cash and take a long-range view of finance, which is good. Social connections become very important financially after the 22nd. You hang out with rich people and they seem supportive. Your financial good (as well as other goods) depend on the good graces of others – so your social skills are ultra-important now.

Parents or parent figures in your life should stay out of harm's way from the 5th to the 12th. Mars is involved in dynamic aspects with Pluto and Uranus. It won't hurt to keep children and children figures out of harm's way during this period either.

Health becomes more delicate after the 22nd. Enhance health in the ways mentioned in the yearly report. The important thing is to get enough rest. Keep the energy levels high.

On the 22nd the planetary power begins to shift yet again. This time it moves from the lower half of the Horoscope to the upper half. This shift will become much stronger next month but you start to feel the pull of your ambitions. Career gradually becomes more important again.

Leo

♌

THE LION

Birthdays from
21st July to
21st August

Personality Profile

LEO AT A GLANCE

Element – Fire

Ruling Planet – Sun
   Career Planet – Venus
   Love Planet – Uranus
   Money Planet – Mercury
   Planet of Health and Work – Saturn
   Planet of Home and Family Life – Pluto

Colours – gold, orange, red

Colours that promote love, romance and social harmony – black, indigo, ultramarine blue

Colours that promote earning power – yellow, yellow-orange

Gems – amber, chrysolite, yellow diamond

Metal – gold

Scents – bergamot, frankincense, musk, neroli

Quality – fixed (= stability)

Quality most needed for balance – humility

Strongest virtues – leadership ability, self-esteem and confidence, generosity, creativity, love of joy

Deepest needs – fun, elation, the need to shine

Characteristics to avoid – arrogance, vanity, bossiness

Signs of greatest overall compatibility – Aries, Sagittarius

Signs of greatest overall incompatibility – Taurus, Scorpio, Aquarius

Sign most helpful to career – Taurus

Sign most helpful for emotional support – Scorpio

Sign most helpful financially – Virgo

Sign best for marriage and/or partnerships – Aquarius

Sign most helpful for creative projects – Sagittarius

Best Sign to have fun with – Sagittarius

Signs most helpful in spiritual matters – Aries, Cancer

Best day of the week – Sunday

Understanding a Leo

When you think of Leo, think of royalty – then you'll get the idea of what the Leo character is all about and why Leos are the way they are. It is true that, for various reasons, some Leo-born do not always express this quality – but even if not they should like to do so.

A monarch rules not by example (as does Aries) nor by consensus (as do Capricorn and Aquarius) but by personal will. Will is law. Personal taste becomes the style that is imitated by all subjects. A monarch is somehow larger than life. This is how a Leo desires to be.

When you dispute the personal will of a Leo it is serious business. He or she takes it as a personal affront, an insult. Leos will let you know that their will carries authority and that to disobey is demeaning and disrespectful.

A Leo is king (or queen) of his or her personal domain. Subordinates, friends and family are the loyal and trusted subjects. Leos rule with benevolent grace and in the best interests of others. They have a powerful presence; indeed, they are powerful people. They seem to attract attention in any social gathering. They stand out because they are stars in their domain. Leos feel that, like the Sun, they are made to shine and rule. Leos feel that they were born to special privilege and royal prerogatives – and most of them attain this status, at least to some degree.

The Sun is the ruler of this sign, and when you think of sunshine it is very difficult to feel unhealthy or depressed. Somehow the light of the Sun is the very antithesis of illness and apathy. Leos love life. They also love to have fun; they love drama, music, the theatre and amusements of all sorts. These are the things that give joy to life. If – even in their best interests – you try to deprive Leos of their pleasures, good food, drink and entertainment, you run the serious risk of depriving them of the will to live. To them life without joy is no life at all.

Leos epitomize humanity's will to power. But power in and of itself – regardless of what some people say – is neither good nor evil. Only when power is abused does it become evil. Without power even good things cannot come to pass. Leos realize this and are uniquely qualified to wield power. Of all the signs, they do it most naturally. Capricorn, the other power sign of the zodiac, is a better manager and administrator than Leo – much better. But Leo outshines Capricorn in personal grace and presence. Leo loves power, whereas Capricorn assumes power out of a sense of duty.

Finance

Leos are great leaders but not necessarily good managers. They are better at handling the overall picture than the nitty-gritty details of business. If they have good managers working for them they can become exceptional executives. They have vision and a lot of creativity.

Leos love wealth for the pleasures it can bring. They love an opulent lifestyle, pomp and glamour. Even when they are not wealthy they live as if they are. This is why many fall into debt, from which it is sometimes difficult to emerge.

Leos, like Pisceans, are generous to a fault. Very often they want to acquire wealth solely so that they can help others economically. Wealth to Leo buys services and managerial ability. It creates jobs for others and improves the general well-being of those around them. Therefore – to a Leo – wealth is good. Wealth is to be enjoyed to the fullest. Money is not to be left to gather dust in a mouldy bank vault but to be enjoyed, spread around, used. So Leos can be quite reckless in their spending.

With the sign of Virgo on Leo's 2nd money house cusp, Leo needs to develop some of Virgo's traits of analysis, discrimination and purity when it comes to money matters. They must learn to be more careful with the details of finance (or to hire people to do this for them). They have to be more cost-conscious in their spending habits. Generally, they need to manage their money better. Leos tend to chafe under financial constraints, yet these constraints can help Leos to reach their highest financial potential.

Leos like it when their friends and family know that they can depend on them for financial support. They do not mind – and even enjoy – lending money, but they are careful that they are not taken advantage of. From their 'regal throne' Leos like to bestow gifts upon their family and friends and then enjoy the good feelings these gifts bring to everybody. Leos love financial speculations and – when the celestial influences are right – are often lucky.

Career and Public Image

Leos like to be perceived as wealthy, for in today's world wealth often equals power. When they attain wealth they love having a large house with lots of land and animals.

At their jobs Leos excel in positions of authority and power. They are good at making decisions – on a grand level – but they prefer to leave the details to others. Leos are well respected by their colleagues and subordinates, mainly because they have a knack for understanding and relating to those around them. Leos usually strive for the top positions even if they have to start at the bottom and work hard to get there. As might be expected of such a charismatic sign, Leos are always trying to improve their work situation. They do so in order to have a better chance of advancing to the top.

On the other hand, Leos do not like to be bossed around or told what to do. Perhaps this is why they aspire so for the top – where they can be the decision-makers and need not take orders from others.

Leos never doubt their success and focus all their attention and efforts on achieving it. Another great Leo characteristic is that – just like good monarchs – they do not attempt to abuse the power or success they achieve. If they do so this is not wilful or intentional. Usually they like to share their wealth and try to make everyone around them join in their success.

Leos are – and like to be perceived as – hard-working, well-established individuals. It is definitely true that they are capable of hard work and often manage great things. But do not forget that, deep down inside, Leos really are fun-lovers.

Love and Relationships

Generally, Leos are not the marrying kind. To them relationships are good while they are pleasurable. When the relationship ceases to be pleasurable a true Leo will want out. They always want to have the freedom to leave. That is why Leos excel at love affairs rather than commitment. Once married, however, Leo is faithful – even if some Leos have a tendency to marry more than once in their lifetime. If you are in love with a Leo, just show him or her a good time – travel, go to casinos and clubs, the theatre and discos. Wine and dine your Leo love – it is expensive but worth it and you will have fun.

Leos generally have an active love life and are demonstrative in their affections. They love to be with other optimistic and fun-loving types like themselves, but wind up settling with someone more serious, intellectual and unconventional. The partner of a Leo tends to be more political and socially conscious than he or she is, and more libertarian. When you marry a Leo, mastering the freedom-loving tendencies of your partner will definitely become a life-long challenge – and be careful that Leo does not master you.

Aquarius sits on Leo's 7th house of love cusp. Thus if Leos want to realize their highest love and social potential they need to develop a more egalitarian, Aquarian perspective on others. This is not easy for Leo, for 'the king' finds his equals only among other 'kings'. But perhaps this is the solution to Leo's social challenge – to be 'a king among kings'. It is all right to be regal, but recognize the nobility in others.

Home and Domestic Life

Although Leos are great entertainers and love having people over, sometimes this is all show. Only very few close friends will get to see the real side of a Leo's day-to-day life. To a Leo the home is a place of comfort, recreation and transformation; a secret, private retreat – a castle. Leos like to spend money, show off a bit, entertain and have fun. They enjoy the latest furnishings, clothes and gadgets – all things fit for kings.

Leos are fiercely loyal to their family and, of course, expect the same from them. They love their children almost to a fault; they have to be careful not to spoil them too much. They also must try to avoid attempting to make individual family members over in their own image. Leos should keep in mind that others also have the need to be their own people. That is why Leos have to be extra careful about being over-bossy or over-domineering in the home.

Horoscope for 2015

Major Trends

Ever since Jupiter entered your sign last July you have been in a cycle of happiness and prosperity. Sure you have some challenges, but you have help in dealing with them. The tone of 2015 is prosperity and joy.

However, along with all this fun, Saturn is in your 5th house of enjoyment for most of the year ahead. Have fun, but don't overdo it. Have fun without evading your true responsibilities.

Prosperity will be good all year, but gets even better from August 11 onwards as Jupiter enters your money house. Jupiter's sojourn in your sign at the beginning of the year is excellent for love. There is serious romance happening this year, although it could have already happened last year too. There's more on this later.

Your health has been basically good over the past year and should get even better in the year ahead as Saturn is moving away from his stressful aspect and makes nice aspects for you. More details later.

Uranus has been in your 9th house for some years now. This shows much change, ruminating about and upgrading of your religious and philosophical beliefs. You seem to be exploring different religions and philosophies these days.

The sexual life is becoming more refined and spiritualized. Mere physical pleasure doesn't seem enough for you. Ever since Neptune moved into your 8th house of transformation and regeneration in 2012 you have been exploring the deeper dimensions of sex.

Your most important interests in the year ahead will be the body, image and personal pleasure (until August 11); finance (from August 11 onwards); home and family (from June 15 to September 18); children, fun and creativity (from January 1 to June 15 and from September 18 onwards); health and work; sex, personal reinvention, occult studies, debt and the repayment of debt; and religion, philosophy, higher education and foreign travel.

Your paths of greatest fulfilment in the year ahead will be the body, image and personal pleasure (until August 11); finance (from August 11 onwards); and communication and intellectual interests (until November 13).

Health

(Please note that this is an astrological perspective on health and not a medical one. In days of yore there was no difference, these perspectives were identical. But now there could be quite a difference. For a medical perspective, please consult your doctor or health practitioner.)

Your 6th house of health has been strong for many years now and will still be strong in the year ahead. You are focused on health and on the ball. You are giving it the attention (perhaps even too much) that it needs.

As we have mentioned, health looks good this year and much improved over last year. The long-term planets are either in harmonious aspect to you or leaving you alone. (Saturn, your health planet, will retrograde back into Scorpio for a few months this year – from June 15 to September 18 – but this is not a serious transit, just a flirtation.

Important foot reflexology points for the year ahead

Try to massage the whole foot on a regular basis, but pay extra attention to the points highlighted on the chart. When you massage, be aware of 'sore spots', as these need special attention. It is also a good idea to massage the ankles and the tops of the feet.

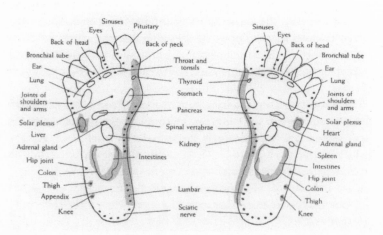

Most of you won't feel this – only those of you born very late in the sign of Leo, from August 19 to August 22.

Good though your health is, you can take steps to make it even better. Pay more attention to the following vulnerable areas in your chart: the heart; the colon, bladder and sexual organs; the spine, knees, teeth, bones, skin and the overall skeletal alignment; and the liver and thighs. The reflex points are highlighted in the chart above.

The heart is always important for a Leo. Eat heart-healthy foods and avoid worry and anxiety, the two emotions that stress the heart. In addition, the colon, bladder and sexual organs have become important over the years. The odd colonic irrigation might be a good idea as the colon needs to be kept clean. Safe sex and sexual moderation is also important these days. In general you benefit from detox regimes.

The spine, knees, teeth, bones, skin and skeletal alignment are other areas always important for Leo, and this year is no different. Regular back and knee massage is beneficial, as are regular visits to a chiropractor or osteopath. Yoga, Pilates, the Alexander Technique and Feldenkrais are excellent therapies for the spine. Give the knees more support when exercising and make sure you're getting enough calcium and vitamin K. If you're out in the sun use a good sun screen.

The liver and thighs have become important since December of last year and will remain so for the next two years. Regular thigh massage will be wonderful. It will also be a good idea to do liver detoxes and there are various herbal ways to do this. Liver action seems more sluggish than usual these days.

Keeping these areas healthy and fit will prevent most problems from happening. For health problems would most likely begin in the above areas.

For the past two years, good emotional health has been very important, and this year too for a few months, from June 15 to September 18. Avoid depression. Do your best to manage your moods and keep them constructive. Through meditation and other spiritual techniques, moods can be mastered and made to serve you.

You are one of the most creative signs in the zodiac, and it is very important that you keep the creative juices flowing. Repression can be a root cause of health problems. It is always good for you to have some creative kind of hobby – something you do for the sheer joy of it. This year it is more important than usual.

Your health planet has been in Scorpio for some years now (and will be there again for a few months this year), while Pluto is in your 6th house of health. Many of you had surgical procedures during the past two years, and surgery could happen this year too. You have a tendency to this. Always get second opinions and investigate whether detoxing the body will do the same job. (It often does, but it does take longer.)

Your weight needs watching this year – especially until August 11 – although diet is less of an issue than it has been for the past two years. It will become important again – briefly – from June 15 to September 18.

Home and Family

Home and family have been important for the past two years. It becomes important again for a few months in the year ahead – from June 15 to September 18. It has been challenging but most of the problems are over with.

Saturn in your 4th house showed a need to take on more family responsibility – this could have been onerous and there was no way to avoid it. The emotional life in general was blocked and you didn't feel safe expressing how you truly felt. The health of family members was perhaps an issue. Many of you wanted to move, felt cramped in the home, but couldn't manage it. Most of this is changing for the better in the year ahead.

Health is still an issue with the family, but this year it's more about the health of your children or the children figures in your life. The emotional life in general is much happier. Regardless of what is going on in the family, your natural Leo optimism cannot be squashed. It just bubbles up.

When Jupiter moves into Virgo on August 11, he will start to make beautiful aspects to your family planet Pluto. Moves or renovations are likely from August 11 onwards and they seem happy. As our regular readers know, when the Horoscope indicates a move it need not be a 'literal' one. It can express itself in a renovation or the purchase of an additional home. The effect is 'as if' a move happened. The home is more expanded and happier.

Leos of childbearing age are much more fertile than usual this year. But you seem to have mixed emotions about this. In general you love children, but this year you seem less enthusiastic about them than usual.

For some years you have been making the home a healthier place to live. Many of you have installed exercise equipment or other kinds of health gadgetry. This trend continues in the year ahead. The home is as much a health spa as a home. However, after August 11 you might start to make the house more of a play ground or entertainment centre too. Most likely you will be buying expensive home theatres, stereo systems and things of this nature.

The family circle expands in the coming year – from August 11 onwards. Generally this happens through birth or marriage, but not always. Sometimes you meet people who are like family to you.

Children (or children figures) seem more of a burden than usual in the year ahead. It will be a challenge to give them the right kind of discipline – neither too much nor too little.

A parent or parent figure is feeling better this year – less pessimistic. He or she starts to prosper and live more of the good life from August onwards. He or she could have moved recently, but if not it can still happen in the year ahead. Siblings or sibling figures will probably not move this year – nor does it seem advisable.

Finance and Career

A beautiful financial year ahead Leo, enjoy!

Jupiter has been in your own sign since July 2014, which is wonderful for finance. This transit does bring enhanced income to be sure, but what it really brings is a higher standard of life. Regardless of how much you actually earn, you live 'as if' you were wealthy. By this we don't mean that you're living like a millionaire, but more according to your own internal standards of the 'good life'. You eat finer foods and in better restaurants. You travel more. You dress better. Expensive personal items such as clothing, jewellery and accessories come to you. You have the wherewithal to enjoy all the leisure activities that you crave.

There is a beautiful spiritual lesson that we see here in your chart. First comes the optimism, the feeling of wealth, the appearance of wealth, the behaviour of wealth – this is Jupiter in your 1st house. Then comes the actual tangible wealth as Jupiter enters your money house. Note the order. One is the natural side effect of the other.

This is also a fortunate transit for speculations. It might not be a bad idea to invest harmless amounts of money on a lottery or some other type of speculation. Don't think that luck has to come in that way though; good luck can manifest in many other ways too. Follow your intuition.

If there is a financial flaw this year it can come from being overly speculative. Reckless. Leos are major risk-takers as it is, and with Jupiter in your sign now these tendencies are greatly magnified. Perhaps it would be advisable to set aside only a certain percentage of your income or assets for speculations of these kinds – 10 per cent maximum, say. This will limit any possible damage, but will allow you to benefit from Lady Luck who is with you this year.

What I like this year is that your chart is showing 'happy money' – money that is earned in enjoyable ways. Perhaps you are at a restaurant and you meet an important financial contact. It can happen at the golf course, tennis court or theatre too. Also it shows that you are enjoying the wealth that you have. You are spending on fun kinds of things.

Children and the children figures in your life seem important on the financial level this year. Probably you are spending more on them, but you can earn from them as well. Children often serve as motivators for their parents. Sometimes children have good financial ideas or connections. (They seem to have connections for you job seekers out there.) Investments in companies or businesses that cater to children seem profitable these days – music, entertainment, toy and games makers, things of this nature.

With fast-moving Mercury as your financial planet, there are many short-term trends in finance that depend on where Mercury is and the aspects he receives. These are best dealt with in the monthly reports.

Favourable financial numbers are 1, 6, 8 and 9.

Though the financial life is very good, this is not an especially strong career year. Your 10th house is basically empty. Only short-term planets will move through there – briefly. Generally this indicates that you are more or less satisfied on the career front and have no need to make major changes.

Career is ruled by another fast-moving planet, Venus. Thus there will be many short-term career trends that we will discuss in the monthly reports.

Love and Social Life

You have been in a banner love and social period since July 2014, and the trend continues in the year ahead until August. After that, your love goals have been more or less attained and there is less emphasis here in the latter months of the year.

Jupiter, the planet of abundance, fun and creativity, in your own sign is making beautiful aspects to your love planet Uranus, as we have mentioned. So there is no question that love is in the air. You have many options. There are many, many opportunities for 'fun' kinds of relationships, and many opportunities for more serious, committed kinds of relationships. You get to choose your preference. Both options are there.

In some cases, something that starts out as a love affair gets more serious. In some cases the committed relationship will have a lot of fun thrown in. In your case, this year, it will be hard to tell the difference between the two.

Singles working towards their first or second marriage have excellent prospects for marriage this year. You might not actually, literally, marry but you will have a relationship that is 'like' a marriage. You will be involved with people that you consider 'marriage material'. The stars impel but they don't compel. People never lose their free will.

Uranus has been in Aries, your 9th house, for some years now. Thus many of the love trends that we have written about in past years are still very much in effect. You are drawn to educated and refined kinds of people, mentor types. You have the aspects of someone who falls in love with the minister, rabbi, imam or professor. Foreigners attract you and love can easily happen in a foreign land. Religious and educational settings are also conducive to romance. You can meet that special someone at college or at a college function, at religious services or religious kinds of functions, or perhaps they are someone you worship with. Ministers or people in your place of worship enjoy playing cupid this year. The same is true with professors.

As in past years, fun and physical intimacy are important, but perhaps just as important is a philosophical compatibility. You and the beloved need to share a similar world view and a similar philosophy of life. You don't need to agree on every point, but you do have to on the basics. If this is lacking, it is doubtful whether the relationship can survive long term.

Those already married or in a relationship can enhance things and smooth over the rough spots by doing fun kinds of things together and through travel. If there are problems, go on some trip – someplace far away. Things should improve. For those of you of a religious bent, it might be good to worship together or to attend spiritual or philosophical classes or lectures as a couple.

Those of you in or working on their third marriage will have an expanded social life this year, but the marriage seems stable. Those working on their fourth marriage have excellent aspects for marriage and romance this year.

Even in a good love year, which you have, some months will be better than others. This is due to the transiting short-term planets and the aspects they make to your love planet. These short-term trends are best dealt with in the monthly reports.

Self-improvement

Saturn's move out of your 4th house this year (for most of the year anyway) not only eases the family situation but helps your spiritual growth as well. For you, more than most, mood is an important element in your spiritual practice. The Moon is your spiritual planet. Unless your feelings are engaged, there will be little success in your prayer or meditative life. In the year ahead you can expect more spiritual growth and more spiritual-type experiences. The dark moods are mostly over with.

Neptune, as we have mentioned, has been in your 8th house of transformation since 2012. Thus the cosmos is calling you (and it will happen in a gradual sort of way) to elevate the sexual act. It is not calling you to abstain from sex, but to raise sex from mere animal passion to an act of worship. Safe sex has been important from a health perspective for some years now. The elevation (or sublimation) of the sexual act is the only real safe sex there is. Condoms may protect you from physical viruses and bacteria, but they don't change the energy vibration. Low vibrations will find other ways to express themselves. You should study the esoteric teachings of sex – tantra and kundalini yoga of the East, or hermetic science in the West – as much as you can.

Neptune in the 8th house has an impact on the finances of the spouse, partner or current love. He or she is being called on to go deeper into the spiritual dimensions of wealth, to tap into the super-natural sources of supply, rather than the natural ones. It would be good to urge the beloved to read as much as possible on the subject and to start to apply it. This will transform their whole financial life.

With Uranus in your 9th house, your religious and philosophical life is very exciting. Modern scientific discoveries are challenging many of your religious and philosophical beliefs. This doesn't necessarily mean that they are wrong. Science is an evolving process and there are many things that the scientists do not yet understand. Still, these challenges are healthy. You are forced to go deeper into your beliefs, to examine them more closely and perhaps revise or discard some of them. In many cases the belief is wrong. And in many cases the belief is right but not in the way that you thought. All of this will bring clarity to this area of life. A revised philosophy of life – a revised world view – will change every other department of life in a positive way.

Month-by-month Forecasts

January

Best Days Overall: 6, 7, 8, 16, 17, 24, 25
Most Stressful Days Overall: 14, 15, 20, 21, 27, 28
Best Days for Love: 1, 6, 7, 12, 13, 16, 17, 20, 21, 22, 24, 25, 31
Best Days for Money: 1, 7, 8, 9, 10, 11, 12, 16, 17, 20, 21, 24, 25, 29, 30
Best Days for Career: 1, 12, 13, 21, 22, 27, 28, 31

You begin your year with the Western, social sector of your chart over-whelmingly dominant. From the 1st to the 15th 80 per cent of the planets are in the West, and this then rises to 90 per cent between the 15th and the 27th. This is quite a challenge for a Leo. You have to forget about yourself and devote yourself to others, to let others have their way (so long as it isn't destructive) and lead by following. The leader, which you are innately, derives his or her power from the consent of the governed and you are learning this in the month ahead. Leadership is a form of service to others. It is not about pomp, ego and personal power. As you focus on others you will find that your own needs will be met.

An important shift happens this month too. The planetary power will move (on the 20th) from the lower half of the Horoscope to the upper half, where it has been for the past six or so months. Symbolically speaking, dawn is breaking in your year. The Sun is coming up. The focus of life is now on the external world and your external goals. Career is starting to become important. You can start to downplay home and family issues now.

On the 20th you enter a yearly love and social peak, which will be much stronger than those of previous years. Uranus, your love planet, receives wonderful aspects. Love is very happy now and the unattached (if there are any of you left) will soon be attached. This is a great love month in a great love year.

Finance also looks strong this month. Jupiter is still in your sign and Mercury, your financial planet, is moving forward until the 21st. With the 6th house of health and work powerful until the 20th job seekers have good fortune. Money can come from second jobs or side jobs – especially until the 5th. After that date, as Mercury moves into your 7th house, your social connections become important financially. You love going to parties anyway, but now there are bottom-line benefits as well. You mingle with rich people and they seem supportive and provide opportunities.

After the 21st you should avoid making major purchases, investments or financial decisions. The financial life should be put under review during Mercury's retrograde. It is time to gain clarity in finances, not for overt action.

Health and energy are good until the 20th, but afterwards rest and relax more. Enhance the health in the ways mentioned in the yearly report. Drive more carefully from the 2nd to the 4th and avoid taking risks or stressful activities then as well. It will not be a good idea to take long trips at that time either.

February

Best Days Overall: 3, 4, 13, 14, 21, 22
Most Stressful Days Overall: 10, 11, 17, 18, 23, 24
Best Days for Love: 1, 2, 3, 4, 10, 11, 13, 14, 17, 18, 20, 21, 22
Best Days for Money: 3, 4, 5, 6, 7, 8, 9, 13, 14, 17, 18, 21, 22, 25, 26
Best Days for Career: 1, 2, 10, 11, 20, 21, 23, 24

Health and energy still needs watching until the 18th, but after that you should see a big improvement. Self-confidence and self-esteem could also be stronger, but there's a silver lining here. Less self-assertion is needed these days. Continue to let others have their way so long as it isn't destructive.

Mercury is still retrograde until the 11th, so be more cautious in financial decision-making. Best to avoid major purchases or investments until after he moves forward again. If you must make an important purchase, do your homework and make sure the vendor has a good returns policy. After the 11th financial clarity and confidence will return. Your financial good comes from the good graces of others and your social skills and social contacts remain important financially. This is the kind of month (and next month too) where you put the financial interests of others ahead of your own. This doesn't mean that you become any sort of victim, but that you have their interest firmly in mind.

Your financial planet spends the month in the sign of Aquarius. This reinforces the social dimension of finance discussed here. It also favours making money online through online businesses or activities. Technology is important financially in general, and you are probably spending more on this these days.

You are still in a yearly love and social peak until the 18th. You are much more popular than usual. You are on the beloved's side, in his or her corner, and he or she feels it and responds to it. There is some exciting sexual encounter between the 1st and the 3rd and from the 23rd to the 27th. On the 18th the Sun enters your 8th house of regeneration, making the rest of the month more sexually active. The tendency is to overdo things, but with Saturn making a square to your sexual planet, more moderation is needed.

On the 18th the spouse, partner or current love enters into a yearly financial peak. You seem very involved with this, taking an active role.

Students should do well this month – especially after the 11th as Mercury goes forward. The mind is sharp and clear. Learning and communication skills are enhanced. College-level students do better after the 20th. They seem serious and focused on their studies.

March

Best Days Overall: 2, 3, 12, 13, 20, 21, 29, 30, 31
Most Stressful Days Overall: 9, 10, 16, 17, 22, 23
Best Days for Love: 2, 3, 12, 13, 16, 17, 20, 21, 22, 23, 29, 30
Best Days for Money: 2, 3, 4, 5, 6, 7, 8, 12, 13, 18, 19, 20, 21, 29, 30, 31
Best Days for Career: 2, 3, 12, 13, 22, 23

Mars makes dynamic aspects with Pluto and Uranus from the 9th to the 12th. Not an especially good period for travel – though you have the urge. Try to schedule trips around this period. Grandchildren (if you have them) should be kept out of harm's way.

Your 8th house became powerful on the 18th of last month and remains so until March 20. On the 13th your financial planet enters this house as well. So, like last month, it is very important to hold the financial interests of others foremost in your mind. You earn as you enrich others. The financial intuition is excellent this month – especially from the 13th onwards. A financial hunch between the 17th and the 19th will prove good, but get verification.

A solar eclipse on the 20th occurs right on the cusp of your 9th house. Technically it occurs in the 8th house, but it is so close to the cusp of the 9th that it impacts on the affairs of the 9th house. You more than most signs, Leo, are strongly affected by every solar eclipse, as the Sun is your ruling planet. So reduce your schedule and stay out of harm's way as much as possible. The things that need to be done should be done, but anything else should be rescheduled.

If you haven't been careful in dietary matters, a physical detox could happen – which is a healthy thing. This is also when you start to redefine yourself – your personality, self-concept and image. Over the next six months you will adopt a new 'look' – a different wardrobe, hairstyle and image. These will more truly reflect who you are now at this stage of your life.

This eclipse affects students at the college or postgraduate level. There can be changes of courses, changes of schools and shake-ups in the current school. The policy of the school changes and it will impact on you. The eclipse also brings dramas in the lives of professors, mentors or ministers. There are shake-ups in your place of worship. This is another period where foreign travel is best avoided.

Since the affairs of the 8th house are also affected by this eclipse, the spouse, partner or current love will be making important financial changes: changes of thinking and strategy. The eclipse will reveal flaws in the old financial thinking.

Health is good this month, but take it easy during the eclipse period.

April

Best Days Overall: 8, 9, 17, 18, 25, 26, 27
Most Stressful Days Overall: 6, 7, 13, 14, 19, 20
Best Days for Love: 1, 2, 8, 9, 13, 14, 17, 18, 21, 22, 26, 27
Best Days for Money: 1, 2, 8, 9, 17, 18, 19, 20, 25, 26, 28, 29
Best Days for Career: 1, 2, 13, 19, 20, 21, 22

A lunar eclipse on the 4th brings change and disruption, but in spite of this, the month ahead is happy and successful. Many, many happy things are happening this month.

On the 20th, as the Sun crosses the Mid-heaven and enters your 10th house, you begin a yearly career peak. There is going to be much career success and progress now.

Also on the 20th, the planetary power starts to shift from the Western, social sector to the independent Eastern sector. And while the East will never be really dominant this year, you have a lot more independence and personal power than before. You no longer need to adapt yourself to situations but can change them or create them to your liking. You are entering a period where you can have things (more or less) your way. You are much more comfortable with a strong Eastern sector than a strong Western one.

Love is also getting red hot this month (it has been good all year). The Sun is travelling with your love planet Uranus until the 7th. This signals an important romantic meeting for singles, and better relations with the spouse or current love for those of you already in relationships. Yes, the eclipse is going to bring out some dirty laundry, but the closeness is there in your relationship. Often an eclipse indicates a marriage, and this could easily happen this month.

The lunar eclipse of the 4th occurs in your 3rd house of communication and affects siblings, sibling figures and neighbours. They have some dramatic, life-changing experiences. Cars and communication equipment get tested. Students not yet at college can change schools or educational plans. There are shake-ups in the administration of their school or in the rules. It will be a good idea to drive more carefully during this period too.

The family is affected by this eclipse, as it makes a stressful aspect to Pluto, your family planet. So, family members should be kept out of harm's way and especially a parent or parent figure. If there are flaws in your home, now is when you find out about them so you can make corrections. Be more patient with family members as they are more temperamental now. There could be some conflict between the beloved and your family during this period.

Health needs more attention from the 20th onwards. Overall, health is good, but this is not one of your better periods. Make sure to get enough rest.

May

Best Days Overall: 5, 6, 14, 15, 23, 24

Most Stressful Days Overall: 3, 4, 10, 11, 16, 17, 30, 31

Best Days for Love: 1, 2, 5, 6, 7, 10, 11, 12, 13, 14, 15, 21, 22, 23, 24, 30, 31

Best Days for Money: 1, 2, 5, 6, 10, 11, 14, 15, 18, 19, 23, 24, 25, 26, 27, 28, 29

Best Days for Career: 1, 2, 12, 13, 16, 17, 21, 22, 30, 31

You are still in a yearly career peak until the 21st and seem very successful. You are where you belong – on top, in charge, above everyone in your world. You are honoured and appreciated, not just for your professional achievements, but for who you are. Personal appearance seems a big issue in the career, so give it attention.

Health needs attention until the 21st and you can enhance your health in the ways mentioned in the yearly report. However, health and overall energy improve dramatically after the 21st.

Technically the Eastern sector of the Horoscope is stronger than the Western sector this month, but not by much. On the 1st and 2nd and from the 16th to the 29th the Eastern, independent sector will have the edge over the Western sector. This is when you will be at your most independent and most able to have things your way. However, from the 3rd to the 15th and from the 29th onwards both sectors will be balanced and neither one will dominate. This shows that your needs and others' needs need to be balanced. You are neither dependent nor independent, but a mixture of the two. If you want to create conditions to suit yourself, the first period is better.

On the 21st your 11th house of friends becomes strong and you enter a social period, although not necessarily a romantic one. (Romance is still very good and is still happening, but your focus is more on friendship and group activities.) This is an excellent period to enlarge your technology skills and knowledge, and for the study of science, astrology and astronomy.

Your financial planet spends the month in the 11th house. You are probably spending out on high-tech things. If so, try to wrap up deals before the 14th when Mercury starts to go backwards again. That bargain that looks so enticing will not seem such a bargain next month. As usual when the financial planet is in retrograde motion, it is time to review your finances and to gain mental clarity about them. Things are not what they seem or the way you think they are.

Finances are still good, in spite of Mercury's retrograde. There could be delays and glitches, but your overall prosperity is strong.

It is always good for you to accessorize with gold – both the metal and the colour. Now, you might want to add some blue too. Blue has been a good colour for you since the beginning of the year.

June

Best Days Overall: 2, 3, 10, 11, 20, 21
Most Stressful Days Overall: 6, 7, 13, 14, 27, 28
Best Days for Love: 1, 2, 3, 6, 7, 10, 11, 20, 21, 29, 30
Best Days for Money: 2, 3, 6, 7, 10, 11, 15, 16, 20, 21, 22, 23, 27, 29, 30
Best Days for Career: 1, 10, 11, 13, 14, 20, 21, 29, 30

Venus enters your sign on the 5th, bringing both career and love opportunities to you. You look and dress 'successful'. People see you as successful and you have this image this month. With Venus joining Jupiter in your sign it's party time – very good for both finance and fun. Technically this is not a yearly personal pleasure peak, that will happen next month, but it's a prelude.

Venus in your sign makes this an excellent month for clothes and accessory shopping. Your sense of style is exceptionally good. Aside from blue and gold, green is a good colour for you this month. After the 24th you might want to accessorize in red too.

Though Saturn moves back into Scorpio on the 15th (a stressful aspect for you), overall health is good and you shouldn't be impacted too much by this transit. The short-term planets are either in harmonious alignment or leaving you alone. You can enhance the health in the ways mentioned in the yearly report.

Your health planet in Scorpio for the next few months re-emphasizes the power of detox regimes for your health. Good emotional health is important too. If there is discord at home resolve it as quickly as you can.

Your 11th house of friends and groups is still powerful until June 11 and you should review last month's discussion of this. The 11th house is a happy house. It is the house where fondest hopes and wishes come true. And this is happening these days. As they happen, new hopes and wishes will arise – it is a never-ending process.

On the 21st as the Sun enters your 12th house you enter into a more spiritual kind of period. Many of you are in the creative arts, and this period brings great inspiration. Leos don't especially like solitude, but at this time you might crave it. Don't worry, there's nothing wrong with you. There are times when we need to be alone and feel our own energies – and connect with our true selves. A vacation from the world is not a bad idea. A spiritual-type retreat would be appealing.

Your financial planet moves forward on the 11th bringing financial clarity and confidence with it. It's fine to buy that new iPad, iPhone or new software now. Online activities boost the bottom line. Friends are also very helpful financially.

July

Best Days Overall: 8, 9, 17, 18, 26, 27, 28
Most Stressful Days Overall: 3, 4, 5, 10, 11, 24, 25, 31
Best Days for Love: 3, 4, 5, 8, 9, 17, 18, 26, 27, 31
Best Days for Money: 7, 8, 9, 17, 18, 19, 20, 27, 28, 29, 30
Best Days for Career: 8, 9, 10, 11, 17, 18, 26

The planetary power is at its maximum Eastern position during this month and the next. You are at the maximum limit of your personal power and independence. This is the time to make those personal changes that you need to make. The only problem is that planetary retrograde activity is at its peak this month too. Progress will tend to be slower. So take your time.

Your 12th house of spirituality is still very powerful until the 21st. This is the preparatory period for your personal new year, which will begin on your birthday. With some this will happen this month and with others next month. The personal new year is a very important time and one should start it on the right footing. Your Solar Return is about to happen and the chart cast for this return will show the patterns for the year ahead. The steps you take now will have a profound influence on the year ahead until your next birthday, so it is a good idea to review the past year and see what has been accomplished, and what still needs to be done. Acknowledge mistakes and correct them. (This is the meaning of atonement.) Pat yourself on the back for the good that was achieved. Most importantly, set goals for the coming year. Review your goals every night before you go to sleep.

There are important spiritual breakthroughs happening this month. Your 12th house is powerful, and, most interestingly, the ruler of the 12th house, the Moon, will be full twice this month. This is a very rare occurrence. You will receive much revelation about your future paths now.

On the 23rd, as the Sun crosses the Ascendant and moves into your 1st house, you enter a yearly personal pleasure peak. You've been living the good life this year anyway, and now even more so. You do need to be careful not to overindulge yourself – especially this month

– as you can easily pile on the pounds. However, this is not only a good period for enjoying all the pleasures of the body, but it's also excellent for getting the body and image into shape.

The month ahead is also prosperous. Your financial planet Mercury is moving very fast, which shows fast financial progress. It shows confidence, someone who covers a lot of financial territory. Until the 8th money comes through friends, through online activities and through involvement with groups and organizations; from the 8th to the 23rd money comes through your intuition. It is a time for 'miracle money' rather than 'natural money'.

On the 23rd Mercury travels with the Sun and crosses the Ascendant, signalling a powerful financial period. Windfalls come to you and there is luck in speculations. Financial opportunity seeks you out.

August

Best Days Overall: 4, 5, 13, 14, 23, 24, 31
Most Stressful Days Overall: 1, 6, 7, 20, 21, 22, 27, 28
Best Days for Love: 1, 4, 5, 13, 14, 23, 24, 27, 28, 31
Best Days for Money: 5, 15, 16, 17, 25, 26, 27
Best Days for Career: 5, 6, 7, 14, 23, 24, 31

Last month the planetary power made an important shift. The lower, subjective sector of the Horoscope started to become powerful. Career goals have more or less been achieved for the time being. Now it is time to build up the forces for your next career push early next year. This is the time, symbolically speaking, to get a good night's sleep, so that the next career push will happen properly. So it is good to focus on your family, the domestic situation and your emotional well-being. If these are right, the career will take care of itself naturally.

The month ahead looks very prosperous. Jupiter enters your money house on the 11th. Your financial planet, Mercury, enters on the 7th and the Sun moves there on the 23rd. You begin a yearly financial peak: for some of you this will be a lifetime peak and for others a multi-year peak. Your money house is filled with beneficent planets this month. There is a cosmic conspiracy to prosper you. There is luck in speculations these days – especially from the 26th to the 28th.

It looks like there is foreign travel happening this month too. Mars, the ruler of your 9th house, which governs travel, moves into your sign on the 9th and spends the rest of the month there. The Sun travels with Jupiter from the 26th to the 28th which also signals travel. These same aspects are very favourable to college-level or postgraduate students. Those applying to college get good news this period.

The love life has been good all year, and particularly so since the 23rd of last month. By now you should be involved in some happy relationship and there is less need to focus here.

Your career planet Venus travels with Jupiter from the 3rd to the 6th. This brings career advancement and opportunity. However, as we mentioned, the focus is starting to shift now. Career opportunities that come should feel emotionally comfortable and should not uproot the family. If not, you can pass on them for now.

Health and energy are excellent these days, in spite of Saturn's stressful aspect. You look good, have plenty of charisma and excel in exercise and athletics. (You are at your personal best this month.)

September

Best Days Overall: 1, 9, 10, 19, 20, 28, 29
Most Stressful Days Overall: 2, 3, 17, 18, 24, 25, 30
Best Days for Love: 1, 9, 10, 19, 20, 24, 25, 28, 29
Best Days for Money: 2, 4, 5, 12, 13, 14, 15, 24, 25, 30
Best Days for Career: 1, 2, 3, 9, 10, 19, 20, 28, 29, 30

There's a lot happening this month. Saturn is moving away from his stressful aspect on the 18th. Mars moves into your money house on the 25th – a good financial signal. And most importantly, there are two eclipses this month. This is guaranteed to shake up the status quo and bring drama and change. Leo loves drama and excitement. A day without drama is like a day without sunshine. You will certainly have plenty this month.

The solar eclipse of the 13th occurs in your money house in the midst of a yearly financial peak. So, important financial changes are happening. My reading of this is that perhaps you have underestimated yourself financially and the eclipse is rectifying things. The financial changes that you make (changes of thinking and strategy) will be good. The eclipse is blasting way financial barriers and blockages. The cosmos will do whatever it takes to remove these things and it can be quite dramatic. There are life-changing events in the lives of the money people in your life.

Every solar eclipse brings a redefinition of your image, personality and self-concept and this one is no different. This will be a six-month process. By the end of it you will dress and accessorize differently. You will project a new 'look'. Solar eclipses are always powerful on you, regardless of where they occur, so reduce your schedule and take it nice and easy during this period – there's no need to tempt fate by indulging in risky or stressful activities.

The lunar eclipse of the 28th (in the Americas it is on the 27th) is more benign for you, but it won't hurt to reduce your schedule anyway. This one occurs in your 9th house. For students – at college level or above – it shows changes of schools, perhaps changes of courses, changes in the educational plans or curriculum. Often there are shake-ups in the college. Often there are rule changes or changes of policy. If you are involved in legal matters, there is a dramatic move forward this period. Action starts to happen here, one way or another. In your chart it looks positive.

Every lunar eclipse affects your spiritual life. Events happen that impel you to change teachers or teachings or your spiritual practice. Sometimes it indicates shake-ups in a charity or spiritual organization that you're involved with. Sometimes it signals life-changing events occurring in the lives of guru or mentor figures in your life. The dream life will tend to be more active under this kind of eclipse, but don't give too much value to it. The astral plane gets stirred up during eclipses and visions are not very reliable. Be more patient with family members this period. They can be more temperamental than usual. Foreign travel is not advisable at this time. If you must travel, schedule your trip around the eclipse period.

October

Best Days Overall: 6, 7, 8, 16, 17, 18, 25, 26

Most Stressful Days Overall: 1, 14, 15, 21, 22, 27, 28

Best Days for Love: 6, 7, 8, 9, 16, 17, 19, 20, 21, 22, 25, 26, 27, 28

Best Days for Money: 1, 2, 3, 9, 10, 11, 12, 13, 19, 20, 22, 23, 27, 28, 29

Best Days for Career: 1, 8, 9, 19, 20, 27, 28

Although you passed your yearly financial peak last month, the money house is still very powerful, and October is a prosperous month. Your financial planet, retrograde since the 17th of last month, starts to move forward again on the 9th so there is financial clarity and confidence. Mars, who is beneficent in your Horoscope, will be in the money house all month and Venus, another beneficent planet, moves in on the 8th.

Money can come to you in many ways. Speculations still prove favourable – especially from the 15th to the 18th and from the 24th to the 27th. Venus's arrival in the money house shows that you have the financial favour of bosses, parents or parent figures, the government and authority figures. They support your financial goals. Pay rises and promotions can happen this month. Money can come from government payments. The government can change rules in a way that benefits you financially.

Though career is not that important these days, success is still happening – especially from the 24th to the 27th. Planetary power below the horizon of your Horoscope doesn't mean that you completely ignore the career, only that you de-emphasize it.

Your 3rd house of communication and intellectual interests became powerful on September 23 and remains powerful until the 23rd of this month. It is good to pursue your intellectual interests both from a personal and from a financial perspective. Mercury, your financial planet, spends the month in the 3rd house. This indicates it is a good month to buy communication equipment – even a car if you need it – and very good for taking courses and attending seminars in subjects that interest you. It would be good to catch up on your reading and to spend money on furthering your education.

Sales, marketing and PR are always important for you, but this month even more so. Those of you involved in these professions should have a successful month.

On the 23rd, the Sun enters your 4th house of home and family. So the focus is on the family – as it should be. However, the 4th house brings other interests – psychological type interests. It is a great period for making psychological breakthroughs, gaining insights into why we feel as we do.

When the 4th house is powerful, old memories come up for review. This is nature's natural healing and digestive process. As we review old memories and look at them from our present vantage point, a redefinition happens. What seemed like a disaster when it happened (perhaps as a child) is seen to be a blessing from one's present state. The pain of an old relationship is seen as good from the perspective of hindsight. It is wonderful that the relationship broke up. The cosmos did you a big favour. So this is a month for psychological and emotional healing.

November

Best Days Overall: 3, 4, 13, 14, 22, 30
Most Stressful Days Overall: 10, 11, 17, 18, 24, 25
Best Days for Love: 3, 4, 6, 7, 13, 14, 17, 18, 21, 22, 26, 27, 30
Best Days for Money: 5, 6, 10, 11, 12, 15, 16, 21, 24, 25, 30
Best Days for Career: 6, 7, 17, 18, 24, 25, 26, 27

Overall your health is excellent, but since the 23rd of last month it has been a bit more delicate. This is not one of your best health periods. Make sure to get enough rest. Enhance your health in the ways mentioned in the yearly report. When your energy is low pre-existing conditions can act up and seem worse than they were before. Raise the energy level and the condition abates. Health and energy will improve dramatically from the 22nd onwards.

Finances are still excellent but not as dominant as they have been the past few months. The money house is less active these days.

Last month on the 23rd the planetary power began to shift from the independent East to the social West. This month the shift gets stronger as Mercury moves from the East to the West on the 2nd. The planetary power is now moving away from you, becoming more distant from you. The energy is flowing towards others and they should be your focus. Self-interest is wonderful (so long as it isn't destructive). Progress, new inventions and new technologies have always come from people pursuing their self-interest. But now you are in a different stage of your cycle. Your good comes through the good graces of others and not so much from personal initiative or effort. It is time to cultivate your social skills. It is more difficult now to change conditions to your liking. Best to adapt to them as best you can. If you have created well in the past few months, conditions should be pleasant for you. If not, note any improvements that can be made, and you can make these changes during your next independent cycle next year.

Your 4th house of home and family continues to be powerful until the 22nd. Review our discussion of this last month.

On the 22nd the Sun enters your 5th house of enjoyment and you begin another of your yearly personal pleasure peaks. Time to party and have fun. It's a kind of Leo paradise. The cosmos urges you to do what you most love to do. Leos of childbearing age have been very fertile for the past two years, and this month – after the 22nd – you are more so than ever.

A happy job opportunity comes on the 29th or 30th. Try to stay out of harm's way that period. Make sure you have a nice easy schedule and avoid confrontations.

December

Best Days Overall: 1, 10, 11, 19, 20, 27, 28, 29
Most Stressful Days Overall: 7, 8, 9, 14, 15, 16, 21, 22
Best Days for Love: 1, 7, 10, 11, 14, 15, 16, 17, 18, 19, 20, 25, 26, 27, 28, 29
Best Days for Money: 1, 2, 3, 4, 12, 13, 21, 22, 30, 31
Best Days for Career: 7, 17, 18, 21, 22, 25, 26

Job seekers had wonderful opportunities last month and there are more good opportunities in the month ahead – especially after the 21st. After the 21st the party period is about over and you take a more serious approach to life (serious in Leo terms). You are in the mood for work and employers pick up on this.

Leos dislike details, but during this period you can handle them better. So if you have detail-oriented tasks to do – arranging files, cleaning the hard drive, doing accounts or bookkeeping – this is a good period to do them in.

Many of you are travelling this month – it is the holiday season after all. But try to avoid making trips between the 5th and the 12th.

Health and energy are good now. After the 21st your attention seems more focused here (hopefully you are not over-focusing). It would be good to initiate health regimes and diets during this period – focus on prevention and healthy lifestyles. You can enhance the health further along the lines mentioned in the yearly report.

Overall you are in a prosperity cycle that will continue well into next year. But until the 20th there could be some bumps along the way this month. The main danger is over-spending. Mercury will conjunct Pluto from the 18th to the 20th. This shows spending on the home and family. Perhaps there are some financial disagreements with a parent or parent figure. However, this aspect is good for borrowing if you need to, and good for paying down debt. Mercury will square Uranus from the 20th to the 21st, indicating some financial upheaval or distur-bance. Perhaps an unexpected expense is incurred that forces financial change. You seem in some financial disagreement with the spouse, partner or current love now too. But this is a short-term problem. Overall prosperity is not affected. As Mercury moves away from his square to Uranus he will start making good aspects to Jupiter after the 21st. This brings prosperity and financial increase. You will not lack for any material thing this month.

Love has been wonderful all year and is still excellent until the 21st. After that more compromise is necessary with the beloved. You seem in disagreement over things.

Your love planet, Uranus, has been retrograde for many months. However, on the 26th it starts moving forward again, bringing more clarity in love. The love life will get much smoother next month.

Virgo

ɱ

THE VIRGIN

Birthdays from
22nd August to
22nd September

Personality Profile

VIRGO AT A GLANCE

Element – Earth
  Ruling Planet – Mercury
  Career Planet – Mercury
  Love Planet – Neptune
  Money Planet – Venus
  Planet of Home and Family Life – Jupiter
  Planet of Health and Work – Uranus
  Planet of Pleasure – Saturn
  Planet of Sexuality – Mars

Colours – earth tones, ochre, orange, yellow

Colour that promotes love, romance and social harmony – aqua blue

Colour that promotes earning power – jade green

Gems – agate, hyacinth

Metal – quicksilver

Scents – lavender, lilac, lily of the valley, storax

Quality – mutable (= flexibility)

Quality most needed for balance – a broader perspective

Strongest virtues – mental agility, analytical skills, ability to pay attention to detail, healing powers

Deepest needs – to be useful and productive

Characteristic to avoid – destructive criticism

Signs of greatest overall compatibility – Taurus, Capricorn

Signs of greatest overall incompatibility – Gemini, Sagittarius, Pisces

Sign most helpful to career – Gemini

Sign most helpful for emotional support – Sagittarius

Sign most helpful financially – Libra

Sign best for marriage and/or partnerships – Pisces

Sign most helpful for creative projects – Capricorn

Best Sign to have fun with – Capricorn

Signs most helpful in spiritual matters – Taurus, Leo

Best day of the week – Wednesday

Understanding a Virgo

The virgin is a particularly fitting symbol for those born under the sign of Virgo. If you meditate on the image of the virgin you will get a good understanding of the essence of the Virgo type. The virgin is, of course, a symbol of purity and innocence – not naïve, but pure. A virginal object has not been touched. A virgin field is land that is true to itself, the way it has always been. The same is true of virgin forest: it is pristine, unaltered.

Apply the idea of purity to the thought processes, emotional life, physical body and activities and projects of the everyday world, and you can see how Virgos approach life. Virgos desire the pure expression of the ideal in their mind, body and affairs. If they find impurities they will attempt to clear them away.

Impurities are the beginning of disorder, unhappiness and uneasiness. The job of the Virgo is to eject all impurities and keep only that which the body and mind can use and assimilate.

The secrets of good health are here revealed: 90 per cent of the art of staying well is maintaining a pure mind, a pure body and pure emotions. When you introduce more impurities than your mind and body can deal with, you will have what is known as 'dis-ease'. It is no wonder that Virgos make great doctors, nurses, healers and dieticians. They have an innate understanding of good health and they realize that good health is more than just physical. In all aspects of life, if you want a project to be successful it must be kept as pure as possible. It must be protected against the adverse elements that will try to undermine it. This is the secret behind Virgo's awesome technical proficiency.

One could talk about Virgo's analytical powers – which are formidable. One could talk about their perfectionism and their almost superhuman attention to detail. But this would be to miss the point. All of these virtues are manifestations of a Virgo's desire for purity and perfection – a world without Virgos would have ruined itself long ago.

A vice is nothing more than a virtue turned inside out, misapplied or used in the wrong context. Virgos' apparent vices come from their inherent virtue. Their analytical powers, which should be used for healing, helping or perfecting a project in the world, sometimes get misapplied and turned against people. Their critical faculties, which should be used constructively to perfect a strategy or proposal, can sometimes be used destructively to harm or wound. Their urge to perfection can turn into worry and lack of confidence; their natural humility can become self-denial and self-abasement. When Virgos turn negative they are apt to turn their devastating criticism on themselves, sowing the seeds of self-destruction.

Finance

Virgos have all the attitudes that create wealth. They are hard-working, industrious, efficient, organized, thrifty, productive and eager to serve. A developed Virgo is every employer's dream. But until Virgos master some of the social graces of Libra they will not even come close to fulfilling their financial potential. Purity and perfectionism, if not handled correctly or gracefully, can be very trying to others. Friction in human relationships can be devastating not only to your pet projects but – indirectly – to your wallet as well.

Virgos are quite interested in their financial security. Being hard-working, they know the true value of money. They do not like to take risks with their money, preferring to save for their retirement or for a rainy day. Virgos usually make prudent, calculated investments that involve a minimum of risk. These investments and savings usually work out well, helping Virgos to achieve the financial security they seek. The rich or even not-so-rich Virgo also likes to help his or her friends in need.

Career and Public Image

Virgos reach their full potential when they can communicate their knowledge in such a way that others can understand it. In order to get their ideas across better, Virgos need to develop greater verbal skills and fewer judgemental ways of expressing themselves. Virgos look up to teachers and communicators; they like their bosses to be good communicators. Virgos will probably not respect a superior who is not their intellectual equal – no matter how much money or power that superior has. Virgos themselves like to be perceived by others as being educated and intellectual.

The natural humility of Virgos often inhibits them from fulfilling their great ambitions, from acquiring name and fame. Virgos should indulge in a little more self-promotion if they are going to reach their career goals. They need to push themselves with the same ardour that they would use to foster others.

At work Virgos like to stay active. They are willing to learn any type of job as long as it serves their ultimate goal of financial security. Virgos may change occupations several times during their professional lives, until they find the one they really enjoy. Virgos work well with other people, are not afraid to work hard and always fulfil their responsibilities.

Love and Relationships

If you are an analyst or a critic you must, out of necessity, narrow your scope. You have to focus on a part and not the whole; this can create a temporary narrow-mindedness. Virgos do not like this kind of person. They like their partners to be broad-minded, with depth and vision. Virgos seek to get this broad-minded quality from their partners, since they sometimes lack it themselves.

Virgos are perfectionists in love just as they are in other areas of life. They need partners who are tolerant, open-minded and easy-going. If you are in love with a Virgo do not waste time on impractical romantic gestures. Do practical and useful things for him or her – this is what will be appreciated and what will be done for you.

Virgos express their love through pragmatic and useful gestures, so do not be put off because your Virgo partner does not say 'I love you' day-in and day-out. Virgos are not that type. If they love you, they will demonstrate it in practical ways. They will always be there for you; they will show an interest in your health and finances; they will fix your sink or repair your video recorder. Virgos deem these actions to be superior to sending flowers, chocolates or Valentine cards.

In love affairs Virgos are not particularly passionate or spontaneous. If you are in love with a Virgo, do not take this personally. It does not mean that you are not alluring enough or that your Virgo partner does not love or like you. It is just the way Virgos are. What they lack in passion they make up for in dedication and loyalty.

Home and Domestic Life

It goes without saying that the home of a Virgo will be spotless, sanitized and orderly. Everything will be in its proper place – and don't you dare move anything about! For Virgos to find domestic bliss they need to ease up a bit in the home, to allow their partner and children more freedom and to be more generous and open-minded. Family members are not to be analysed under a microscope, they are individuals with their own virtues to express.

With these small difficulties resolved, Virgos like to stay in and entertain at home. They make good hosts and they like to keep their friends and families happy and entertained at family and social gatherings. Virgos love children, but they are strict with them – at times – since they want to make sure their children are brought up with the correct sense of family and values.

Horoscope for 2015

Major Trends

Ever since Jupiter entered your 12th house in July 2014 you have been in an intense spiritual period. You are growing in a spiritual kind of way – internally. Your capacities are being enlarged. Many of the goals that seemed unattainable in the past are now seen as very attainable. Your understanding of life and yourself is greatly increased. This is not yet seen on the surface. It is all secret. But come August 11, these inner changes will start to become visible. You enter a multi-year prosperity cycle.

When a spiritual kind of breakthrough happens (and you've had many last year and will have more in the coming year) it is a most joyous kind of experience. The soul is liberated. The whole outlook on life changes. Certain oppressive thoughts or feelings are overcome and will never trouble you again. Thus you become free to attain personal and financial goals.

Saturn has been in your 3rd house of communication and intellectual interests for some years now, which is a difficult aspect for students. They needed to work harder in their studies. Learning has not been a joy (as it is supposed to be) but a discipline and a chore. Happily, this year, Saturn has left this position and learning should go easier.

Saturn's move into Sagittarius late last year signals a need to watch your energy more. Energy levels are not what you are used to. More details on this later.

Neptune has been in your 7th house of love since July 2012. This transit refines and elevates the whole love life. The love life is being spiritualized. There's more on this later.

Uranus has been in your 8th house of transformation for some years now. Thus there is much sexual experimentation going on these days. The rule books are getting thrown out and you learn, by trial and error, what works for you.

Your important areas of interest this year are the body, image and personal pleasure (from August 11 onwards); communication and intellectual interests (from June 15 to September 18); home and family (January 1 to June 15 and September 18 onwards); children, fun and creativity; love and romance; sex, personal reinvention, occult studies, debt and the repayment of debt; and spirituality (until August 11).

Your paths of greatest fulfilment this year are spirituality (until August 11); the body, image and personal pleasure (from August 11 onwards); and finance (until November 13).

Health

(Please note that this is an astrological perspective on health and not a medical one. In days of yore there was no difference, these perspectives were identical. But now there could be quite a difference. For a medical perspective, please consult your doctor or health practitioner.)

Virgos are always focused on health, but this year less so than usual. Your 6th house is not a house of power.

Saturn, as we mentioned, is for most of the year in stressful aspect with you. Neptune too. By themselves these planets are not enough to cause sickness, but when they are joined by the short-term planets you become more vulnerable to problems. This year, your most vulnerable periods will be February 18 to March 20, May 21 to June 20 and November 22 to December 21. Be sure to rest and relax more those periods. Spend more time in health spas and treat yourself to massage or reflexology treatments.

The important thing is to maintain high energy levels. The body, as we understand it in astrology, is a dynamic energy system. It responds to and obeys the laws of energy. Because this is so, the energy changes caused by the movement of the planets affect the body either positively or negatively. When the cosmic energy is lower than usual we just need more rest. The cosmos forces us to make tough decisions – to focus on the things that are really important and to let lesser things go. The idea is to maximize your energy and not fritter it away on inessentials.

There is much that can be done to enhance the health and prevent problems from developing. Give more attention to the following areas: the small intestine; the ankles and calves; the head and face; and the adrenals. Reflex points for these areas are shown in the diagram above.

Important foot reflexology points for the year ahead

Try to massage the whole foot on a regular basis, but pay extra attention to the points highlighted on the chart. When you massage, be aware of 'sore spots', as these need special attention. It is also a good idea to massage the ankles and the tops of the feet.

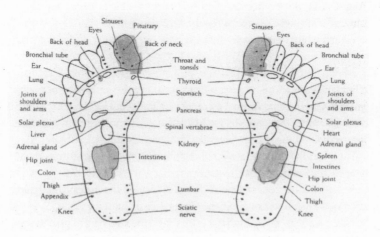

The small intestine is ruled by Virgo and is always important for you. Detoxing the small intestine is always a beneficial health thing for you to do. The ankles and calves likewise are important for Virgo. These should be regularly massaged. Give the ankles more support when exercising.

Regular scalp and face massage will be wonderful. Craniosacral therapy will also be good. When you massage the head and face you are not only strengthening these areas but the whole body as well, as the head and face contain reflexes to the entire body.

To keep the adrenals healthy you should try to avoid anger and fear, as these two emotions particularly stress the adrenals.

Your health planet Uranus is in your 8th house of regeneration this year. Thus safe sex and sexual moderation are also important these days. Generally the tendency is to overdo it. But if you listen to your body (and not your mind) you will know when enough is enough.

This transit also signals the power of detox regimes, and you respond very well to these things. The 8th house also rules surgery and you seem to have a tendency towards this – but detoxing will often achieve the same thing, although it takes longer. Get second opinions.

Home and Family

Your 4th house of home and family is prominent this year – and challenging. This area is perhaps the most challenging in your Horoscope.

Saturn moved into your 4th house very late last year and will spend most of the year ahead here (although it will retrograde back into your 3rd house for a few months). You are taking on more family responsibilities this year. The responsibilities seem heavy – burdensome – and you can't really avoid them. You must just smile and lift the load. These responsibilities can come from children or children figures in your life. Virgos of childbearing age become unusually fertile after August 11.

There seems to be a love-hate relationship with a parent or parent figure. On the one hand this parent figure is very devoted to you and seems generous (especially after August 11). On the other hand he or she brings more responsibilities – and perhaps more control.

Though there will be opportunities to move in the coming year – after August 11 – a move doesn't seem advisable just yet. Perhaps you feel cramped for space, but it is better to use your existing space more creatively than to move. A move seems to have better aspects a few years down the road.

The cosmos is bringing right order to the whole family and domestic situation this year. This will go on well into next year too. Family relationships are getting reorganized, as is the domestic routine.

The family situation doesn't seem like much fun this year, so it is understandable that you are trying to inject some fun in the home. You seem to be buying entertainment gadgetry, and perhaps sports equipment. You are working to make the home an entertainment centre as much as a home.

A parent or parent figure could be moving in with you or close to you after August 11. The marriage of a parent or parent figure seems stressed this year and is getting a severe testing.

Children or children figures in your life are very restless these days and could have multiple moves. Siblings or sibling figures could move this year – they have good opportunities for this. Grandchildren (if you have them) could also be moving this year. The moves seem happy.

Finance and Career

The year ahead seems prosperous Virgo, enjoy.

The north node of the Moon will spend most of the year ahead in your money house. This shows that financial activities bring fulfilment this year. Sometimes it also indicates 'excess' – but this is a nice problem to have.

The spouse, partner or current love could be feeling the opposite – deficiency in earnings or in the financial state. He or she seems unstable in this department, taking major risks, going in new directions, and this can produce a feeling of insecurity.

There are other indicators of prosperity in your chart too. Jupiter, as we have mentioned, will enter your sign on August 11. By itself this doesn't produce tangible wealth, but it produces the feeling of wealth, the lifestyle of wealth (each according to their stage and status in life) or the image of wealth. One lives on a grander scale. One lives 'as if' one were rich. And, generally, the wherewithal for this comes. You will dress and accessorize more expensively. You will project an image of wealth and others will perceive you as prospering.

Family support seems strong from August 11 onwards. A parent or parent figure seems generous.

Venus is your financial planet. And, as our regular readers know, she is a fast-moving planet. In the course of a year she will move through all the signs and houses of your Horoscope. Thus money and financial opportunities come to you in many ways and through many people and situations. It all depends on where Venus is at a given time and the aspects she receives. These short-term trends are best dealt with in the monthly reports.

Venus will make a rare retrograde from July 25 to September 6. She only does this once every two years or so. These retrogrades are not so good for overt financial actions or decision-making, but they are excellent for a review of the financial situation. Then, when mental clarity has been attained, you will be ready to move forward when Venus does. The financial decisions will then be much better and more realistic.

There will be a lunar eclipse in your money house on April 4. This will produce necessary financial changes – generally though an upheaval or crisis. The cosmos tends to force you to make any changes that have long been needed.

The spouse, partner or current love will be making many financial changes in the coming year. Their earnings, as we mentioned above, will be unstable and erratic. Sometimes they will be sky high – much more than was envisioned, but sometimes there will be serious lows too. He or she will need to learn to 'smooth out' earnings, to set aside money from the good times to cover the bad times.

Job seekers have had excellent aspects since July last year and this trend continues into the year ahead – especially until August 11. If a new – and good – job hasn't yet materialized, it can still happen in the year ahead. Job seekers should look to family and family connections – this seems to be the source. It might also be good to get involved in charities or good causes as they too can lead to employment.

Career seems fairly static this year – some years are like that. You seem content with things as they are.

Love and Social Life

Twenty thirteen – especially the latter part – and 2014 were excellent love years for you. Many of you entered into serious kinds of relationships. Many of you married. This year, your relationship will get tested. Saturn is making stressful aspects to your love planet Neptune most of the year. There will be some respite (a little) from June 15 to September 18, when Saturn is retrograde, but basically Saturn impacts on your love planet for most of the year ahead.

These testings are seldom pleasant, but they are good. They tend to destroy relationships that were unsound or shaky to begin with. This is good. Only the best will do for you. The stress testing will reveal if love is real. And, if love isn't real, why should we mourn when it dissolves? If love is real the testing will only make it stronger. The stress will show the weak areas so that they can be corrected. Fundamentally sound relationships will only get better.

Singles will probably not date as much as usual. You seem more picky than is usual for you, which is probably a good thing. Your focus will be on quality rather than quantity. Social activity in general is less than usual and for the same reasons.

If you are involved in business kinds of partnerships these too will get tested in the year ahead; shaky ones can dissolve.

Singles are not likely to marry in the coming year, and probably it is not advisable at this time. Love, if it is real, needs time to develop – give it the time that it needs. There's no rush.

By nature you are attracted to spiritual and creative kinds of people. You like the poet, the musician, the actor or dancer. You like the psychic or the yogi. But ever since Neptune moved into Pisces in 2012 this attraction has become even stronger.

You are always idealistic in love. You have always searched for the perfect love. And these days your idealism is much stronger than usual. The problem here is that your standards are so high that few mortals can live up to them. Thus there is always this subtle feeling of dissatisfaction even in basically good relationships. This problem too is exacerbated these days. The cosmos has put an exclamation mark on it.

Singles are likely to meet many who seem ideal these days. The good news is that Saturn will show – pretty quickly – whether the potential partner is really ideal or not.

Favourable numbers for love are 1, 12 and 18.

Self-improvement

We mentioned earlier that you are in a very spiritual period this year, as you were last year too. So, if you are not yet on a spiritual path, this is a good time to start. Those already on such a path will make enormous progress this year. Those not involved in spirituality are likely to be more involved with drugs or alcohol – the false proxies for spiritual development.

The dream life this year will be overactive and in many cases prophetic. Pay attention to your dreams; write them down in the morning when you get up. You are being instructed in your dreams on many important issues.

There will be increased extrasensory perception (ESP) and psychic phenomena this year. Those on a spiritual path will understand these things as they are quite common. But those not yet on a path will have what they call 'strange coincidences'. You think of someone and five minutes later they call. You have an urge to avoid a certain road and later you find out there was an accident there. You open a book and you find the exact page you're looking for. The invisible world is letting you know that it's around. There's more to life than what you see with your eyes.

Many people feel blocked from following their dreams. In some cases it is lack of money, sometimes lack of connections, sometimes a feeling of lack of ability. The beauty of the spiritual breakthroughs that are happening this year is that you will see that these so-called obstructions were nothing more than beliefs you held in your mind. These manifested as physical obstructions. When you let go of these limiting beliefs, the outer obstructions disappear.

Virgo naturally gravitates to the solar approach to spirituality. The esoteric side of Christianity is especially appealing. This is good, but this year there is a need to exalt the feelings, to get the feelings engaged in the spiritual practice. When you are in a right mood, Divine contact will be easy.

The love life will go better if you take a more realistic view of perfection. Here on Earth, perfection is not given to us on a silver platter. It is something we have to create. If love isn't yet perfect, do things that will improve the situation. Little by little you will get closer to your ideal. You will be on the road to perfection – and this is what is important. If the love life is better today than it was yesterday, you are successful, though the ideal still seems far off.

Saturn in the 4th house most of the year often shows tendencies to repression of feeling. And this generally leads to depression. In many cases you feel unsafe expressing what you really feel. Repression is not the right way to go about things. If you have access to a counsellor or therapist, that would be wonderful. If not, it is useful to learn safe ways to express negative feelings. Refer to my book *A Technique For Meditation* for various ways to do this.

Month-by-month Forecasts

January

Best Days Overall: 9, 10, 18, 19, 27, 28
Most Stressful Days Overall: 2, 3, 16, 17, 22, 23, 29, 30
Best Days for Love: 1, 4, 12, 13, 14, 21, 22, 23, 31
Best Days for Money: 1, 7, 8, 11, 12, 13, 16, 17, 21, 22, 24, 25, 31
Best Days for Career: 4, 14, 22, 23, 31

Your personal solar cycle is in its waxing (growing) phase. The universal solar cycle is also waxing. Almost all of the planets are moving forward. This is an excellent month to start new projects or launch new products into the world. The 1st to the 5th would be the best days, but after the 21st is also very acceptable. You will have strong cosmic support and momentum for your launch.

You begin your year with the Western, social sector of your chart totally dominant. The vast majority of the planets are in the West. The planetary power is distant from you and favours others. So, you are in an 'unselfish' stage of your cycle. Others come first. Your way is probably not the best way these days. Let others have their way, so long as it isn't destructive. If conditions irk you, make note of improvements that can be made and when your cycle of personal independence comes later on in the year, it will be easier to make the changes. This is a time for taking a vacation from yourself and your personal interests and needs.

You begin your year in the midst of a yearly personal pleasure peak. (You will have another near your next birthday.) So until the 20th have fun; explore the rapture side of life.

Your 6th house of health and work is powerful this month – especially after the 20th. Half of the planets are either there or moving through there this month. This is good news for job seekers. There are many opportunities happening now. Virgos are always productive workers but this month even more so.

Most of the planets are below the horizon in the lower half of your chart this month. Mercury, your career (and personal) planet is retrograde from the 21st onwards. Keep the focus on the family and your emotional well-being. The career can take a back seat for a while. If emotional issues are resolved the career will fall into place.

Health and energy are good this month, although they are better before the 20th than after it. Virgo is always focused on health but this month more so than usual. The real danger now is hypersensitivity to health issues. Be careful you don't create problems where none really exist.

February

Best Days Overall: 5, 6, 7, 15, 16, 23, 24
Most Stressful Days Overall: 13, 14, 19, 20, 25, 26
Best Days for Love: 1, 2, 10, 11, 19, 20, 21
Best Days for Money: 1, 2, 3, 4, 8, 9, 10, 11, 13, 14, 20, 21, 22
Best Days for Career: 8, 9, 17, 18, 25, 26

Health and energy become more delicate this month after the 18th. Make sure you get enough sleep. Review our health discussion in the yearly report. When energy is low pre-existing conditions can flare up and become more severe. Raise the energy level and these conditions abate.

Though your energy is not what it should be or will be in the future, many nice things are happening this month. On the 18th you enter a yearly love and social peak. This means more dating, more parties, more gatherings, more romance. There is an especially interesting romantic or social meeting occurring between the 23rd and the 27th. This seems something spiritual – something meaningful – but there's no need to rush into anything. Let love develop as it will.

Children and children figures in your life seem more temperamental this month. They too need to pay more attention to their health.

On the 18th the planetary power shifts from the lower to the upper half of your Horoscope. Hopefully, over the past six months you have put your family and emotional life in right order. Now it is time to begin to focus on your outer, worldly goals. On the 11th the career planet Mercury starts moving forward, so there is more clarity about the career path. Your career planet will be in your 6th house the whole month – a clear message. Achieve your career goals the old-fashioned way, through work and productivity. Your work ethic impresses the authority figures in your life.

Venus, your financial planet, spends most of the month in Pisces, her most exalted position. Thus, earning power is strong. The financial intuition is excellent. Apply your spiritual understanding to your financial life. Your financial good – like almost everything in your life these days – happens through the good graces of others. Social skills and social contacts seem very important. Keep the financial interests of others in mind. Focus more on their interest than on your own and your own financial needs will be met naturally.

On the 20th Venus moves into your 8th house of regeneration, signalling a great period for some financial spring cleaning. Get rid of waste. Get rid of possessions that you no longer need or use. Clear the decks for the new good that wants to come. This is also a good period for paying down debt or for making debt – depending on your need.

March

Best Days Overall: 4, 5, 6, 14, 15, 22, 23
Most Stressful Days Overall: 12, 13, 18, 19, 24, 25, 26
Best Days for Love: 1, 2, 3, 9, 10, 12, 13, 18, 19, 22, 23, 27
Best Days for Money: 2, 3, 7, 8, 12, 13, 20, 21, 22, 23
Best Days for Career: 7, 8, 18, 19, 24, 25, 26, 29, 30, 31

Your spiritual life has been prominent since July 2014. Much progress has been made and even more will be made in the coming months. A solar eclipse on the 20th precipitates spiritual changes. My feeling is that new revelation will come that alters your practice, attitude and perhaps even teachings.

Those of you born very late in the sign of Virgo are affected most strongly by this eclipse – those of you born from September 20 to September 23. If you fall into this category take it nice and easy during this period. Avoid risky or stressful activities. It won't hurt for all of you to reduce your schedules, but it is especially important to those of you most affected by the eclipse.

This eclipse occurs right on the cusp of the 8th and 7th houses. Thus the affairs of both houses are affected. The current relationship or marriage has been undergoing testing all year, but this period more so than normal. It doesn't necessarily mean a break up, but a flawed relationship could end. There are dramatic events in the lives of the spouse, partner, current love and friends. They are making big financial changes and perhaps face some financial crisis. There could be health scares too. If you are involved in estate or insurance issues, they start to move forward in a dramatic way.

Health and energy still needs watching until the 20th. Review our discussion of this in the yearly report. Health will improve after the 20th.

Mars makes some dynamic aspects with Pluto and Uranus from the 9th to the 12th. Avoid confrontations at work or with the neighbours. People can overreact to things during this period. It will be a good idea to drive more defensively and carefully too.

Like last month you prosper by prospering others. The financial interest of others should be your first consideration. The spouse, partner or current love enters a yearly financial peak on the 20th and you seem very involved with this. He or she is more generous. As we mentioned above, there are important financial changes for the beloved.

Your financial planet will conjunct Uranus and square Pluto from the 3rd to the 6th. This can bring sudden, unexpected financial changes – perhaps some unexpected expense. The money for this will be found, however, and the problem is short term.

You mix with influential people from the 17th to the 19th. There is opportunity for an office or workplace romance.

April

Best Days Overall: 1, 2, 10, 11, 12, 19, 20, 28, 29
Most Stressful Days Overall: 8, 9, 15, 16, 21, 22
Best Days for Love: 1, 2, 6, 7, 13, 15, 16, 21, 22, 23, 24
Best Days for Money: 1, 2, 3, 4, 5, 8, 9, 13, 17, 18, 21, 22, 25, 26
Best Days for Career: 8, 9, 19, 20, 21, 22, 28, 29

The lunar eclipse of the 4th appears to be a powerful one, so take it easy this period, a few days before and after the event. It occurs in your money house so major financial changes are afoot. Changes that long needed to be made get made. The eclipse forces the issue. The changes will be good but generally not so pleasant while they happen. This eclipse affects Uranus and Pluto, the rulers of your 6th and 3rd houses respectively. Thus there can be job changes or changes in the conditions of work. If you employ others there is employee instability and perhaps staff turnover now. Cars and communication equipment get tested and often need replacement or repair. Be more careful driving. Siblings and sibling figures can have dramatic, life-changing kinds of experiences and the same is true for friends. Be more patient with them during this period, they are probably rather edgy.

Though you are making financial changes, the financial life looks good. Until the 11th your financial planet Venus is in your 9th house – a beneficent house. Earning power is strong. Financial opportunities can come from abroad or through foreign investments. Foreigners in general are playing a prominent role in the financial life. Your financial judgement is very solid this period. Venus is in Taurus, her natural home. On the 11th Venus crosses the Mid-heaven and enters your

10th house of career. This is good in that it shows a strong focus on finance. It is high on your priorities. Often this kind of aspect shows money that happens through pay rises, from the government and from your good professional reputation. Guard that professional reputation now. There are bottom-line consequences here. You have the financial favour of elders, bosses, parents and parent figures these days. They seem supportive.

Venus squares Neptune on the 19th and 20th. This can bring financial disagreements with the spouse, partner or current love. Financial deals – major purchases or investments – need more homework then. Things are not what they seem. The spouse, partner or current love is still in a yearly financial peak until the 20th and still seems generous with you.

Health and energy are good all month, but get even better after the 20th. You still have two long-term planets in stressful alignment, but the short-term planets are helping you.

Love is still complicated and being tested, but things go easier after the 20th.

Your 9th house becomes powerful after the 20th. Half of the planets are either there or moving through there. This is wonderful for college-level students: they seem focused on their studies and should do well. Foreign lands call to you this month. Travel is in the air.

There are interesting spiritual breakthroughs happening early in the month between the 1st and the 7th.

May

Best Days Overall: 8, 9, 16, 17, 25, 26, 27
Most Stressful Days Overall: 5, 6, 7, 12, 13, 18, 19
Best Days for Love: 1, 2, 3, 4, 12, 13, 21, 22, 30, 31
Best Days for Money: 1, 2, 5, 6, 12, 13, 14, 15, 21, 22, 23, 24, 28, 29, 30, 31
Best Days for Career: 1, 2, 10, 11, 18, 19, 28, 29

May is a very active and hectic sort of month, but a successful one.

Career is the main headline now. Your 10th house is easily the most powerful this month with 50 per cent of the planets there or moving through there. Family and your emotional well-being are important, but now is the time to focus on the career. On the 21st you enter a yearly career peak. This is when you make the most progress for the year. Perhaps you won't attain your career goals in their entirety, but you will see good progress made towards their fulfilment. You will be closer to your objectives than you were a month ago.

The only career complication is the retrograde of your career planet Mercury on the 14th. This will not stop your progress but it will slow things down a little. Try to be perfect in your communications – in giving or receiving instructions, in conversations with bosses. Miscommunication is the main career danger now.

With the Sun moving through the career house from the 21st onwards you can advance your career by getting involved in charitable activities. Mars in your 10th house from the 12th onwards indicates a lot of hard work and aggressiveness in career matters. You are facing competition from others and you have to work harder. Bosses can be more impatient. They want things done yesterday.

All this makes health more delicate this month – especially from the 21st on. Pursue career goals by all means, but do so in a calmer kind of way. Make sure to schedule in rest and relaxation periods. Let go of lesser things and keep your focus on what is really important. Health can be enhanced in the ways mentioned in the yearly report. Aches, pains and other symptoms can be caused by low energy levels. Raise the energy level and they will disappear.

Finances are more delicate this month. You have to work harder to achieve your goals. Venus will spend most of the month in your 11th house of friends. This indicates the importance of social connections in finance. Basically you have the financial favour of friends. It will be very advantageous to be involved with trade or professional organizations from the 7th onwards. Online activities bring profits.

Venus makes dynamic aspects with both Uranus and Pluto from the 21st to the 26th. This is a turbulent financial period. There can be sudden expenses and sudden changes in your financial plans. But these are short-term problems, not trends for the year ahead.

Foreign travel is not advisable during this period.

June

Best Days Overall: 4, 5, 13, 14, 22, 23
Most Stressful Days Overall: 2, 3, 8, 9, 15, 16, 29, 30
Best Days for Love: 1, 8, 9, 10, 11, 17, 18, 20, 21, 27, 28, 29, 30
Best Days for Money: 1, 2, 3, 10, 11, 20, 21, 24, 25, 29, 30
Best Days for Career: 6, 7, 15, 16, 24, 25

Continue to watch your health and energy levels early in the month. Little by little improvements will happen. On the 15th Saturn will move away from his stressful aspect to you, and by the 21st the Sun will start to make harmonious aspects. Health and overall energy are good after the 21st.

You are still in a yearly career peak until the 21st. Things are still hectic there. Overwork is the main problem. By the 24th things should calm down as Mars leaves the career house.

A parent or parent figure needs to be more careful until the 24th (and this was true all of last month too). He or she should avoid haste and watch the temper. People can overreact to this. Haste can lead to accident or injury.

By June 21 your career goals are more or less achieved, and even if they are not completely achieved, good progress to that end has been made. Your interest starts to shift to friends, groups and group activities. The online world calls to you. Social networking is more interesting. This is a period where you expand your knowledge of technology, computers, science and astrology.

The love life is also very nice this period. Neptune is receiving positive aspects and Saturn is moving away from his stressful aspect to the love planet. A current relationship improves. Singles have romantic meetings. Being involved with groups helps the love life. Online kinds of love also happen.

The month ahead looks prosperous. On the 5th Venus starts travelling with Jupiter, the planet of abundance. The aspect will be most exact from the 28th to the 30th. This signals a nice payday. The financial intuition is excellent from the 5th onwards. This, as our regular readers know, is the short cut to wealth. The financial planet in the 12th house of spirituality signals a good time to go deeper into the spiritual dimensions of wealth. A good time to access the supernatural, rather than the natural, sources of supply. Family members – and especially a parent or parent figure – are more prosperous this month and seem more supportive. A parent or parent figure seems less pessimistic.

Last month the planetary power began to shift from the West to the East and the shift gathers momentum this month. Now you are entering into a cycle of personal independence and power. Make those changes that need to be made. Create happiness for yourself; take the actions needed for this. You have the support of the cosmos. Other people are always important but if necessary you can go it alone this month. You don't need their approval.

July

Best Days Overall: 1, 2, 10, 11, 19, 20, 29, 30
Most Stressful Days Overall: 6, 7, 12, 13, 26, 27, 28
Best Days for Love: 6, 7, 8, 9, 14, 15, 16, 17, 18, 24, 25, 26
Best Days for Money: 8, 9, 17, 18, 22, 23, 26, 27, 28
Best Days for Career: 7, 8, 12, 13, 17, 18, 29, 30

For the next two months the planetary power will be at its maximum Eastern position for the year. This is the period where personal independency and personal power are strongest. Good to take advantage of this. You won't see this again for another year. You can have life on your own terms now (more or less). You have the power to create conditions to your liking. You don't need to depend on others for your good or happiness. Your self-interest is as important as anyone else's and the cosmos is supporting it. The only problem with this is that many planets are retrograde this month – the maximum number this year. Change might happen more slowly than you'd like, but it will happen.

Job opportunities have been abundant all year and many of you landed very nice jobs in the past year. If not, the prospects for the month ahead are still excellent.

Finances are good but complicated this month. Venus, your financial planet, spends most of the month in your 12th house, signalling good financial intuition and a good understanding of the spiritual dimensions of wealth. You are more generous with your money this month, more charitable. In general you spend more freely (you can afford to). On the 19th Venus crosses the Ascendant and enters your 1st house – a very good financial aspect. Venus actually camps out on the Ascendant from the 19th onwards. This brings money, clothing and personal accessories to you. You spend on yourself. You feel rich and look rich (more than usual). The only problem is that Venus will start to retrograde on the 25th. Maybe some of this personal spending needs more homework. The financial life should be being reviewed from the 25th onwards. This is not a good period for big ticket purchases or major investments. Venus will re-cross the Ascendant in a few months time (on October 8) and that might be a better time to spend on yourself.

Venus camping out on your Ascendant is good for the love life. You look good. You have a sense of style. You exude more grace and charm. The opposite sex takes notice. With Mercury making nice aspects to the love planet Neptune after the 8th there is harmony with the beloved, and if you are unattached there are happy romantic meetings.

Health and energy are good and will get even better next month.

Watch the driving from the 14th to the 17th. Avoid arguments as well (although this will be difficult). Avoid confrontations at the workplace between the 24th and the 27th too.

August

Best Days Overall: 6, 7, 15, 16, 17, 25, 26
Most Stressful Days Overall: 2, 3, 8, 9, 23, 24, 29, 30
Best Days for Love: 2, 3, 5, 10, 11, 14, 20, 21, 23, 24, 29, 30, 31
Best Days for Money: 5, 14, 15, 18, 19, 23, 24, 25, 31
Best Days for Career: 5, 8, 9, 15, 16, 26, 27

An eventful and happy month, Virgo. Enjoy.

On the 11th Jupiter moves into your sign and will be there for the rest of the year ahead and well into next year. You begin a multi-year cycle of prosperity. Lady Luck sits beside you. You catch the lucky breaks in life. You are experiencing the good life – the physical and sensual delights – and the wherewithal will come to enjoy it all.

Since you are in a long-term cycle of prosperity, now would be a good period to attain clarity on your financial goals and plans. Venus, your financial planet, is retrograde all month. There can be a delayed reaction to your prosperity, but it is still happening.

Venus will travel with Jupiter from the 3rd to the 6th. This shows financial good fortune, but it might be delayed. This transit also gives a tendency to overspend, which might not be advisable just yet.

Mercury travels with Jupiter from the 6th to the 8th. This brings financial good and career success. But it might also signal a tendency to overspend. A parent or parent figure has a nice financial payday.

On the 23rd the Sun crosses your Ascendant and enters your 1st house. You begin one of your yearly personal pleasure peaks. The body gets indulged. The only problem here is weight – there is tendency now (and for the rest of the year) to put on the pounds.

As we have mentioned, Virgos of childbearing age are very fertile now, and especially this month.

You have been in a strong spiritual period since July 2014, and last month and this, until the 23rd, this becomes even more apparent. Your dream life is probably more exciting than your waking life and it might be hard to rouse yourself from it. Supernatural experiences have been happening all year, but they increase during this period. Spiritual breakthroughs are happening and these are most joyous things. Your financial limits are not what they seem. Your ability to achieve is greatly expanded. You are very conscious of a Higher Power guiding your affairs.

Health and energy are excellent this month – the best they have been all year.

September

Best Days Overall: 2, 3, 12, 13, 22, 23, 30
Most Stressful Days Overall: 4, 5, 6, 19, 20, 26, 27
Best Days for Love: 1, 7, 9, 10, 17, 19, 20, 26, 27, 28, 29
Best Days for Money: 1, 2, 9, 10, 12, 14, 15, 19, 20, 28, 29, 30
Best Days for Career: 4, 5, 6, 14, 15, 24, 25

The cosmos has ordained a long-term cycle of happiness and prosperity for you. So it is fitting that the blockages to this (internal or external) get blasted away. Two eclipses this month will clear your path.

The solar eclipse of the 13th is the stronger of the two and it occurs in your own sign. Take it nice and easy that period. This is going to produce a redefinition of your personality and image. You are going to think differently about yourself and will want others to think differently too. Thus, over the next six months, you will change the way you dress, wear your hair and the overall image that you present to others. You will project a richer, more successful type of image. Every solar eclipse brings spiritual changes and this one is no different. The many revelations you've had over the past few months are behind it. You change your spiritual practice, attitudes, teachers and perhaps teachings. Part of it has to do with dramatic events that can occur in the life of your guru or mentor. Sometimes it is due to shake-ups in a spiritual or charitable organization you're involved with.

The lunar eclipse of the 28th (in the Americas it happens on the 27th) occurs in your 8th house of transformation and regeneration. It will be a good idea to reduce your schedule during this period. This eclipse can bring encounters with death – although not necessarily physical death. They can be near-death kinds of experiences – close calls – or the deaths of people you know. Often people have dreams of death. The dark angel comes calling. He lets you know that he is around. He is there to remind you that life here on Earth is short (especially in cosmic terms) – a blink of the eye. There is no time to waste; we must be doing something meaningful with our lives. Sometimes surgery happens or is recommended under this kind of eclipse. As always be sure to get a second opinion.

Every lunar eclipse tests friendships and brings dramas to the lives of friends. This too is part of the cosmic reshuffling going on. The chess pieces are being moved on the board. A new phase of the game is commencing for you. Computers and high-tech equipment also get tested and often need repair or replacement. It would be a good idea to have your important files backed up before the eclipse period begins, and make sure your anti-virus and anti-hacking software is up to date.

Overall, health and energy are still good this month, but Saturn moves back into his stressful aspect with you on the 15th. Don't burn the candle at both ends, there's no need.

October

Best Days Overall: 1, 9, 10, 19, 20, 27, 28
Most Stressful Days Overall: 2, 3, 16, 17, 18, 23, 24, 29, 30
Best Days for Love: 4, 5, 8, 9, 14, 15, 19, 20, 23, 24, 27, 28, 31
Best Days for Money: 1, 8, 9, 10, 11, 12, 13, 19, 20, 27, 28
Best Days for Career: 2, 3, 11, 12, 13, 21, 22, 29, 30

Last month, on the 23rd, you entered a yearly financial peak, which continues until the 23rd of this month. It's a prosperous month ahead. In addition to your financial peak, your financial planet, Venus, now moving forward again, crosses your Ascendant and enters your 1st house. This shows windfalls. You look rich. You feel rich. People see you that way. Money is seeking you out, financial opportunities likewise. The spiritual planet, the Sun, in your money house shows excellent financial intuition (some call this 'gut feeling' but intuition is much more that). Mercury in your money house (moving forward on the 9th) shows the financial favour of bosses, elders, parents and parent figures. Your good professional reputation is important in your earnings. Your financial planet travels with Jupiter from the 24th to the 27th – a classic indicator of financial success. There will be a nice payday that period.

Venus crossed your Ascendant a few months back but then she went into retrograde motion. Now she is moving forward again, signalling an excellent time to buy clothing, jewellery and personal accessories.

Venus in your sign tends to be good for love. You look good. You exude more grace and charm. You are attractive to the opposite sex. Yet, for you, the love life is more complicated. Your love planet Neptune is retrograde and you seem distant from the beloved. The problems in your relationship have nothing to do with your personal appearance or magnetism.

Singles will have many romantic opportunities this month, but none of them look serious.

Health and energy are good this month and you can enhance it further in the ways mentioned in the yearly report.

Last month the planetary power began to shift from the upper to the lower half of your Horoscope. By October 8 up to 80 per cent of the planets will be below the horizon of your chart. Career goals are more or less achieved for now. It is time now to build up the energy for your next career push, beginning next March. Now is the time to the get the family and emotional life in right order.

November

Best Days Overall: 5, 6, 15, 16, 24, 25
Most Stressful Days Overall: 13, 14, 19, 20, 26, 27
Best Days for Love: 6, 7, 10, 17, 18, 19, 20, 26, 27, 28
Best Days for Money: 5, 6, 7, 8, 9, 15, 16, 17, 18, 24, 25, 26, 27
Best Days for Career: 10, 11, 21, 26, 27, 30

Mars was in your sign all last month and is still there until the 12th of this. Both Venus and Jupiter have also been in your sign. Excessive giddiness could lead to carelessness on the physical plane. This can cause accidents or injury. Enjoy your life, but be mindful. Also haste and impatience – caused by Mars – could cause injury if you're not mindful. Watch the temper as well.

Though your yearly financial peak ended last month, finances still look strong. Venus enters the money house on the 8th and Mars on the 12th. Mars in the money house shows the generosity of the spouse, partner or current love. It shows that money can come from estates, trust funds, or insurance claims. Spare cash should be used to pay down debt, but if you need to borrow, the aspects are good for that too.

You can earn through creative financing and through buying undervalued properties that are troubled. Foreigners are important in the financial life too this month; foreign investments as well.

Your 3rd house of communication and intellectual interests became strong on the 23rd of last month and is still strong until the 22nd. This is a nice transit for students (below college level). They are focused on their studies and should do well. A nice transit for siblings and sibling figures as well. They have more energy, self-confidence and self-esteem. They seem more successful on the worldly level as well and happy career opportunities come to them.

For you this is a good month to attend lectures, seminars and courses in subjects that interest you. Good to catch up on your reading. Good to give the mental body the nutrition and exercise it needs.

Health and energy need more attention from the 22nd onwards. This is not your best health period. This doesn't mean sickness, just a need for more preventative care. Review our discussion of this in the yearly report and make sure you get enough rest.

Love is bittersweet this month. There is a nice romantic meeting on the 6th or 7th, and Neptune, the love planet, receives good aspects until the 22nd. But afterwards the testing of the current relationship intensifies. This is when one learns whether love is real or not.

The planetary momentum is overwhelmingly forward this month: 90 per cent of the planets are moving forward from the 18th onwards. Your personal solar cycle is in its waxing phase. This would be a good time to start new projects or launch new products into the world. However, after the New Year might be even better. Much depends on your need.

December

Best Days Overall: 2, 3, 4, 12, 13, 21, 22, 30, 31
Most Stressful Days Overall: 10, 11, 17, 18, 23, 24
Best Days for Love: 7, 8, 17, 18, 25, 26
Best Days for Money: 2, 3, 4, 5, 6, 7, 12, 13, 17, 18, 21, 22, 25, 26, 30, 31
Best Days for Career: 1, 12, 21, 22, 23, 24, 30, 31

Your 4th house of home and family became very powerful on November 22 and remains powerful until December 22. This signals the importance of family and emotional well-being. These should be the focus now. The planetary power is at its low point in your chart and, symbolically, it is midnight in your year. Outer activity is lessened. Inner activity is more prominent. The victories in life are won in the midnight hour; this is when they actually occur – they only become visible, manifest, during the day.

When there is power in the 4th house we have opportunities for emotional healing and cleansing. It is a period when we can come to terms with the past. The traumas and pains of the past need not shape our future. In many cases the so-called trauma was only a child's interpretation of an event. When it is looked at from the present, adult consciousness, the trauma loses its power. This is why the cosmos has arranged things so that the past can be looked at – reviewed – in natural ways and every year this happens. Even if you're not seeing a therapist, old memories will arise spontaneously this month.

There is method to this apparent madness. You're supposed to look at these things and resolve them. Most of the time, you will reinterpret the event from your present consciousness. A cosmic digestion of the experience is happening. The nutrition (the wisdom) from the experience will be extracted and the waste (the pain and false interpretations) will get eliminated. This is a month for psychological-type breakthroughs.

Health still needs watching this month – even more than last month. But if you make sure you get enough rest, and schedule in some massages or other natural treatments, you should get through with little problem. Health and energy will improve dramatically after the 22nd.

On the 22nd, as the ruler of the solar system, the Sun, moves into your 5th house of fun and enjoyment, you begin another one of your yearly personal pleasure peaks. It's party time in your year.

Love is still being tested – this is a long-term trend – but it gets much easier after the 22nd. The holidays and New Year should be socially happy.

Venus, your financial planet, spends most of the month in Scorpio and the ruler of your 8th house of regeneration, Mars, spends the month in your money house. This is a very clear message. Reduce waste and redundancy. Get rid of old possessions that you no longer need or use. Rid yourself of material that obstructs the financial life. Pay down debt. (However, if you do need to borrow, this is a good time too – your line of credit will probably be increased this month.) Keep the financial interests of others foremost in your mind.

Libra

THE SCALES

Birthdays from
23rd September to
22nd October

Personality Profile

LIBRA AT A GLANCE

Element – Air

Ruling Planet – Venus
   Career Planet – Moon
   Love Planet – Mars
   Money Planet – Pluto
   Planet of Communications – Jupiter
   Planet of Health and Work – Neptune
   Planet of Home and Family Life – Saturn
   Planet of Spirituality and Good Fortune – Mercury

Colours – blue, jade green

Colours that promote love, romance and social harmony – carmine, red, scarlet

Colours that promote earning power – burgundy, red-violet, violet

Gems – carnelian, chrysolite, coral, emerald, jade, opal, quartz, white marble

Metal – copper

Scents – almond, rose, vanilla, violet

Quality – cardinal (= activity)

Qualities most needed for balance – a sense of self, self-reliance, independence

Strongest virtues – social grace, charm, tact, diplomacy

Deepest needs – love, romance, social harmony

Characteristic to avoid – violating what is right in order to be socially accepted

Signs of greatest overall compatibility – Gemini, Aquarius

Signs of greatest overall incompatibility – Aries, Cancer, Capricorn

Sign most helpful to career – Cancer

Sign most helpful for emotional support – Capricorn

Sign most helpful financially – Scorpio

Sign best for marriage and/or partnerships – Aries

Sign most helpful for creative projects – Aquarius

Best Sign to have fun with – Aquarius

Signs most helpful in spiritual matters – Gemini, Virgo

Best day of the week – Friday

Understanding a Libra

In the sign of Libra the universal mind – the soul – expresses its genius for relationships, that is, its power to harmonize diverse elements in a unified, organic way. Libra is the soul's power to express beauty in all of its forms. And where is beauty if not within relationships? Beauty does not exist in isolation. Beauty arises out of comparison – out of the just relationship between different parts. Without a fair and harmonious relationship there is no beauty, whether it in art, manners, ideas or the social or political forum.

There are two faculties humans have that exalt them above the animal kingdom: their rational faculty (expressed in the signs of Gemini and Aquarius) and their aesthetic faculty, exemplified by Libra. Without an aesthetic sense we would be little more than intelligent barbarians. Libra is the civilizing instinct or urge of the soul.

Beauty is the essence of what Librans are all about. They are here to beautify the world. One could discuss Librans' social grace, their sense of balance and fair play, their ability to see and love another person's point of view – but this would be to miss their central asset: their desire for beauty.

No one – no matter how alone he or she seems to be – exists in isolation. The universe is one vast collaboration of beings. Librans, more than most, understand this and understand the spiritual laws that make relationships bearable and enjoyable.

A Libra is always the unconscious (and in some cases conscious) civilizer, harmonizer and artist. This is a Libra's deepest urge and greatest genius. Librans love instinctively to bring people together, and they are uniquely qualified to do so. They have a knack for seeing what unites people – the things that attract and bind rather than separate individuals.

Finance

In financial matters Librans can seem frivolous and illogical to others. This is because Librans appear to be more concerned with earning money for others than for themselves. But there is a logic to this financial attitude. Librans know that everything and everyone is connected and that it is impossible to help another to prosper without also prospering yourself. Since enhancing their partner's income and position tends to strengthen their relationship, Librans choose to do so. What could be more fun than building a relationship? You will rarely find a Libra enriching him- or herself at someone else's expense.

Scorpio is the ruler of Libra's solar 2nd house of money, giving Libra unusual insight into financial matters – and the power to focus on these matters in a way that disguises a seeming indifference. In fact, many other signs come to Librans for financial advice and guidance.

Given their social grace, Librans often spend great sums of money on entertaining and organizing social events. They also like to help others when they are in need. Librans would go out of their way to help a friend in dire straits, even if they have to borrow from others to do so. However, Librans are also very careful to pay back any debts they owe, and like to make sure they never have to be reminded to do so.

Career and Public Image

Publicly, Librans like to appear as nurturers. Their friends and acquaintances are their family and they wield political power in parental ways. They also like bosses who are paternal or maternal.

The sign of Cancer is on Libra's 10th career house cusp; the Moon is Libra's career planet. The Moon is by far the speediest, most change-able planet in the horoscope. It alone among all the planets travels through the entire zodiac – all twelve signs and houses – every month. This is an important key to the way in which Librans approach their careers, and also to what they need to do to maximize their career potential. The Moon is the planet of moods and feelings – Librans need a career in which their emotions can have free expression. This is why so many Librans are involved in the creative arts. Libra's ambitions wax and wane with the Moon. They tend to wield power according to their mood.

The Moon 'rules' the masses – and that is why Libra's highest goal is to achieve a mass kind of acclaim and popularity. Librans who achieve fame cultivate the public as other people cultivate a lover or friend. Librans can be very flexible – and often fickle – in their career and ambitions. On the other hand, they can achieve their ends in a great variety of ways. They are not stuck in one attitude or with one way of doing things.

Love and Relationships

Librans express their true genius in love. In love you could not find a partner more romantic, more seductive or more fair. If there is one thing that is sure to destroy a relationship – sure to block your love from flowing – it is injustice or imbalance between lover and beloved. If one party is giving too much or taking too much, resentment is sure to surface at some time or other. Librans are careful about this. If anything, Librans might err on the side of giving more, but never giving less.

If you are in love with a Libra, make sure you keep the aura of romance alive. Do all the little things – candle-lit dinners, travel to exotic locales, flowers and small gifts. Give things that are beautiful, not necessarily expensive. Send cards. Ring regularly even if you have nothing in particular to say. The niceties are very important to a Libra. Your relationship is a work of art: make it beautiful and your Libran lover will appreciate it. If you are creative about it, he or she will appreciate it even more; for this is how your Libra will behave towards you.

Librans like their partners to be aggressive and even a bit self-willed. They know that these are qualities they sometimes lack and so they like their partners to have them. In relationships, however, Librans can be very aggressive – but always in a subtle and charming way! Librans are determined in their efforts to charm the object of their desire – and this determination can be very pleasant if you are on the receiving end.

Home and Domestic Life

Since Librans are such social creatures, they do not particularly like mundane domestic duties. They like a well-organized home – clean and neat with everything needful present – but housework is a chore and a burden, one of the unpleasant tasks in life that must be done, the quicker the better. If a Libra has enough money – and sometimes even if not – he or she will prefer to pay someone else to take care of the daily household chores. However, Librans like gardening; they love to have flowers and plants in the home.

A Libra's home is modern, and furnished in excellent taste. You will find many paintings and sculptures there. Since Librans like to be with friends and family, they enjoy entertaining at home and they make great hosts.

Capricorn is on the cusp of Libra's 4th solar house of home and family. Saturn, the planet of law, order, limits and discipline, rules Libra's domestic affairs. If Librans want their home life to be support-ive and happy they need to develop some of the virtues of Saturn – order, organization and discipline. Librans, being so creative and so intensely in need of harmony, can tend to be too lax in the home and too permissive with their children. Too much of this is not always good; children need freedom but they also need limits.

Horoscope for 2015

Major Trends

Saturn has been in your money house for the past two years. This has meant finances have been stressed. There was a need to reorganize the financial life and often this isn't pleasant. Happily, Saturn is out of the money house for most of the year and you should see a big improve-ment in this area this year. More details later.

Uranus has been in your 7th house of love for many years now. This makes for social and romantic instability. No doubt there have been many divorces and romantic break-ups in the past few years. The instability continues in the year ahead. There is a need to learn how to deal with this, and there's more on this later.

Pluto has been in your 4th house of home and family for many years and he will be there in the year ahead. Many of you have experienced the death of family members of late. In some cases this wasn't actual deaths but near-death kinds of experiences, or surgery. The family relationships are experiencing a cosmic detox and these things are not usually pleasant. But the end result is good. The family circle will become more ideal, but through all kinds of dramas.

Neptune has been in your 6th house of health and work since July 2012. This indicates an interest in spiritual healing and this interest will continue for many more years. Job seekers have to work harder to find work in the year ahead. The work is there, but more effort is needed to find it. More on this later.

Jupiter will enter your 12th house of spirituality on August 11. This will initiate a strong spiritual period for you, a period of inner growth. The dream life and your extrasensory perception (ESP) faculties will be greatly enhanced. You will be more involved with charitable activities too.

Your most important areas of life this year will be finances (from June 15 to September 18); communication and intellectual interests (from January 1 to June 15 and September 18 for the rest of the year); home and family; health and work; love, romance and social activities; friends, groups and group activities (until August 11); and spirituality (from August 11 onwards).

Your paths of greatest fulfilment this year are the body, image and personal pleasure (until November 13); friends, groups and group activities (until August 11); and spirituality (August 11 onwards).

Health

(Please note that this is an astrological perspective on health and not a medical one. In days of yore there was no difference, these perspectives were identical. But now there could be quite a difference. For a medical perspective, please consult your doctor or health practitioner.)

Health is still delicate this year. Two powerful planets, Uranus and Pluto, are making stressful aspects to you. This has been going on for some years now. Happily, your 6th house of health is strong this year and you are paying attention. This extra attention is a positive for health.

As our regular readers know, there is much that can be done to enhance the health and prevent problems from developing. The first and most important thing is to maintain high energy levels. This is the first defence against disease. A strong aura – a strong energy field – will repel most diseases. Thus it is good to rest and relax more. Make sure you get enough sleep. A little planning of your day will enable you to do more with less energy. Delegate tasks whenever possible. It might be a good idea to spend some time in a health spa and get more massages or reflexology treatments. Things that increase overall energy are good.

Aside from this it would be good to focus on the following areas – the vulnerable areas of the Horoscope this year: the heart; the kidneys and hips; and the feet. The reflexes for these are shown in the chart above.

Right diet often helps with heart problems, but more important than that is avoiding worry and anxiety. According to many spiritual healers these are the root causes of heart problems.

The kidneys and hips are always important for Libra. Kidney detoxing – and there are many herbal ways to do this – would be good. As would regular hip massage.

The feet too are always important for Libra, but more so since 2012. Keep the feet warm in the winter. Wear shoes that fit and that don't

Important foot reflexology points for the year ahead

Try to massage the whole foot on a regular basis, but pay extra attention to the points highlighted on the chart. When you massage, be aware of 'sore spots', as these need special attention. It is also a good idea to massage the ankles and the tops of the feet.

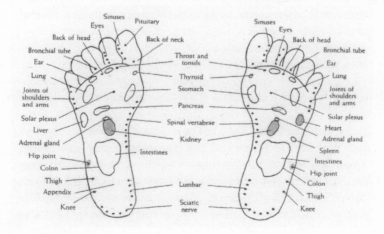

knock you off balance. Libra is very much into fashion, but as far as shoes are concerned, comfort is more important, although if you can have both, so much the better. Regular foot massage is always powerful for you, but especially now. Foot hydrotherapy is also powerful and there are many gadgets for this on the market which you might want to invest in.

Your health planet, Neptune, is in his own sign and house these days. Thus he is more powerful on your behalf (which is another positive for health). Neptune is the most spiritual of all the planets, and his role as your health planet gives us many messages. You will respond well to spiritual-type therapies – meditation, reiki, the laying on of hands and the manipulation of subtle energies. If problems arise (God forbid) see a spiritual healer. Generally he or she should be able to take care of the problem.

It is always a good idea to stay in a state of grace with the Higher Power within you. But for you it is an actual health issue. Health problems could arise from a disconnection from the Higher Power. (All health problems have their origin in this, but for you it is more dramatic.) Spiritual healing is always a strong interest for you, but now you are going deeper into this. Read all you can on the subject and apply what you read.

Your health planet rules the oceans and he is in a water sign. Thus you have a very strong connection with the healing powers of the water element. From a health perspective it is very good to spend more time near oceans, rivers and lakes. Boating, swimming and water sports are healthy kinds of exercises. Yoga and tai chi would also be good. If you feel under the weather, have a soak in the tub for an hour or so. The body will relax and you'll feel much better.

Home and Family

As we have mentioned, Pluto has been in your 4th house of home and family for some years now, and he will be there for many more. This is a very long-term transit. Pluto's slow movement shows his thoroughness. He will not rest until your family situation is ideal. Whatever has to be done to achieve this ideal – even if it involves major dramas – he will do. He will revamp the physical home until it is where he wants it

– even if it means destroying the old one, or causing major renovations to be needed.

The same is true for family relationships. Pluto is ruthless. If family members don't have the right attitudes or mind set, he will send dramas – near-death kinds of experiences – to get them back on track. He knows how to do his job.

When Pluto moves through the 4th house, the current family pattern will die. And since death is always followed by resurrection, it will be reborn on a higher and better level. The end results of Pluto's actions are always good, and things will be vastly improved over the way they were, but it will not be so pleasant while he's at work.

You are giving birth to a new family relationship and a new dynamic. No matter how much modern technology sanitizes it, childbirth is a messy business. There is a lot of blood and gore. Yet, when the child is born, the mother rejoices. She deems it worthwhile to have undergone all the pain. And so it is with your family and domestic situation these days. This is a long-term process, but it is what the cosmos is planning for you.

So, in many cases family members have literally died. In other cases they have had near-death experiences or medical crises. The home has undergone serious renovations (and these can still happen in the year ahead and in coming years). In some cases the family unit has broken up, either through death or divorce or quarrels. But have no fear – things will get patched up on a better level.

Pluto is also your financial planet, and his position in the 4th house gives many signals on this level too. You are spending more on the home and on the family. A parent or parent figure is prominent in the financial life. Many of you are starting home-based businesses or working from home. Family connections play an important role in finances.

The entire year is good for renovation or construction work in the home. But if you're redecorating in a cosmetic sort of way – painting, or buying objects for the home – January 1–3, February 20 to March 17, June 5 to July 19 and December 29–31 are good times.

A move is not likely in the year ahead.

A parent or parent figure seems to be paying more attention to a sibling than to you. This same parent figure has been restless for many years and has either had multiple moves or has lived in different places for long periods of time. This trend continues in the year ahead. Siblings or sibling figures could have moved in the past two years, but this year they stay put. Children and children figures have a stable kind of home and family year. Moves don't seem likely. Grandchildren could move (a happy move) after August 11.

Finance and Career

Uranus has been impacting on your financial planet for some years now and has brought major and dramatic financial changes. Disruptive sorts of changes. Things are quieter and less dramatic this year as Uranus has moved away from his square aspect. (He is still affecting Pluto, but not as directly as in previous years.)

Finances are OK until August 11 – nothing special one way or another. There are no disasters, but no special prosperity either. However, after August 11, as Jupiter enters Virgo, he will start to make very nice aspects to your financial planet. Earnings should increase; overall wealth likewise. The latter half of the year is going to be much more prosperous than the early part.

With Pluto as your financial planet you are someone who likes to make other people rich, someone who looks out for the financial interests of others, someone who is good at managing other people's money. You can see value where others see only death and decay. Thus you are someone who can profit from troubled companies or properties, turning them around and making them successful once again.

Those of you of the appropriate age are doing more estate planning. Many of you are inheriting money or being named in someone's will. (This could have happened in recent years too.)

Your financial planet's long sojourn in the sign of Capricorn indicates a conservative approach to wealth and to spending. I consider this a positive thing. You have sound financial judgement. You are not a speculator or a risk-taker. You have a long-term perspective on wealth. You have a good sense of what something will be worth many years from now. You manage your money well.

This is a wonderful position for disciplined financial regimes – for savings and investment plans and for living within one's means. These habits lead to wealth over the long haul.

The financial planet in the 4th house shows good family support, as we have mentioned, and someone who spends on the family. It signals someone who invests in family members and who earns through family connections and a family-type business.

This aspect is also good for real estate – both commercial and residential. (Residential property is ruled by the 4th house, but commercial real estate comes under Capricorn's rule.)

When Jupiter starts to make his fortunate aspect with your financial planet, he will do so from the 12th house of spirituality. This shows a sound financial intuition which should be trusted. It also shows someone who is exploring the spiritual dimensions of wealth. This is not natural money, but supernatural money – miracle money. It seems to happen naturally, but you know, deep down inside, that it is miraculous. Read as much as you can on the spiritual aspects of wealth.

Jupiter rules your 3rd house of communications. Thus earnings can come from retailing, trading, buying and selling. Good use of the media becomes important financially. People need to know of your products or service. A positive buzz needs to be built around them. A sibling or sibling figure in your life seems helpful financially – neighbours too.

Love and Social Life

We have mentioned that the love life has been complicated and highly unstable for some years now. This trend continues in the year ahead.

There is good news and bad news about this. On the one hand the love life is freer now than it has ever been. You are meeting new and exciting kinds of people, unusual kinds of people, and you seem to like this these days. Love can happen for you in the most unexpected ways. Any time. Any place. Every time you meet someone you think is ideal, you soon meet another who is more the ideal. It will be difficult to settle down these days.

The bad news is that many of you have been experiencing break-ups in your marriages or serious relationships. This is never fun. Uranus in your 7th house is taxing even the social genius of Libra.

If you are single, marriage or a serious relationship isn't likely – and is probably not advisable either. You and the beloved need as much elbow room as possible. You need your social freedom (and so does he or she).

If you are married, your relationship is being severely tested (especially if this is your first marriage). I have seen marriages survive this kind of transit, but it takes a *lot* of work and commitment. Most people are not willing to pay this kind of price.

This is a year to enjoy your relationships as they are without trying to project too much on to them. People come and go, but love always remains. Your love and non-attachment will draw to you all your needs in love. The faces may change, but the needs will be met.

You are attracted by unconventional people. This has been a trend for some years now. Plain vanilla is not for you. Your love has to be a genius – a high-tech programmer or engineer, a scientist or mathematician fits the bill, as do astrologers, astronomers, inventors and media people. The online world is conducive to romantic opportunity this year.

Though romance is complicated the overall social life – especially friendships – seems very happy. Jupiter has been in your 11th house of friends since last July and will remain there until August 11. So you are meeting new and significant people. You are making long-term friendships now. The friends you meet now are like siblings to you – and perhaps siblings or other sibling figures make the introductions.

Self-improvement

Spiritual healing, as we mentioned, will be a major focus this year and for many years to come. There is going to be much revelation on this subject. In your case, there is no health regime that is complete unless the spiritual dimension is dealt with.

Spiritual healing is a bit different from mind-body healing. Mind-body healing is very good but it has its limitations. Since it is the mind that has created the health problem in the first place, we are in a situation where the sick mind must heal itself. The thing that created the problem is trying to solve the problem.

Spiritual healing is about invoking a power that is above the mind – above the mental process – and allowing it to heal the mind and eventually the body. The mind is used to make the initial connection with the power, but after that it should remain still – the less mental interference the better. It is important to understand that though you set the power into motion it is not you or your mind that is doing the work.

The spiritual dimensions of finance will become important after August 11, as we said. This too is a big subject. As with physical healing it is about invoking a power that is above the mind and allowing it to operate in your financial affairs.

In theory, everyone has equal access to the spiritual, supernatural supply. In practice, however, it is not so. Much psychological clutter – false teachings, beliefs and internal denials – have to be cleared out in order to have access to this supply. This takes some spiritual work, but it is worth it. A good understanding of the nature of spiritual supply – or Providence as some call it – will not only solve personal financial problems, but the financial problems in the world at large.

Napoleon Hill's *Think And Grow Rich* is a classic in the field and a good book for you to read, but still it mostly deals with the mind aspects of wealth. Spiritual supply is something above that. The spiritual approach to wealth is about recognizing one and only one source of supply – the Divine. When you invoke the Divine supply no one else is involved. The transaction is strictly between you and the Divine. If it grants (and it does) nothing and no one can stop it – it can only be blocked by you yourself, by your disbelief or denial. The Divine will often work through human instruments to bring your supply to you, but not necessarily. It can act directly with little or no 'outside' help if need be.

Read all you can on the subject and, more importantly, be attentive to the inner revelation that will come in the year ahead through your dreams, intuitions and hunches.

Month-by-month Forecasts

January

Best Days Overall: 2, 3, 11, 12, 13, 20, 21, 29, 30
Most Stressful Days Overall: 4, 5, 18, 19, 24, 25, 31
Best Days for Love: 1, 2, 3, 12, 13, 14, 21, 22, 23, 24, 25, 31
Best Days for Money: 7, 8, 9, 10, 14, 15, 16, 17, 18, 19, 24, 25, 27, 28
Best Days for Career: 1, 4, 5, 9, 10, 20, 21, 29, 30, 31

The planetary momentum is forward this month – overwhelmingly so; until the 21st 90 per cent of the planets are moving forward (and after then it's still 80 per cent). Your personal solar cycle is waxing (growing), as is the universal solar cycle. This is an excellent time to start a new project or business, or to launch a new product into the world. The 1st to the 5th and the 20th are the best days for this, and even after the 21st the prospects are very good.

You begin this year with the planetary power mostly below the horizon of your chart. The lower hemisphere is where the power is. Thus you are in a period where family and emotional wellness is important. Outer career goals can be downplayed at the moment. They are important, but if your domestic and emotional situation is good, those things will take care of themselves. This is the period where you build and strengthen the psychological foundations of future career success.

Last month on the Winter Solstice, the planetary power shifted from the independent East to the social West – your favourite sector. Your period of personal independence is over with and you will now have to adapt more to situations. It is more difficult to create conditions that suit your own interests. Now (and for the next six or so months) you can hone and cultivate your already strong social skills.

Until the 20th your 4th house of home and family is very strong. This is where your focus needs to be. The past will sneak up on you now. Old memories and experiences will arise spontaneously during this period. This is nature's way of digesting the past – of extracting the nutrition from past experiences and eliminating the waste. Look at these things as they arise and view them from your present state of understanding. This will naturally resolve many negative things. If you are seeing a therapist, there will be much progress this month.

On the 20th you enter one of your yearly personal pleasure peaks. It's party time; time to explore the fun side of life. After you've satisfied these urges, you will be in a better frame of mind to get down to business next month.

Your health and energy levels are stressed until the 20th. Make sure to get enough rest and sleep. Enhance the health in the ways mentioned in the yearly report. This month, from the 12th onwards, make sure to get enough exercise. Head and face massage will be powerful this month too.

February

Best Days Overall: 8, 9, 17, 18, 25, 26
Most Stressful Days Overall: 1, 15, 16, 21, 22, 27, 28
Best Days for Love: 1, 2, 10, 11, 20, 21, 22
Best Days for Money: 3, 4, 5, 6, 7, 10, 11, 13, 14, 15, 16, 21, 22, 23, 24
Best Days for Career: 1, 8, 9, 17, 18, 27, 28

The month ahead is still excellent for starting new projects, business ventures or for launching new products. Between 80 and 90 per cent of the planets are moving in a forward direction this month. From the 18th onwards would be the best time to start such ventures this month – the Moon will be waxing then.

It is basically a happy month ahead. You are still in the midst of a yearly personal pleasure cycle – a peak period for this. Health and energy are much improved over last month too. If there have been long-standing health problems they seem in abeyance now. With more energy all kinds of new possibilities open up to you, things that weren't possible when your energy was low.

Finances also seem much improved. Saturn is now out of your money house and your financial planet Pluto is moving forward and receiving good aspects all month, especially after the 18th. Job seekers have good fortune from the 18th onwards too. There are many opportunities for job seekers. A happy job opportunity comes early in the month too – but there could be delays involved here.

Librans dislike details. Yet, they are part of life. With your 6th house of health and work strong after the 18th it is a good period to tackle those important 'detail' kinds of tasks such as the accounts, bookkeeping, filing, cleaning up the hard drive, etc.

The love life seems happy this month. Both Mars and Venus enter your 7th house of love on the 20th. It seems that you are pursuing someone, and by the 21st you will catch him or her. The only issue here is the stability of this relationship – Uranus has been in your 7th house for some years now. Mars travelling with Venus is a classic love indicator – and especially in your chart. Venus is your personal planet and Mars is your love planet. Next month both these planets will move over Uranus and the relationship will get tested.

Libra is always socially popular, but these days more so than ever. The planetary power is mostly in the social West and Venus moves into your 7th house of love on the 20th. You are devoted to others. You put their interests ahead of your own. You are totally on the side of the beloved (and friends in general). You are there for them. This makes for popularity.

March

Best Days Overall: 7, 8, 16, 17, 24, 25, 26
Most Stressful Days Overall: 1, 14, 15, 20, 21, 27, 28
Best Days for Love: 2, 3, 12, 13, 20, 21, 22, 23, 30, 31
Best Days for Money: 2, 3, 4, 5, 6, 9, 10, 11, 12, 13, 14, 15, 20, 21, 22, 23
Best Days for Career: 1, 10, 11, 18, 19, 20, 27, 28, 29, 30

A solar eclipse on the 20th occurs right on the cusp of the 7th house, although technically it is in the 6th house. The affairs of both houses are affected. Thus there are shake-ups in love. Good things – a marriage, engagement or new relationship – often cause as much disruption as bad things. A current relationship gets tested. Dirty laundry – unresolved issues – comes up for cleansing. There can be job changes as well – either within your present company or with another one. There are disturbances in the work environment. Important changes happen in your health regime too.

Every solar eclipse tests friendships and this one is no different. Sometimes it is the actual relationship that contains flaws and now you find out about the problem. Sometimes the friend experiences some life-changing event and this complicates the relationship. Computers, software and high-tech equipment get tested now too. Often they need replacement. It would be a good idea to have your important files backed up and your anti-virus, anti-hacking software up to date. Technology is wonderful when it works as it should, but a total nightmare when glitches arise.

This solar eclipse is most powerful on those of you born early in the sign of Libra – those of you with birthdays from September 22–24. If you fall into this category take it nice and easy during this period. Do your best to stay out of harm's way.

The solar eclipse coincides with the beginning of a yearly love and social peak. So the love life is exciting this month, although turbulent and unstable. There will be many ups and downs, and never a dull moment. Aside from the eclipse, Venus travels with Uranus from the 3rd to the 6th. Often this creates changes in the affections. The darling of yesterday becomes the dog of today and vice versa. Your love planet Mars moves over the eclipse point from the 9th to the 12th, causing more of the same. On the other hand, the surprises in love can be pleasant ones. Someone new comes into the picture out of the blue. Again the only issue is the stability of these things.

You are always a risk-taker in love, and this month even more so. You jump into relationships quickly – perhaps too quickly. You are a love at first sight person these days (much more than usual).

Health and energy are not what they should be from the 20th onwards, so make sure you get enough rest. Review our discussion of health in the yearly report. In addition to what is written there, you can enhance the health by giving more attention to the lungs, small intestine, arms, shoulders and respiratory system. Arm and shoulder massage is powerful.

April

Best Days Overall: 3, 4, 5, 13, 14, 21, 22

Most Stressful Days Overall: 10, 11, 12, 17, 18, 23, 24

Best Days for Love: 1, 2, 10, 11, 12, 13, 17, 18, 19, 20, 21, 22, 28, 29

Best Days for Money: 1, 2, 6, 7, 8, 9, 10, 11, 12, 17, 18, 19, 20, 25, 26, 28, 29

Best Days for Career: 8, 9, 18, 19, 23, 24, 28

The lunar eclipse of the 4th occurs in your own sign and thus affects you very strongly. Avoid stressful or risk-taking activities around that period. Your overall health and energy levels are stressed anyway, and especially during the eclipse period. It might be a good idea to spend quiet time at home or arrange for a massage that day.

If you have not been careful in dietary matters, a physical detox can happen. This is not disease, though the symptoms are sometimes similar – just the body getting rid of unwanted material. The eclipse also announces a redefinition of the personality and your self-concept – and often this is forced upon you. Others are defining you in a way that is not pleasant, and you must redefine yourself for yourself. Over the next six months you will present a new image, a new look, to the world. You will dress and accessorize differently.

Every lunar eclipse impacts on the career, Libra. The eclipsed planet, the Moon, is your career planet. So career changes are afoot. There are changes in the hierarchy of your company, industry or profession. The rules can be changed. Bosses, elders, parents or parent figures can have dramatic, life-changing experiences. (They should be encouraged to reduce their schedules over the eclipse period too.)

This particular lunar eclipse is stronger than usual in that two powerful planets are involved here – Uranus and Pluto. Thus there are financial dramas and changes happening for you. Flaws in your financial thinking and strategy are revealed and you are forced to adjust. If you are involved with estate, tax or insurance issues, there are dramatic turns now. They move forward, one way or another. You are forced to deal with these things. The impact on Uranus shows that children and children figures in your life are affected. They too are redefining themselves now. They should also reduce their schedule during the eclipse period.

Last month on the 21st the planetary power began to shift from the lower to the upper half of your Horoscope. Symbolically speaking, it is morning in your year. Time to be up and about and focused on your worldly outer goals. Start taking action on your career goals now. Hopefully you've had a good night's sleep and have the energy for a new career push now.

May

Best Days Overall: 1, 2, 10, 11, 18, 19, 28, 29
Most Stressful Days Overall: 8, 9, 14, 15, 21, 22
Best Days for Love: 1, 2, 9, 12, 13, 14, 15, 18, 19, 21, 22, 28, 29, 30, 31
Best Days for Money: 3, 4, 5, 6, 8, 9, 14, 15, 16, 17, 23, 24, 25, 26, 30, 31
Best Days for Career: 8, 9, 17, 18, 21, 22, 28, 29

Health and energy are much better than last month. You still need to be careful as two major planets are stressing you, but the worst is over.

Career has become important since the planetary shift in power last month and you seem very successful these days. Venus crosses your Mid-heaven and enters your 10th house of career on the 7th. You are on top now. Reaching the heights of what you imagine for yourself. People see you as successful. You dress and look the part. Personal appearance and overall demeanour are important careerwise. You are honoured and appreciated these days, not just for your career achievements but for who you are.

Career is good and you haven't even reached your peak for the year! This will begin next month.

Last month on the 20th the Sun entered your 8th house of regeneration and will be there until the 21st of this month. This is a wonderful period for weight-loss regimes and detox programmes. It is a sexually active kind of period as well. Whatever your age or stage in life, the libido is stronger than usual.

The 8th house is all about renewal and resurrection. But these things don't happen unless impurities are cleansed from the mind and body. So this is a month for getting rid of old possessions that you no longer need and for getting rid of old thought and emotional patterns that no longer serve your interest. Those of you who are interested in past life regression will find such activities successful.

The love life looks happy this month, especially from the 12th onwards. Mars in your 9th house shows an expansion of the social life: more dating, more opportunities. Until the 12th the physical aspects of love are important – especially sexual magnetism. But wealth is also very alluring. After the 12th you are attracted to mentor types – people you can learn from; it is the college professor or the minister (or these types of people) that attract you. Romantic opportunities happen in educational or worship settings – at your place of worship, at some religious festival or gathering, or at a college or university function. Love can happen in foreign lands or with foreigners too.

Be more patient with family members (especially a parent or parent figure) from the 13th to the 16th and the 22nd to the 24th. He or she seems stressed out.

Avoid risk-taking activities from the 21st to the 26th.

June

Best Days Overall: 6, 7, 15, 16, 24, 25
Most Stressful Days Overall: 4, 5, 10, 11, 17, 18, 19
Best Days for Love: 1, 8, 9, 10, 11, 17, 18, 19, 20, 21, 27, 28, 29, 30
Best Days for Money: 2, 3, 4, 5, 10, 11, 13, 14, 20, 21, 22, 23, 27, 28, 29, 30
Best Days for Career: 6, 7, 15, 16, 17, 18, 19, 27

The main headline this month is your career. It seems very active and successful. You enter a yearly career peak on the 21st and this will go on until July 23. Family is important but now you need to focus on the career. The demands are strong. You're working very hard. There is competition to be dealt with. A promotion could have happened last month, but, if not, it can happen this month too. The spouse, partner or current love is also successful this month and seems supportive of your own career. Friends are also supportive.

You are always good on the social scene; this month will be good to achieve career goals through social means. Good to attend or host the right parties and gatherings. You are meeting (especially after the 24th) just the right people who can help you. This will not replace hard work and performance, but it opens doors for you.

Career is wonderful this month, but finances are more challenging. Your financial planet Pluto has been retrograde since April 17 and receives stressful aspects after the 21st of this month. Saturn retrogrades back into your money house on the 15th. You're not yet finished with reorganizing your finances. Extra expenses and financial delays force you to reorganize. If you shift things around a little, you will have what you need. These problems are short-term things. They will pass.

The love life is good this month. Your love planet spends most of the month in the 9th house and you should review our discussion of this last month. On the 24th Mars crosses your Mid-heaven and enters your 10th career house. This shows a change in your love attitudes. You are attracted by power and prestige now. You mix with the high and mighty. You are attracted to people who can help you careerwise. Romance can happen with bosses or with people involved in your career. You have the aspects for an office romance now. The Mid-heaven is the most powerful point in the chart – even stronger than the Ascendant. Thus the love planet's position there shows that your social magnetism and allure is unusually powerful – another positive for love.

Health and energy become more stressful after the 21st, so make sure you get enough sleep and rest. Enhance the health in the ways mentioned in the yearly report. Yes, career is hectic and demanding. It is very important, but you can approach it in a calmer way. Alternate work with rest periods. Delegate tasks wherever possible. Let go of lesser concerns and focus on what is really important to you.

July

Best Days Overall: 3, 4, 5, 12, 13, 22, 23, 31
Most Stressful Days Overall: 1, 2, 8, 9, 14, 15, 16, 29, 30
Best Days for Love: 6, 7, 8, 9, 14, 15, 16, 17, 18, 24, 25, 26
Best Days for Money: 1, 2, 9, 10, 11, 18, 19, 20, 24, 25, 27, 28, 29, 30
Best Days for Career: 6, 7, 14, 15, 16, 26

It might be a good idea to go on holiday this month. Retrograde activity is at its maximum for the year, with 50 per cent of the planets moving backwards by the end of the month. Even Venus, your personal planet, will make a rare retrograde on the 25th. This means that there will not be much happening in the world or in many areas of your life in July and not much you can do to speed things up. A holiday is advisable for other reasons too – health and energy are still stressed (especially until the 23rd) and more rest is called for. Many things in your life will straighten themselves out of their own accord in the coming months. There's no need to force things and increase your stress levels.

One of the problems with a holiday is that you are in a yearly career peak until the 23rd. However, with today's technology one can keep in touch with work from anywhere. It might be feasible.

Finances improve after the 23rd but still seem slow. The two planets involved in finance – Saturn and Pluto – are both retrograde. The important thing now is to gain mental clarity in this area. This comes from doing your homework, getting the facts, resolving the doubts. Then your financial decisions will be sound.

Love is still high on the agenda. Many of the trends of last month are still in effect now. The love planet, Mars, spends the month in your 10th house. The spouse, partner or current love is succeeding and is supportive of your career goals. In many cases, this transit signals that love itself – the current relationship – is the career and the main priority. In many cases it shows the advancement of the career through social means. Singles are still attracted to people of power and prestige. Like last month, power is your aphrodisiac. Like last month, office romances are likely.

One of the problems with this position is that it is easy to get into a relationship of convenience rather than of real love. Convenience might give some comfort but it is not love.

Last month the planetary power began to make an important shift from the West to the East of the Horoscope – from the social to the independent sector. This month the shift is even stronger. It is now time to focus on number one, time to please yourself rather than trying to please others, time to make those changes in your life that need to be made. Personal independence and power are going to increase day by day. The only problem with this is the retrograde of Venus. You need to be clear on exactly what should be changed. This seems confusing at the moment, so start thinking and making your plans now. When Venus moves forward in a couple of months' time, the changes will be easier to make.

August

Best Days Overall: 1, 8, 9, 18, 19, 27, 28
Most Stressful Days Overall: 4, 5, 10, 11, 12, 25, 26, 31
Best Days for Love: 3, 4, 5, 13, 14, 23, 24, 31
Best Days for Money: 5, 6, 7, 15, 16, 20, 21, 22, 25, 26
Best Days for Career: 4, 5, 10, 11, 12, 13, 14, 25

Jupiter has been in your 11th house of friends and group activities since July 2014. Over half of the planets are either in or moving through this house this month, so it is a strong social month. In the past year you've made new and significant friends, and this month even more. Your knowledge of computers, science and technology has greatly expanded over the same period too. When the 11th house is this strong people often get their horoscopes done. Your knowledge of astrology and astronomy is greatly increased. The 11th house is where 'fondest hopes and wishes' come to pass. It is a happy kind of month.

Jupiter enters your spiritual 12th house on August 11. Mercury entered it on the 7th, while the Sun moves there on the 23rd. This signals that the month ahead (and the rest of the year) is very spiritual.

Be prepared for all kinds of experiences that can't be explained rationally. You will start reading more books on spirituality, psychic phenomena and ESP (extrasensory perception). You will start to explore your own abilities here. Many of you are already on a spiritual path. In those cases, your innate spiritual gifts will become even stronger. Many will even be involved in teaching others.

Finances are still not what they should, or will, be, but they are improving. Saturn starts to move forward on the 2nd. Jupiter makes fabulous aspects to your financial planet Pluto after the 11th. You are entering a prosperity period, but it has not yet reached its fullness. Pluto is still retrograde. Continue to gain mental clarity on finance. Things are actually much better than they seem at the moment.

Health and energy are much improved this month, and next month they will be even better. Enhance the health in the ways mentioned in the yearly report.

Your love planet, Mars, leaves the 10th house of career on the 9th and enters the 11th house. This brings a shift in love attitudes. Where once you were attracted by power and prestige, now you want friendship and equality. You want someone you can have fun with. This month you have the aspects for an online romance. Singles will find good romantic opportunities online. Romantic opportunities will come at group activities and events too. Friends are playing Cupid.

September

    Best Days Overall: 4, 5, 6, 14, 15, 24, 25
    Most Stressful Days Overall: 1, 7, 8, 22, 23, 28, 29
    Best Days for Love: 1, 9, 10, 19, 20, 28, 29, 30
    Best Days for Money: 2, 3, 12, 13, 17, 18, 22, 23, 30
    Best Days for Career: 2, 3, 7, 8, 12, 13, 24

We have two eclipses this month, which will bring disturbance and changes in the world and in your life. In spite of all the excitement, many nice positive things are happening for you.

First off, Saturn moves out of your money house on the 18th, greatly easing the financial pressures. Venus, the ruler of your Horoscope, starts moving forward on the 6th, bringing clarity to your personal affairs. And on the 23rd the Sun crosses the Ascendant and enters your 1st house, initiating a yearly personal pleasure peak. Health and energy are good this month as well.

The solar eclipse of the 13th occurs in your 12th house, bringing about change in your spiritual life – your outlook, opinions, attitudes and practice. Jupiter moved into this house last month, so these changes are not surprising. New revelation, new understanding comes to you and this change is just natural. The eclipse also indicates shake-ups in a charity or spiritual organization that you are involved with. The spiritual people in your life experience life-changing dramas. Friendships get tested too. Every solar eclipse does this. Computers, software and high-tech gadgets also get tested and might need replacement – back up your important files and make sure your anti-virus, anti-hacking software is up to date. This solar eclipse is basically benign for you, but it won't hurt to reduce your schedule a bit: it might not be so benign for the people around you.

The lunar eclipse of the 28th (in the Americas it is on the 27th) affects you more strongly. Here you should definitely reduce your schedule and take it easy for a few days. Stressful activities, especially if they are elective, would be better off rescheduled. This eclipse occurs in your 7th house and tests your marriage or current love relationship. Unresolved issues – things that have been swept under the rug – now come up for cleansing. If there are hidden flaws in your relationship, you find out about them now and can take steps to correct them. Good relationships will survive this, but flawed ones can go down the tubes. Be more patient with the beloved (and friends) during this period. They are more high strung and temperamental.

Every lunar eclipse affects your career. Thus there are major changes happening here too. Often an eclipse indicates shake-ups at the top in the corporate hierarchy. Often there are changes in your industry or profession. Sometimes the government agency that regulates your industry or profession changes the rules and its policy. People involved in your career experience life-changing kinds of dramas – bosses, parents or parent figures likewise.

All of this will work out in the end, but while the events happen, it can be uncomfortable.

October

> Best Days Overall: 2, 3, 11, 12, 13, 21, 22, 29, 30
> Most Stressful Days Overall: 4, 5, 19, 20, 25, 26, 31
> Best Days for Love: 1, 8, 9, 10, 19, 20, 25, 26, 27, 28
> Best Days for Money: 1, 9, 10, 14, 15, 19, 20, 27, 28
> Best Days for Career: 2, 3, 4, 5, 12, 13, 21, 22, 29, 30, 31

On August 11 you began a yearly cycle of prosperity. This month it intensifies. Late last month Pluto, your financial planet, started to move forward after months of retrograde motion. Saturn, which has been stressing finances, moved out of the money house on September 18. On the 23rd, the Sun enters your money house, initiating a yearly financial peak. Moreover, from the 24th to the 27th Venus will travel with Jupiter, bringing a nice payday or financial windfall. A prosperous month in a prosperous year.

Last month you entered a yearly personal pleasure peak, and this is in effect until the 23rd. This is a time for enjoying all the pleasures of the body – for indulging the body. The opportunities for this will come. It is a very good period to get the body and image in right shape.

Venus is moving forward again and the planetary power is at its maximum Eastern position. You are at your maximum point of personal power and independence. Libra tends to be too social and too reliant on others. It is good periodically to practise standing on your own two feet and becoming more self-reliant. By now your personal goals are much clearer. Now is the time to make them happen. There's no need to worry too much about what others will think: they will more or less go along too.

The planetary momentum is forward this month – 80 per cent of the planets are moving forward. Your birthday, which many of you are having this month, marks the beginning of your personal solar cycle. If you have a pressing need to start a new project or business, or to launch a new product, this is a good month to do it. (From the 13th to the 27th is best.) If you have free will in the matter, it would be better to wait until after the New Year though.

Health and energy are good this month. The planetary stresses of the past few months are much eased up. You can enhance the health further in the ways mentioned in the yearly report.

Love seems happy this month. Late last month (on the 25th) your love planet Mars changed signs and houses. It moved into your spiritual 12th house and will be there all of this month. Love is idealistic now. You are attracted to creative and spiritual types – the musician, the poet, the dancer, the spiritual channel or yogi. Practicality in love is now out the window. All you care about is the passion of the moment – the feeling of love. Once again you seem to be pursuing someone and by the end of the month you catch him or her. Love and social opportunities happen in spiritual settings – at charity functions, the yoga studio, the spiritual retreat, lecture or seminar.

November

Best Days Overall: 8, 9, 17, 18, 26, 27
Most Stressful Days Overall: 1, 15, 16, 22, 28, 29
Best Days for Love: 6, 7, 8, 17, 18, 21, 22, 26, 27
Best Days for Money: 5, 6, 10, 11, 15, 16, 24, 25
Best Days for Career: 1, 10, 11, 21, 22, 28, 29, 30

Last month you were the pursuer in love; this month the situation seems reversed. Love pursues you and will find you. There's nothing special that you need to do, love will find you. Just go about your daily business. The beloved seems very devoted to you this month – from the 12th onwards. He or she puts your interest ahead of their own. The beloved is totally on your side and supportive. You are having love on your terms this month.

Venus enters your sign on the 8th. If you are female this indicates more beauty and grace to the image. You always have a wonderful sense of style, but this period even more so. If you are male it signals more association with young women.

The two love planets in your chart – Mars and Venus – are in your sign from the 12th onwards. So, male or female, you are more attractive to the opposite sex. This is a great period for buying clothes and accessories or for beautifying the body.

The planetary power shifts this month. The shift began last month, but now it is confirmed. The lower half of the Horoscope is now dominant. By now career goals have more or less been achieved, and if they have not been completely achieved, good progress towards them has been made. Now it is time to prepare for your next career push which will happen next year. It is time to prepare the psychological foundations of future success. Time to get the home, family and emotional life in right order. If these are right, career will take care of itself.

You are still in a yearly financial peak until the 22nd. Jupiter is still making nice aspects to your financial planet, which is still moving forward. A prosperous month. The Sun in your money house (since October 23) flags the importance of online activities and technology in general. It's good to spend on these things. Good to be up to date. Mercury in the money house from the 2nd to the 20th shows the importance of sales, marketing and good PR. It also shows financial opportunity from foreign sources – foreign people or companies. Since Mercury rules your 9th house, in your chart he behaves like Jupiter – he is an expander. He shows increased earnings.

Health is good this month but there are a few warning signals. Mars in your sign from the 12th onwards can make you impatient and hasty. This can lead to accident or injury. Make haste by all means but in a mindful kind of way. Venus makes some dynamic aspects with Pluto and Uranus from the 19th to the 24th. Avoid risk taking and be more mindful on the physical plane.

December

Best Days Overall: 5, 6, 14, 15, 16, 23, 24
Most Stressful Days Overall: 12, 13, 19, 20, 25, 26
Best Days for Love: 5, 6, 7, 14, 15, 16, 17, 18, 19, 20, 23, 24, 25, 26
Best Days for Money: 2, 3, 4, 7, 8, 9, 12, 13, 21, 22, 30, 31
Best Days for Career: 1, 10, 11, 20, 25, 26, 30, 31

Mars, the love planet, makes dynamic aspects with Pluto and Uranus from the 5th to the 12th. Be more patient with the beloved during that time, as he or she could be having personal dramas. The beloved should stay out of harm's way then. Confrontations, temper tantrums and risky activities should be avoided. But love still seems good and the beloved still seems devoted to you.

The month ahead looks prosperous. On the 5th Venus enters your money house and stays there until the 30th. This shows a personal focus on finance. You want to look and appear wealthy. You dress more expensively. A very nice job opportunity occurs between the 10th and the 12th. Your financial planet Pluto will start receiving positive aspects from the 22nd onwards. Next month will be even better.

Your 3rd house of communication and intellectual interests became powerful on November 22 and remains so until the 22nd of this month. Time to give your mind the nutrition it needs. It is good to catch up on your reading and take courses, seminars or workshops on subjects that interest you. This is a nice aspect for students below college level. School work has been a struggle this year, but this month things go easier.

Health needs more attention after the 22nd. As always, make sure you get enough rest. Enhance the health in the ways discussed in the yearly report.

Many people report a sense of depression around the holidays. There are various reasons for this – much depends on their astrological sign and what is happening in the heavens – but aside from that, the holidays tend to rake up old, unresolved memories. The old family baggage gets an airing. This could be your experience too. The Sun moves into your 4th house of home and family on the 22nd. Rather than getting depressed, this resurfacing of the family baggage can be made to help you. Look at the memories that come up. Observe your opinions and judgements about them. Be an impartial observer. If the emotions are too strong and you find you lose your objectivity, write out your feelings (without censoring yourself) and then throw the paper away. You will feel much better and the old memories will lose their power.

Scorpio

ṃ

THE SCORPION

Birthdays from
23rd October to
22nd November

Personality Profile

SCORPIO AT A GLANCE

Element – Water

Ruling Planet – Pluto
  Co-ruling Planet – Mars
  Career Planet – Sun
  Love Planet – Venus
  Money Planet – Jupiter
  Planet of Health and Work – Mars
  Planet of Home and Family Life – Uranus

Colour – red-violet

Colour that promotes love, romance and social harmony – green

Colour that promotes earning power – blue

Gems – bloodstone, malachite, topaz

Metals – iron, radium, steel

Scents – cherry blossom, coconut, sandalwood, watermelon

Quality – fixed (= stability)

Quality most needed for balance – a wider view of things

Strongest virtues – loyalty, concentration, determination, courage, depth

Deepest needs – to penetrate and transform

Characteristics to avoid – jealousy, vindictiveness, fanaticism

Signs of greatest overall compatibility – Cancer, Pisces

Signs of greatest overall incompatibility – Taurus, Leo, Aquarius

Sign most helpful to career – Leo

Sign most helpful for emotional support – Aquarius

Sign most helpful financially – Sagittarius

Sign best for marriage and/or partnerships – Taurus

Sign most helpful for creative projects – Pisces

Best Sign to have fun with – Pisces

Signs most helpful in spiritual matters – Cancer, Libra

Best day of the week – Tuesday

Understanding a Scorpio

One symbol of the sign of Scorpio is the phoenix. If you meditate upon the legend of the phoenix you will begin to understand the Scorpio character – his or her powers and abilities, interests and deepest urges.

The phoenix of mythology was a bird that could recreate and reproduce itself. It did so in a most intriguing way: it would seek a fire – usually in a religious temple – fly into it, consume itself in the flames and then emerge a new bird. If this is not the ultimate, most profound transformation, then what is?

Transformation is what Scorpios are all about – in their minds, bodies, affairs and relationships (Scorpios are also society's transformers). To change something in a natural, not an artificial way, involves a transformation from within. This type of change is radical change as opposed to a mere cosmetic make-over. Some people think that change means altering just their appearance, but this is not the kind of thing that interests a Scorpio. Scorpios seek deep, fundamental change. Since real change always proceeds from within, a Scorpio is very interested in – and usually accustomed to – the inner, intimate and philosophical side of life.

Scorpios are people of depth and intellect. If you want to interest them you must present them with more than just a superficial image. You and your interests, projects or business deals must have real substance to them in order to stimulate a Scorpio. If they haven't, he or she will find you out – and that will be the end of the story.

If we observe life – the processes of growth and decay – we see the transformational powers of Scorpio at work all the time. The caterpillar changes itself into a butterfly; the infant grows into a child and then an adult. To Scorpios this definite and perpetual transformation is not something to be feared. They see it as a normal part of life. This acceptance of transformation gives Scorpios the key to understanding the true meaning of life.

Scorpios' understanding of life (including life's weaknesses) makes them powerful warriors – in all senses of the word. Add to this their depth, patience and endurance and you have a powerful personality. Scorpios have good, long memories and can at times be quite vindictive

- they can wait years to get their revenge. As a friend, though, there is no one more loyal and true than a Scorpio. Few are willing to make the sacrifices that a Scorpio will make for a true friend.

The results of a transformation are quite obvious, although the process of transformation is invisible and secret. This is why Scorpios are considered secretive in nature. A seed will not grow properly if you keep digging it up and exposing it to the light of day. It must stay buried - invisible - until it starts to grow. In the same manner, Scorpios fear revealing too much about themselves or their hopes to other people. However, they will be more than happy to let you see the finished product - but only when it is completely unwrapped. On the other hand, Scorpios like knowing everyone else's secrets as much as they dislike anyone knowing theirs.

Finance

Love, birth, life as well as death are Nature's most potent transformations; Scorpios are interested in all of these. In our society, money is a transforming power, too, and a Scorpio is interested in money for that reason. To a Scorpio money is power, money causes change, money controls. It is the power of money that fascinates them. But Scorpios can be too materialistic if they are not careful. They can be overly awed by the power of money, to a point where they think that money rules the world.

Even the term 'plutocrat' comes from Pluto, the ruler of the sign of Scorpio. Scorpios will - in one way or another - achieve the financial status they strive for. When they do so they are careful in the way they handle their wealth. Part of this financial carefulness is really a kind of honesty, for Scorpios are usually involved with other people's money - as accountants, lawyers, stockbrokers or corporate managers - and when you handle other people's money you have to be more cautious than when you handle your own.

In order to fulfil their financial goals, Scorpios have important lessons to learn. They need to develop qualities that do not come naturally to them, such as breadth of vision, optimism, faith, trust and, above all, generosity. They need to see the wealth in Nature and in life, as well as in its more obvious forms of money and power. When they develop generosity their financial potential reaches great heights, for Jupiter, the Lord of Opulence and Good Fortune, is Scorpio's money planet.

Career and Public Image

Scorpio's greatest aspiration in life is to be considered by society as a source of light and life. They want to be leaders, to be stars. But they follow a very different road than do Leos, the other stars of the zodiac. A Scorpio arrives at the goal secretly, without ostentation; a Leo pursues it openly. Scorpios seek the glamour and fun of the rich and famous in a restrained, discreet way.

Scorpios are by nature introverted and tend to avoid the limelight. But if they want to attain their highest career goals they need to open up a bit and to express themselves more. They need to stop hiding their light under a bushel and let it shine. Above all, they need to let go of any vindictiveness and small-mindedness. All their gifts and insights were given to them for one important reason – to serve life and to increase the joy of living for others.

Love and Relationships

Scorpio is another zodiac sign that likes committed clearly defined, structured relationships. They are cautious about marriage, but when they do commit to a relationship they tend to be faithful – and heaven help the mate caught or even suspected of infidelity! The jealousy of the Scorpio is legendary. They can be so intense in their jealousy that even the thought or intention of infidelity will be detected and is likely to cause as much of a storm as if the deed had actually been done.

Scorpios tend to settle down with those who are wealthier than they are. They usually have enough intensity for two, so in their partners they seek someone pleasant, hard-working, amiable, stable and easy-going. They want someone they can lean on, someone loyal behind them as they fight the battles of life. To a Scorpio a partner, be it a lover or a friend, is a real partner – not an adversary. Most of all a Scorpio is looking for an ally, not a competitor.

If you are in love with a Scorpio you will need a lot of patience. It takes a long time to get to know Scorpios, because they do not reveal themselves readily. But if you persist and your motives are honourable, you will gradually be allowed into a Scorpio's inner chambers of the mind and heart.

Home and Domestic Life

Uranus is ruler of Scorpio's 4th solar house of home and family. Uranus is the planet of science, technology, changes and democracy. This tells us a lot about a Scorpio's conduct in the home and what he or she needs in order to have a happy, harmonious home life.

Scorpios can sometimes bring their passion, intensity and wilfulness into the home and family, which is not always the place for these qualities. These traits are good for the warrior and the transformer, but not so good for the nurturer and family member. Because of this (and also because of their need for change and transformation) the Scorpio may be prone to sudden changes of residence. If not carefully constrained, the sometimes inflexible Scorpio can produce turmoil and sudden upheavals within the family.

Scorpios need to develop some of the virtues of Aquarius in order to cope better with domestic matters. There is a need to build a team spirit at home, to treat family activities as truly group activities – family members should all have a say in what does and does not get done. For at times a Scorpio can be most dictatorial. When a Scorpio gets dictatorial it is much worse than if a Leo or Capricorn (the two other power signs in the zodiac) does. For the dictatorship of a Scorpio is applied with more zeal, passion, intensity and concentration than is true of either a Leo or Capricorn. Obviously this can be unbearable to family members – especially if they are sensitive types.

In order for a Scorpio to get the full benefit of the emotional support that a family can give, he or she needs to let go of conservatism and be a bit more experimental, to explore new techniques in childrearing, be more democratic with family members and to try to manage things by consensus rather than by autocratic edict.

Horoscope for 2015

Major Trends

Saturn has been in your sign for the past two years, which was a challenging aspect. Overall energy was not what it should have been. Perhaps you felt pessimistic about life and yourself. You felt older than your years, and even young people were thinking about old age. Self-esteem and self-confidence were not what they should have been. It was necessary to take a low personal profile. Happily, this is mostly over with. Saturn moved out of your sign in December 2014 and will spend most of the year ahead in Sagittarius. Although he will retrograde briefly back into your sign from June 15 to September 18, the worst of the transit is over with. You are more optimistic and energetic this year.

Saturn's move into Sagittarius is a very nice transit for overall health. If you've had health problems, you should hear good news this year. If you've been healthy, then your health will become even better. There's more on this later.

Pluto, the ruler of your Horoscope, has been in Capricorn, your 3rd house of communication, for some years now. He will be there for many more years. This shows a focus on communication and intellectual activities. It's a very nice aspect for students. They should do well in their studies. This is also a nice aspect for those of you involved in sales, marketing, journalism and PR. You should do well this year.

When Jupiter entered Leo in July 2014 you entered a cycle of career success. This trend continues in the year ahead. More details later.

Neptune has been in your 5th house of fun and creativity since 2012, and remains there for many more years. This is a very nice transit for those of you involved in the creative arts. You are unusually inspired and original these days.

Uranus has been in your 6th house of health and work for some years and will be there in the year ahead. Thus there has been much job instability – multiple job changes. There have also been many changes in the conditions of the workplace. More on this later.

Your most important areas of interest this year will be the body and image (from June 15 to September 18); finance (from January 1 to June 15 and September 18 onwards); communication and intellectual interests; children, fun and creativity; health and work; career (until August 11); and friends, groups and group activities (from August 11 onwards).

Your paths of greatest fulfilment this year will be career (until August 11); friends, groups and group activities (from August 11 onwards); and spirituality (until November 13).

Health

(Please note that this is an astrological perspective on health and not a medical one. In days of yore there was no difference, these perspectives were identical. But now there could be quite a difference. For a medical perspective, please consult your doctor or health practitioner.)

Health is much improved over the past few years. Saturn, the planet that was stressing you out, is mostly out of your sign. And when he returns from June 15 to September 18, he will only affect those born late in the sign of Scorpio – those of you with birthdays from November 19 to November 22. Saturn in your sign was very good for weight-loss regimes, if you needed them (and this still holds for Saturn's return between June and September).

Uranus has been in your 6th house of health for many years now, as we have mentioned. This shows an experimentalism in health matters, a willingness to try new and untested therapies, new and cutting-edge health technologies.

It also shows, and we have mentioned this in past years, that your job now is to learn how you function personally – learn what works for you. We are all wired up very differently. Each person is a law unto themselves when it comes to health, and this is the time to learn.

Good though your health is, you can make it even better. Give more attention to the following areas – the vulnerable areas in the year ahead: the colon, bladder and sexual organs; the head, face and scalp; the adrenals; the muscles; and the ankles and calves. The reflexes for these areas are shown in the diagram overleaf.

The colon, bladder and sexual organs are always important for you and this year is no different. Libido has been more sluggish the past two years – the elimination system as well. There should be improvements here in the year ahead. Regular colonic irrigation is a good idea. Safe sex and sexual moderation is always important.

Regular scalp and face massage will be good to help the important areas of the head and face, as will be craniosacral therapy. Try to avoid fear and anger, the two emotions that stress out the adrenals.

Good muscle tone is always important for you. Thus vigorous physical exercise is good. Make sure you give the ankles good support when you're exercising, though. Ankles and calves should be regularly massaged.

Good emotional health is desirable for everyone, but it is especially important for you. If there is discord in the family or on the domestic front, the physical health is affected. But also, you don't feel healthy even though there might not be physical symptoms. Good health for you means physical fitness and good emotional health. Make sure your moods are constructive and positive. Don't let yourself become a victim of mood, but always be the master. Meditation will be a big help.

With your aspects, health problems can be coming from the memory body – they might not be what they are diagnosed to be. If memories get

Important foot reflexology points for the year ahead

Try to massage the whole foot on a regular basis, but pay extra attention to the points highlighted on the chart. When you massage, be aware of 'sore spots', as these need special attention. It is also a good idea to massage the ankles and the tops of the feet.

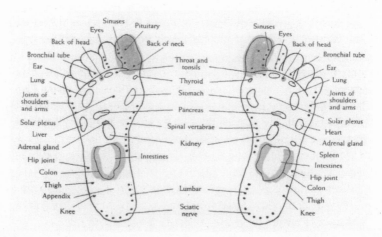

stimulated in a negative way, real symptoms can be produced. These symptoms feel real, but the way to treat them is to clean the negative memory. Past life regression might be a good therapy in these cases.

Home and Family

Your 4th house of home and family is not a house of power this year. Normally this would show a status quo kind of year. However, this year (and during the latter part of last year) your family planet Uranus is receiving wonderful aspects from Jupiter. So there are important and positive developments happening.

The family situation hasn't been happy the past few years. Pluto, the ruler of your Horoscope, and Uranus have been in stressful aspect. This shows conflict with the family and most especially with a parent or parent figure. This conflict has been intense at times. There could have been a break between you and the family. This person wants to serve you, but not in the way that you would like. Happily, things are much easier this year. The stressful aspect – though still in effect – is not as strong as it was in past years. And, as we have mentioned, Jupiter is making nice aspects to your family planet. Is there peace now? Perhaps not. But there's less conflict than before.

Finance seems to play a role in the better condition. Either you or the parent figure is being supportive financially. There seems to be good financial co-operation between you.

A move could happen this year – a happy one. The home is enlarged. The family circle is expanded – generally through birth or marriage. This plays a role in the better condition as well. Uranus has been in your 6th house of health and work for some years, indicating someone working from home, in a home office or home-based business. This has been the trend for many years and it continues. This aspect also shows that you are making the home more healthy. You could be installing exercise or spa equipment in the home, or making the home a healthier environment by removing toxic paints, or asbestos or toxic deposits around the home.

Renovations are good all year, but especially from February 20 to April 1. If you're decorating in a cosmetic kind of way – repainting or buying objects of beauty for the home – February 20 to March 17 is good.

A parent or parent figure has a wonderful social life this year. If he or she is single, there is romantic opportunity. A move is not likely this year.

You seem close with siblings and sibling figures this year – especially with the oldest. He or she could have had multiple moves in the past few years and the trend continues in the year ahead.

The spouse, partner or current love could have moved last year, and if not this could still happen in the year ahead. Children or children figures in your life are having quiet kind of family year. The same is true for grandchildren, if you have them.

Finance and Career

As we mentioned, the main financial headline is Saturn's move from your own sign into Sagittarius, your money house. He will spend most of the year there and will be there for the next two years – a long-term trend.

How will you experience this Saturn transit? Much depends on you and your personal circumstances. Saturn is going to reorganize and reorder the finances in a better, more cosmic kind of way. His methodology is pressure. Stress. He gives the financial life a 'stress test'. In this stress test weaknesses get revealed and thus you are able to correct them.

We really don't know our financial health in the good times. When the breaks come our way and Lady Luck sits beside us, many things get overlooked. Perhaps we are overpaying for that phone package or that internet connection. Perhaps we are unconcerned that debt is too high relative to earnings. Or that we overspent on that wardrobe or holiday. As long as the money is rolling in, these are considered trifles and we don't bother. But when the times get tougher, when the breaks are not happening, when extra expenses and responsibilities arise, then these seemingly little things become important and we must do something about them. The way you manage your money becomes important. And this is Saturn's function.

Dealing with this pressure is seldom pleasant. But the end result will be good. We will be financially healthier than before. Saturn gives you the stress, gives you the crisis, but he also shows solutions. No matter how grave the financial situation seems to be there is always a solution.

Your experience of this transit will also depend on how responsible you have been in your financial life. For those who have been responsible, Saturn will put on the stress, but you will come out richer than before. For those who have been irresponsible, this is a time where the bills come due. It can be quite traumatic. There can be law suits and bankruptcies. Past misdeeds have to be dealt with. But these kinds of traumas too will lead, eventually, to better financial health and better financial attitudes.

The good news here is that your financial planet, Jupiter, is in your 10th career house and is the most elevated (for most of the year) of all the planets. This shows a strong focus here. And when times are tough the focus is necessary. We get what we focus on. Finance needs your attention. This transit also shows good financial support from elders, bosses, parent figures and authority figures. Good relations with the government are important. The government seems to play a huge role in earnings. Pay rises and promotions are likely this year. You seem successful in your career.

There is luck in speculations until August 11. But you shouldn't rely on this. The financial luck still needs good financial management.

On August 11 your financial planet moves into Virgo, your 11th house. Friends are prospering and seem more supportive. It will be very good to be involved with groups and organizations – there is a good bottom-line benefit. Be sure to stay up to date with the latest technology, it seems important in your financial life. This transit favours online kinds of businesses or earning from online activities.

Jupiter's move into Virgo is wonderful for finance. It shows prosperity. You have extra responsibilities, but the money for them will come. The important thing is to make it through to August.

Love and Social Life

Your 7th house is not a house of power this year and this tends to a status quo kind of year, romance-wise. Those of you who are married will most likely stay married and singles will tend to stay single. It shows a kind of contentment with things as they are. There is no compelling cosmic push to make changes. (However, there is nothing against you making changes, if you choose.)

Though the romantic life is fairly static, the overall social life will become more active after August 11 with Jupiter's move into your 11th house of friends. You will be meeting new and significant people – and they seem wealthy. A lot of your socializing will involve money – perhaps the promotion of some product or service – or business-type functions. This area of life seems happy.

Since fast-moving Venus is your love planet there are many short-term trends in love, depending of where Venus is at a given time and the aspects she receives. These are best dealt with in the monthly reports.

Venus will make one of her rare retrogrades this year – from July 25 to September 6. This tends to produce glitches and delays in love. Sometimes relationships seem to go backwards instead of forwards. Sometimes the social judgement is not up to par and there is a lack of social confidence. This is a good time to review your love life or marriage and see where positive improvements can be made. It is not a time for major love decisions one way or another.

Venus will spend an unusual amount of time in the sign of Leo (your 10th house of career) this year, approximately four months. Her usual transit is less than a month. So there are love opportunities with bosses, elders and authority figures in the year ahead. You will gravitate to people who are above you in status and who can be helpful in your career. Power becomes the ultimate aphrodisiac. These tendencies are prominent this year.

The love life of a parent or parent figure is much improved this year. If this person is married the marriage will become happier. If he or she is single a significant relationship is happening. Siblings and sibling figures are having a status quo love year. However, they seem more sexually active this year.

Children and children figures are having a very happy love and social year – from August 11 onwards. If they are of the appropriate age, marriage or a serious relationship is likely.

Self-improvement

We discussed Saturn's move into your money house earlier. Extra financial responsibilities will come. The tendency (a very human kind of thing) is to try to avoid and evade them. But this is not advisable this year. Face them. Confront them. Accept them. Especially if you know in your heart that the responsibilities are legitimate. They may seem huge. More than you can handle. But as you accept them, help will come. You will discover that you have the power to handle these things. Saturn gives you the challenge and also the power to handle it. Things are not the way you imagined them to be. There is a spiritual growth that happens when you co-operate with Saturn and you don't want to miss this.

This is not a year to play games with the government. You need their favour in your financial life.

When your financial planet moves into your 11th house on August 11, you will learn that wealth is much more than just physical, tangible things. Those are only part of the story. Wealth of friendships is also wealth. Who you know is perhaps just as important as how much you actually have.

Children and children figures in your life are under very intense spiritual energies these days. This has been the case since 2012. They are more sensitive, more easily hurt. Watch your voice tone when you talk to them. Their physical bodies are becoming more refined as well – and this is a long-term trend. They should avoid alcohol and drugs these days as they can react badly to them. They will have dreams and see visions. They will have all kinds of supernatural-type experiences. If they confide in you, don't deny these things. Just listen without judgement. They are more attuned to invisible energies these days. School work could suffer because of this. The mundane world seems uninteresting and unimportant to them. So, they will need to work harder in school for the next few years.

Month-by-month Forecasts

January

Best Days Overall: 4, 5, 14, 15, 22, 23, 31
Most Stressful Days Overall: 6, 7, 8, 20, 21, 27, 28
Best Days for Love: 1, 12, 13, 21, 22, 27, 28, 31
Best Days for Money: 7, 8, 16, 17, 24, 25
Best Days for Career: 1, 6, 7, 8, 9, 10, 20, 21, 29, 30

You begin your year with the planetary power at the nadir (low point) of your chart. Your 4th house of home and family is much stronger than the 10th house of career. Half of the planets are either in or moving through your 4th house this month – a clear message. Career is important and successful this year, but now it is time to get the family and domestic situation straight. Now is the time to build up your interior forces for your next career push in about four months. Work on the career by the inner, subjective methods – visualize, imagine, dream about where you want to be and what you want to achieve. Enter, as best you can, into the feeling of being where you want to be. Right now, never mind how this will be done. The best way to get to your goals is to 'be there' in your consciousness. The 'how' will unfold in due course.

You are in an excellent period for starting new projects and new activities. The planetary momentum is overwhelmingly forward this month. Your personal solar cycle and the universal solar cycle are in their waxing phases. You will have a lot of momentum and support behind you. The best days for starting new projects are from the 1st to the 5th and on the 20th. In a pinch anytime after the 20th is acceptable.

On the 20th the planetary power shifts from the Eastern, independent sector to the Western, social sector of the Horoscope. Your cycle of personal independence is over with for now and it is time to develop your social skills. Hopefully you made the personal changes you needed to make over the past six months. Now it is time to live with them. If you created well, life is pleasant. If there are mistakes, adapt to them as best you can. Changes are more difficult to make for the next few months. Your way is not the best way these days. Many of the problems and challenges that people face arise precisely because they got their own way. Let others have their way now, so long as it isn't destructive.

Finances are more stressful than usual this month. Saturn is in your money house, creating feelings of being squeezed and bringing extra financial responsibilities. Your financial planet Jupiter is retrograde all month, slowing down financial progress. After the 20th he receives stressful aspects to boot. You just have to work harder to achieve your financial goals this month. Good financial management is important all year, but especially in the month ahead.

On an overall level health is much better than last year. But after the 20th you are not in your best health period. Enhance your health in the ways mentioned in the yearly report. Until the 20th your health can be improved through calf and ankle massage. Avoid depression and negative states. Diet is more of an issue. After the 20th give more attention to the feet. Regular foot massage will be powerful.

February

    Best Days Overall: 1, 10, 11, 19, 20, 27, 28
    Most Stressful Days Overall: 3, 4, 17, 18, 23, 24
    Best Days for Love: 1, 2, 10, 11, 20, 21, 23, 24
    Best Days for Money: 3, 4, 13, 14, 21, 22
    Best Days for Career: 3, 4, 8, 9, 17, 18, 27, 28

Finances are pretty much like last month until the 18th. You just need to work harder. If you put in the work, you should prosper. Jupiter, your financial planet, is still retrograde, so avoid making major financial changes, investments or purchases. (Of course you shop for groceries and other necessities, but we refer to major purchases.) The financial life is under review. The important thing is to gain mental clarity in this area – to resolve your doubts. This is a time for fact gathering. Later when Jupiter moves forward you can implement your plans. You should see some improvement after the 20th, but finances are still not what they should be or will be.

Health still needs watching until the 18th. Refer to our discussion last month. The feet are still important healthwise until the 20th. After then give more attention to the kidneys and hips. Hip massage will be beneficial, especially from the 20th to the 24th. A kidney detox might be a good idea. It will also be important to maintain love and social harmony at this time as disharmony here can create physical problems. Health will improve after the 18th.

On the 18th, as the Sun enters your 5th house, you begin one of your yearly personal pleasure peaks. This will be a fun period, a creative kind of period, a cosmic vacation. This is great period to be more involved with the children or children figures in your life. In fact this seems your cosmic mission during this time. A happy career opportunity comes to a child or child figure between the 23rd and the 27th. You are involved here.

Love seems happy this month. Your love planet Venus travels with Neptune from the 1st to the 3rd. This shows a happy romantic meeting, something fun. Venus will be in the sign of Pisces until the 20th, her most exalted position. Thus your social grace – your 'drawing' power – your attractiveness – is at its height. Venus in Pisces is her most sensitive position. Thus you experience nuances in love that most people never experience. Love is very idealistic now. And, sometimes, with this position we project our ideals on the beloved when it isn't warranted. On the other hand, seeing the ideal in another tends to enhance the love experience. You bring out their highest and best.

The beloved will be much more sensitive than usual until the 20th, so be careful of voice tone or body language. He or she can overreact to this. Singles find love opportunities in the usual places until the 20th – at parties, sporting events and places of entertainment. After the 20th romantic opportunities happen at the workplace or as you pursue your health goals. Health professionals and people involved in your health are very alluring after the 20th.

March

Best Days Overall: 1, 9, 10, 18, 19, 27, 28
Most Stressful Days Overall: 2, 3, 9, 10, 16, 17, 22, 23, 29, 30, 31
Best Days for Love: 2, 3, 12, 13, 22, 23
Best Days for Money: 2, 3, 12, 13, 20, 21
Best Days for Career: 1, 2, 3, 10, 11, 18, 19, 20, 29, 30, 31

A solar eclipse on the 20th shakes things up on a world level but seems basically benign to you. It straddles your 5th and 6th houses and impacts on both these areas of life. Children and children figures in your life are redefining themselves and will start to project a new image to the world. This is basically a healthy thing. We are never the same from day to day and periodically we should take stock of ourselves. Speculations are not favourable during this period. Children and children figures should avoid risky, stressful kinds of activities.

This eclipse also announces job and career changes. These will be good, but can be disruptive. (Good things can be just as disruptive as bad things.) Barriers to your career success are coming down. There can be shake-ups in your company, industry and profession – in the hierarchies there. Changes of policy can also happen. The rules of the game change. Job changes can even happen before the eclipse – from the 9th to the 12th. There is instability at the workplace and if you hire others there can be some staff turnover now. The conditions of work change. The good news here is that job seekers have plenty of job opportunities from the 20th onwards, and those who employ others will easily find new recruits.

The Sun's move into Aries on the 20th vastly improves the financial picture. The Sun and your financial planet, Jupiter, go into 'mutual reception' – this means that each is a guest in the sign and house of the other. This indicates good co-operation between these two planets. Thus, you have the financial favour of bosses, elders, parents and parent figures. They are supportive of your financial goals and seem eager to prosper you. Pay rises and promotions could happen. A new job will bring more money (whether it is in your present company or with another one). Money can come from the government too. If you have issues with the government this would be a good time to resolve them. However, Jupiter is still retrograde, so continue to put the financial life under review. Earnings are happening but with delays and glitches. Make sure all the little details of your financial transactions are perfect. Minor mistakes can cause major delays.

Be more patient with the beloved from the 3rd to the 6th. He or she seems more temperamental. A current relationship gets tested. Love improves after the 17th. You seem more in harmony with the beloved.

For the unattached there are happy romantic meetings happening from the 17th onward – the 28th to the 30th seems especially good.

Overall health and energy are good this month. You are focused here too. You can enhance the health further in the ways mentioned in the yearly report.

April

Best Days Overall: 6, 7, 15, 16, 23, 24
Most Stressful Days Overall: 13, 14, 19, 20, 25, 26, 27
Best Days for Love: 1, 2, 13, 19, 20, 21, 22
Best Days for Money: 8, 9, 17, 18, 25, 26
Best Days for Career: 8, 9, 18, 19, 25, 26, 27, 28

Eclipses are cosmic announcements that change is imminent. They are like giant billboards in the sky, telling you to get ready. The lunar eclipse of the 4th is no different.

Many, many changes are happening now. On the 8th, Jupiter, your financial planet, starts moving forward for the first time this year. On the 20th, the planetary power shifts to the upper half of your Horoscope, signalling a psychological shift for you. You are getting ready for your major career push for the year. Time to let go (temporarily) of home and domestic concerns and focus on your outer goals. If you do right you will feel right. Serve your family by being successful in the world.

Also on the 20th you enter a yearly love and social peak.

The lunar eclipse of the 4th is a strong one. Many planets besides the Moon are affected. Thus many areas of life are affected. You should reduce your schedule during this period. The eclipse occurs in your 12th house of spirituality, indicating dramatic changes in your spiritual life – your practice, your attitudes, the teachings that you follow. There are shake-ups in spiritual, religious or charitable organizations that you are involved with. Often there are dramas in the lives of gurus or mentors – the spiritual people in your life. Every lunar eclipse activates the dream life, but this one more so than usual. However, it's not advisable to pay too much attention your dreams during this period, as much of what is happening is flotsam and jetsam stirred up by the eclipse.

Career changes happen as well and these seem positive. But the circumstances that bring them about can be dramatic. Generally there are shake-ups in the corporate hierarchy, or in your industry or profession. Policies can change dramatically. The government agency that regulates your industry or profession can make changes in their rules. There can be life-changing dramas in the lives of bosses, elders, parents or parent figures. Uranus, your home and family planet, is involved in this eclipse so there are dramas in the lives of family members. Flaws in the home are revealed and you must make the corrections. Passions run high in the family. You have had a tense relationship with certain family members for some time and things flare up again.

In your chart the eclipsed planet, the Moon, is ruler of your 9th house. Foreign travel is not advisable at this time. College students can change institutions or courses or make other changes to their educational plans. If you are involved in legal issues, they move forward now – one way or another – and you are forced to spend time on these things.

May

Best Days Overall: 3, 4, 12, 13, 21, 22, 30, 31
Most Stressful Days Overall: 10, 11, 16, 17, 23, 24
Best Days for Love: 1, 2, 12, 13, 16, 17, 21, 22, 30, 31
Best Days for Money: 5, 6, 7, 14, 15, 23, 24
Best Days for Career: 8, 9, 17, 18, 23, 24, 28, 29

Health and energy became more stressful on the 20th of last month, and will remain so until the 21st of this. Make sure you get enough rest. This month you can enhance your health by giving more attention to the neck and throat until the 12th. Regular neck massage is advisable. Don't allow tension to build up there. If you feel under the weather restore harmony in the marriage and love life as quickly as possible. After the 12th pay attention to the lungs, arms, shoulders and respiratory system. Don't allow tension to build up in the shoulders and massage them regularly. Detox regimes are helpful. If you feel under the weather, get out in the fresh air and breathe deeply. Health and energy improve after the 21st.

Finances are much improved these days. You have had to work harder for earnings since the 20th of last month and this is the case until May 21. But things are picking up. The log jam is over. Financial confidence is good. You are prospering. You still have the financial favour of those in authority in your life, and their favour will be stronger after the 21st.

Love is happy this month. Until the 20th you are in a yearly love and social peak. The social life and your social magnetism are at their strongest. The only problem is that this social focus can be a distraction from your financial life. Each vies with the other for supremacy – for your attention. You are mixing with authority figures these days, people above you in status and power. The good news is that this helps the career. You meet just the right people who can help you. It is also good to advance your career by social means. The social contacts (and your social skills) are very important careerwise.

On the 21st your 8th house of transformation becomes very powerful – easily the most powerful in the Horoscope at this time: 50 per cent of the planets are either there or moving through there this month. Now most people are not comfortable with a strong 8th house. The affairs it deals with – death, decomposition, detoxification, taxes, the underworld – are not pleasant interests. But for you this is Scorpio heaven. These are the areas most interesting to you and you excel in them.

Scorpios are sexually active even under normal circumstances; this period even more so. If you are involved in research projects, learning about secret things, there is success this month. If you are of the appropriate age, it would be good to do your estate and tax planning now. It is also a good time for any kind of detox or weight-loss regime.

June

Best Days Overall: 8, 9, 17, 18, 19, 27, 28
Most Stressful Days Overall: 6, 7, 13, 14, 20, 21
Best Days for Love: 1, 10, 11, 13, 14, 20, 21, 29, 30
Best Days for Money: 2, 3, 10, 11, 20, 21, 29, 30
Best Days for Career: 6, 7, 15, 16, 20, 21, 27

Boudoir Sdn. Bhd.
(898821-U)
2F-11, Bangsar Village II,
Jalan Telawi 1
Kuala Lumpur
Tel: 03-22823128
Fax: 03-22873128

Seat #   : 5
Bill #   : 019619
Customer : Jen Gill Kaur
Cashier   : director
Date   : 21-10-2014
Time   : 13:37

Receipt

Qty	Items	Amount
1	F.Affair-P	80.00

Item Total(RM):	80.00
Serv. Charge(RM):	0.00
Round Up(RM):	0.00
Sub Total(RM):	80.00
Pay. Amt(RM):	100.00

Cash:100.00
Change: 20.00

Thank you
Please come again

Saturn retrogrades back into your sign on the 15th, but for most of you the effect will be slight. However, if you were born late in Scorpio – from November 19 to November 22 – you will feel this very strongly. You might feel pessimistic, older than your years, and you might seem distant and cold to others. You will have to consciously project more warmth and love to those around you.

Health and energy are affected by Saturn's retrograde but the short-term planets are easing the stress and health should be good this month. Until the 24th, continue to give more attention to the lungs, arms, shoulders and respiratory system. Make sure you are getting enough fresh air. Detox regimes are still very good. After the 24th pay more attention to the stomach. Diet will become then too. Women should give more attention to the breasts. Moods and emotions always play a role in health, but this period more so and more dramatically. Work to keep your mood positive and constructive. There's a lot of water in the Horoscope from the 21st onwards, so moods and emotions – positive or negative – are more powerful and have more impact than usual.

Career energy is getting stronger day by day and you haven't yet reached your peak. Continue to focus there and let home and family issues go for a while. You probably can't completely ignore them, but you can downplay them for a while. On the 5th Venus crosses the Mid-heaven and enters your career house. Thus the two beneficent planets of the zodiac – Jupiter and Venus – will be in this house. This signals success, but also happiness and satisfaction. Success happens in happy ways.

Your love planet in the 10th house gives many messages. First, it reinforces the importance of social skills in the career. Your personal competence is important, no question about that, but the likeability factor might be more important these days. It's not just about doing your job, but your ability to get along with others that matters. Enhance the career by attending or hosting the right kinds of parties and gatherings. You are meeting people who can be very helpful in your career.

Venus in the 10th house is also good for the love life. Romance is high on your agenda (love and money seem the most important things this period) and you focus on it. This focus brings success. There are opportunities for office romances. You are attracted to people of power and prestige. A very happy love meeting happens between the 28th and the 30th. (This is also a good financial period.)

July

Best Days Overall: 6, 7, 14, 15, 16, 24, 25
Most Stressful Days Overall: 3, 4, 5, 10, 11, 17, 18, 31
Best Days for Love: 8, 9, 10, 11, 17, 18, 26
Best Days for Money: 9, 18, 26, 27, 28
Best Days for Career: 6, 7, 14, 15, 16, 17, 18, 26

Retrograde activity is strong this month – it's at its maximum for the year. Things are moving more slowly. There are delays. Many will attribute this to the summer season, but it is the increased retrograde activity that is causing this. It is good to understand these things.

Success – both financial and careerwise – is happening for you this month, but perhaps at a slower pace than you would like. Also, much of the success is happening behind the scenes and so you might not be aware of it at the moment. Rest assured that it is happening.

On the 23rd, you enter your yearly career peak. Half of the planets are either in or moving through your 10th house this month. This is a lot of power. So career goals are being achieved (or good progress is made towards their achievement). Pay rises and promotions can happen. (They could have happened earlier too, but are more likely this month.) The money people and the authority figures in your life are supporting your career goals.

The spouse, partner or current love also seems successful this period and he or she is also supportive.

Health and energy become more delicate – and need attention – from the 23rd onwards. Enhance the health in the ways mentioned in the yearly report. Also, like last month, give more attention to the stomach and your general diet. Women should give more attention to the breasts. Review our discussion of this last month. The most important thing is to get enough rest. When energy is low pre-existing conditions can flare up or get worse. Even if there are no pre-existing conditions, you are more vulnerable to opportunistic infections and the like.

Venus, your love planet, makes one of her rare retrogrades on the 25th. This will not stop the love life. Singles will still date. Social invitations will still happen. But things slow down. A current relationship can seem to go backward. The normal social confidence and judgement are not there. There can be problems due to poor romantic choices. Affections shift. The love life should reviewed from the 25th onwards. No important long-term decisions should be made during this time. The important thing is to gain mental clarity about your needs in love and the kind of relationship that you're in. Decision-making should come later when Venus moves forward, in two months' time.

August

Best Days Overall: 2, 3, 10, 11, 12, 20, 21, 22, 29, 30
Most Stressful Days Overall: 1, 6, 7, 13, 14, 27, 28
Best Days for Love: 5, 6, 7, 14, 23, 24, 31
Best Days for Money: 5, 15, 23, 24, 25
Best Days for Career: 4, 5, 13, 14, 25

Last month, on the 23rd, the planetary power began to shift. The Eastern, independent sector is now powerful. The planetary power is moving towards you rather than away from you. It is time to focus on your own interests and desires. It is wonderful to get on with others; wonderful to be concerned about their needs. But your own needs are no less important. And you are in the cycle where these should be dealt with. Now is the time to stand on your own two feet, to practise self-reliance, to take personal responsibility for your happiness. People skills are wonderful, but now is the time to develop personal initiative. For the next five months or so, your personal power and independence are strong. Use this time to create conditions of happiness. If others don't go along initially with you (eventually they will), act independently.

You are still in a yearly career peak until the 23rd. And the focus should still be there. You seem to be working very hard this month, fending off the competition, meeting deadlines, putting in long hours. But it pays off. Your social graces are still important in your career, but less so than last month. Now it is your work ethic that impresses superiors. Uncles or aunts (or these kinds of figures in your life) seem very helpful in the career this month.

Health and energy are still stressful until the 23rd. Like last month, enhance the health by giving more attention to the stomach, breasts and diet, until the 9th. Keep moods positive and constructive. Do your best to maintain family harmony (it won't be easy but do your best). After the 9th give more attention to the heart.

By the 23rd you will have made satisfactory progress in your career and the focus shifts to friends and group activities. Jupiter moves into your 11th house of friends on the 11th and the Sun follows suit on the 23rd. Being involved in group activities helps the career. But the other message of the Horoscope is that your mission now is to be there for your friends. (Your own interests are the most important at the moment, but when these are filled, be there for your friends.) An important new friendship materializes between the 6th and the 8th. And you will be making many more new friends after the 11th. It is a social period, but not necessarily a romantic one.

Your love planet remains retrograde all month. Between the 3rd and the 6th there is a happy romantic meeting, but don't leap into anything serious just yet. Take love slowly and let things develop.

September

Best Days Overall: 7, 8, 17, 18, 26, 27
Best Stressful Days Overall: 2, 3, 9, 10, 24, 25, 30
Best Days for Love: 1, 2, 3, 9, 10, 19, 20, 28, 29, 30
Best Days for Money: 2, 12, 19, 20, 30
Best Days for Career: 2, 3, 9, 10, 12, 13, 24

Mars spends most of the month (until the 25th) in your 10th house of career and Venus spends the entire month there. So you are still working long hours and fending off the competition. Two things matter in the career now – your social connections and your work ethic. Both seem equally important.

We have two eclipses this month and this more or less guarantees that there will be much change and upheaval. People (and nations)

were given the gift of free will. Too often this free will gets abused –
plans, projects or institutions are made that are not in line with the
cosmic will. The function of the eclipses is to shatter these things, so
that the cosmic will can manifest.

The solar eclipse of the 13th occurs in your 11th house of friends.
Friendships will get tested. Sometimes it is the actual relationship that
is flawed and sometimes the testing is because of dramatic events in
the lives of friends. Be more patient with them this period. Computers
and high-tech equipment gets tested too and often needs replacement
or repair. Computer crashes are more likely at this time. It's a good
idea to have your files backed up and your anti-virus, anti-hacking
software up to date. A good idea to have battery back up too: electricity
supply could be unstable.

Every solar eclipse brings career changes of various kinds.
Sometimes the actual career changes – you move to another company
or even change your career path. But most of the time such change
involves alterations in the rules and the approach: shake-ups in the
corporate hierarchy, changes of policy, changes of emphasis. Your
strategy and tactics need to change. Flaws in your present thinking get
revealed now and you are able to make the necessary corrections.
Bosses, parents or parent figures should stay out of harm's way and
avoid risky activities. They are more vulnerable during eclipse
periods.

The lunar eclipse of the 28th (in the Americas it happens on the
27th) occurs in your 6th house of health and work. This signals job
changes, changes in the conditions of work, and instability with
co-workers. Sometimes such an eclipse produces a health scare and
changes in the dietary or health regimes. The job changes can be
within your present company or with a new one. Health looks good
this month (much better than last month), so any health scare is most
likely nothing more than a scare. Enhance the health by giving more
attention to the heart until the 25th and to the intestines afterwards.
Earth-based therapies – crystals, mud baths, mud packs – are powerful
from the 25th onwards.

October

Best Days Overall: 4, 5, 14, 15, 23, 24, 31
Most Stressful Days Overall: 1, 6, 7, 8, 21, 22, 27, 28
Best Days for Love: 1, 8, 9, 19, 20, 27, 28
Best Days for Money: 1, 9, 10, 16, 17, 18, 19, 20, 27, 28
Best Days for Career: 2, 3, 6, 7, 8, 12, 13, 21, 22, 29, 30

The planetary power is now approaching its maximum Eastern position. Day by day you grow in independence and personal power. This has been the case since late July. The problem has been that your ruling planet, Pluto, has been retrograde since April 17. So you have the power to change conditions, but there seemed to be a lack of clarity on what exactly should be changed. Happily this is over with. Pluto started moving forward on the 25th of last month. Your goals are now clear. You know what has to be done and you have the power to do it. Create your personal paradise now. The cosmos is supporting you.

Clarity is happening in the love life too as Venus starts to move forward. Until the 8th Venus is still in your 10th house (she has spent a lot of time in that house this year). For months now you have been attracted to the high and mighty – to people of power and prestige. Office romances probably happened over the past few months, and if not, the opportunities were there. You had a practical attitude towards love. Love was a career move, or career choice, like any other. Things are changing now. On the 8th Venus moves into your 11th house of friends. You are now more attracted to relationships of peers – equals. Romantic opportunities happen online or as you get involved with groups and organizations. Friends play Cupid. Romance is conducted in a high-tech kind of way – through video calls, texts, email, etc.

Venus will spend most of the month in the sign of Virgo. This is not her favourite sign. She cannot function at her best. The problem is that you (and the people you attract) are too mental, too analytical, too much the perfectionist. Romance is about feeling. Analysis tends to kill the feeling. Also, the desire for perfection that Venus in Virgo produces can lead one to be too critical and judgemental. If something is less than perfect, words are spoken, the tone of voice changes, one is critical either in thought or word. Do your best to avoid these traps. If you must criticize, keep it constructive. And, if the beloved is not in a receptive frame of mind, avoid it altogether. Don't allow the mental approach to interfere with romantic moments. Analysis should come later.

A very happy romantic meeting happens between the 24th and the 27th. A happy job opportunity comes from the 15th to the 18th. Be more patient with bosses, parents or parent figures from the 5th to the 7th. Parent figures should stay out of harm's way on the 11th and 12th.

November

Best Days Overall: 1, 10, 11, 19, 20, 28, 29
Most Stressful Days Overall: 3, 4, 17, 18, 24, 25, 30
Best Days for Love: 6, 7, 17, 18, 24, 25, 26, 27
Best Days for Money: 5, 6, 13, 14, 15, 16, 24, 25
Best Days for Career: 1, 3, 4, 10, 11, 21, 22, 30

Saturn has been in your money house for most of the past year and is there for the rest of it too. So you have been taking on extra financial responsibilities. However, Jupiter has moved away from his square to Saturn so finances are much improved. You still need good financial management and still need to reorganize, but your earning power seems equal to the extra responsibility now. Job seekers still have good aspects, especially until the 12th. Job opportunities happen online or through friends until then. After the 12th job seekers might consider volunteering their time to charities or some good cause; this can lead to important job connections.

Health and energy are wonderful this month. There are no planets stressing you out anymore (only the Moon will make short-term stress for you), so you have all the energy you need to achieve any goal. Personal power and independence is reaching its peak this month as well. Create your personal paradise now.

Good though your health is you can enhance it further by paying more attention to the small intestine until the 12th and to the kidneys and hips after that date. Hip massage will be powerful then. Your health planet, Mars, will be in your 12th house from the 12th onwards. Thus you will respond well to spiritual-type therapies – meditation, reiki, the laying on of hands and the manipulation of subtle energy. If you feel under the weather a spiritual healer will be beneficial.

Last month (on the 23rd) the Sun crossed the Ascendant and entered your 1st house. You began one of your yearly personal pleasure peaks (which will last until the 22nd of this month). This is a time for pampering the body and for enjoying all the sensual delights. It is also a good time to get the body and image the way you want it to be. Happy career opportunities have been coming to you and this trend continues until the 22nd. You look successful. People see you this way and you dress and look the part.

On the 22nd, as the Sun enters your money house, you begin a yearly financial peak. You will work hard for earnings – it's not a smooth ride – but if you put in effort, you will see good results.

Venus spends most of the month (from the 8th onwards) in your spiritual 12th house. For many months this year you were very practical about love; now the reverse is true. You couldn't care less about power, prestige, or money. You are ultra idealistic. It is only the feeling of love that matters to you. As long as this is present, prince and pauper are equal. Love and romantic opportunities happen in spiritual settings – at meditation seminars, spiritual lectures, spiritual retreats, prayer or chanting sessions or charity events.

December

Best Days Overall: 7, 8, 9, 17, 18, 25, 26
Most Stressful Days Overall: 1, 14, 15, 16, 21, 22, 27, 28, 29
Best Days for Love: 7, 17, 18, 21, 22, 25, 26
Best Days for Money: 2, 3, 4, 10, 11, 12, 13, 21, 22, 30, 31
Best Days for Career: 1, 10, 11, 20, 27, 28, 29, 30, 31

Many of the trends of last month are still very much in effect. The planetary power is still in the Eastern sector and Pluto is moving forward. You have power to create conditions as you desire them to be, to have your own way in life, to take charge of your own happiness. There's no need to seek the approval of others. They will adjust and will probably support you. This is a time for having life on your own terms. Even love is on your terms this month.

You are still in a yearly financial peak until the 22nd. Wealth and prosperity is happening but you have to work hard for it. The good news is that you are willing to put in the extra work, willing to overcome any challenge – and this tends to success. Financial goals will be achieved (or good progress will be made towards them).

Health and energy are super right now. With more energy all kinds of undreamt of possibilities arise – things you never imagined during low energy times. You can enhance the health even further through spiritual therapies and through spiritual healers.

Avoid confrontations at work or with fellow workers from the 5th to the 12th. They can overreact to things during this period. Uncles and aunts (or those who play this role in your life) should stay out of harm's way that period too. They should arrange nice, easy schedules. Watch the temper then too.

Last month the planetary power shifted to the lower half of your Horoscope. Career goals have been more or less achieved, or good progress towards them has been made. Now is the time to build up your energy for the next career push, which will begin in five or six months' time. It is time now to take care of your inner needs – the emotional and family needs. You are not abandoning your career but approaching things in a different way – through interior methods such as meditation, visualization and controlled dreaming. Imagine that you have already attained your goal and stay in that state as much as possible.

Venus crosses your Ascendant and enters your sign on the 5th. This is wonderful for love. First off, it makes you more attractive to the opposite sex. Males are attracting beautiful women into the life. Females are becoming more glamorous and beautiful. Love seeks you out and there's nothing much you need to do. Just go about your daily business. If you are in a relationship, the current love is very devoted to you these days.

Sagittarius

THE ARCHER

Birthdays from
23rd November to
20th December

Personality Profile

SAGITTARIUS AT A GLANCE

Element – Fire

Ruling Planet – Jupiter
  Career Planet – Mercury
  Love Planet – Mercury
  Money Planet – Saturn
  Planet of Health and Work – Venus
  Planet of Home and Family Life – Neptune
  Planet of Spirituality – Pluto

Colours – blue, dark blue

Colours that promote love, romance and social harmony – yellow, yellow-orange

Colours that promote earning power – black, indigo

Gems – carbuncle, turquoise

Metal – tin

Scents – carnation, jasmine, myrrh

Quality – mutable (= flexibility)

Qualities most needed for balance – attention to detail, administrative and organizational skills

Strongest virtues – generosity, honesty, broad-mindedness, tremendous vision

Deepest need – to expand mentally

Characteristics to avoid – over-optimism, exaggeration, being too generous with other people's money

Signs of greatest overall compatibility – Aries, Leo

Signs of greatest overall incompatibility – Gemini, Virgo, Pisces

Sign most helpful to career – Virgo

Sign most helpful for emotional support – Pisces

Sign most helpful financially – Capricorn

Sign best for marriage and/or partnerships – Gemini

Sign most helpful for creative projects – Aries

Best Sign to have fun with – Aries

Signs most helpful in spiritual matters – Leo, Scorpio

Best day of the week – Thursday

Understanding a Sagittarius

If you look at the symbol of the archer you will gain a good, intuitive understanding of a person born under this astrological sign. The development of archery was humanity's first refinement of the power to hunt and wage war. The ability to shoot an arrow far beyond the ordinary range of a spear extended humanity's horizons, wealth, personal will and power.

Today, instead of using bows and arrows we project our power with fuels and mighty engines, but the essential reason for using these new powers remains the same. These powers represent our ability to extend our personal sphere of influence – and this is what Sagittarius is all about. Sagittarians are always seeking to expand their horizons, to cover more territory and increase their range and scope. This applies to all aspects of their lives: economic, social and intellectual.

Sagittarians are noted for the development of the mind – the higher intellect – which understands philosophical and spiritual concepts. This mind represents the higher part of the psychic nature and is motivated not by self-centred considerations but by the light and grace of a Higher Power. Thus, Sagittarians love higher education of all kinds. They might be bored with formal schooling but they love to study on their own and in their own way. A love of foreign travel and interest in places far away from home are also noteworthy characteristics of the Sagittarian type.

If you give some thought to all these Sagittarian attributes you will see that they spring from the inner Sagittarian desire to develop. To travel more is to know more, to know more is to be more, to cultivate the higher mind is to grow and to reach more. All these traits tend to broaden the intellectual – and indirectly, the economic and material – horizons of the Sagittarian.

The generosity of the Sagittarian is legendary. There are many reasons for this. One is that Sagittarians seem to have an inborn consciousness of wealth. They feel that they are rich, that they are lucky, that they can attain any financial goal – and so they feel that they can afford to be generous. Sagittarians do not carry the burdens of want and limitation which stop most other people from giving generously. Another reason for their generosity is their religious and philosophical idealism, derived from the higher mind. This higher mind is by nature generous because it is unaffected by material circumstances. Still another reason is that the act of giving tends to enhance their emotional nature. Every act of giving seems to be enriching, and this is reward enough for the Sagittarian.

Finance

Sagittarians generally entice wealth. They either attract it or create it. They have the ideas, energy and talent to make their vision of paradise on Earth a reality. However, mere wealth is not enough. Sagittarians want luxury – earning a comfortable living seems small and insignificant to them.

In order for Sagittarians to attain their true earning potential they must develop better managerial and organizational skills. They must learn to set limits, to arrive at their goals through a series of attainable sub-goals or objectives. It is very rare that a person goes from rags to riches overnight. But a long, drawn-out process is difficult for Sagittarians. Like Leos, they want to achieve wealth and success quickly and impressively. They must be aware, however, that this over-optimism can lead to unrealistic financial ventures and disappointing losses. Of course, no zodiac sign can bounce back as quickly as Sagittarius, but only needless heartache will be caused by this attitude. Sagittarians need to maintain their vision – never letting it go – but they must also work towards it in practical and efficient ways.

Career and Public Image

Sagittarians are big thinkers. They want it all: money, fame, glamour, prestige, public acclaim and a place in history. They often go after all these goals. Some attain them, some do not – much depends on each individual's personal horoscope. But if Sagittarians want to attain public and professional status they must understand that these things are not conferred to enhance one's ego but as rewards for the amount of service that one does for the whole of humanity. If and when they figure out ways to serve more, Sagittarians can rise to the top.

The ego of the Sagittarian is gigantic – and perhaps rightly so. They have much to be proud of. If they want public acclaim, however, they will have to learn to tone down the ego a bit, to become more humble and self-effacing, without falling into the trap of self-denial and self-abasement. They must also learn to master the details of life, which can sometimes elude them.

At their jobs Sagittarians are hard workers who like to please their bosses and co-workers. They are dependable, trustworthy and enjoy a challenge. Sagittarians are friendly to work with and helpful to their colleagues. They usually contribute intelligent ideas or new methods that improve the work environment for everyone. Sagittarians always look for challenging positions and careers that develop their intellect, even if they have to work very hard in order to succeed. They also work well under the supervision of others, although by nature they would rather be the supervisors and increase their sphere of influence. Sagittarians excel at professions that allow them to be in contact with many different people and to travel to new and exciting locations.

Love and Relationships

Sagittarians love freedom for themselves and will readily grant it to their partners. They like their relationships to be fluid and ever-changing. Sagittarians tend to be fickle in love and to change their minds about their partners quite frequently.

Sagittarians feel threatened by a clearly defined, well-structured relationship, as they feel this limits their freedom. The Sagittarian tends to marry more than once in life.

Sagittarians in love are passionate, generous, open, benevolent and very active. They demonstrate their affections very openly. However, just like an Aries they tend to be egocentric in the way they relate to their partners. Sagittarians should develop the ability to see others' points of view, not just their own. They need to develop some objectivity and cool intellectual clarity in their relationships so that they can develop better two-way communication with their partners. Sagittarians tend to be overly idealistic about their partners and about love in general. A cool and rational attitude will help them to perceive reality more clearly and enable them to avoid disappointment.

Home and Domestic Life

Sagittarians tend to grant a lot of freedom to their family. They like big homes and many children and are one of the most fertile signs of the zodiac. However, when it comes to their children Sagittarians generally err on the side of allowing them too much freedom. Sometimes their children get the idea that there are no limits. However, allowing freedom in the home is basically a positive thing – so long as some measure of balance is maintained – for it enables all family members to develop as they should.

Horoscope for 2015

Major Trends

The major headline this year is Saturn's move into your own sign. This began in December of last year. Saturn will be in your sign for most of the year ahead (although he will retrograde briefly into Scorpio from June 15 to September 18), and will be a presence in your sign for the next two years (approximately). Thus, the happy-go-lucky Sagittarian is now in a more serious period. You are more serious about life. You are thinking of old age and the conditions that will prevail then. Many of you feel your age and even older than your actual years. You are confronted with your physical limitations and need to adjust your lifestyle to these limitations. Overall energy is not up to its usual standards. Perhaps your spouse, partner or current love sees you as cold, aloof or distant. You will have to work harder to project love and warmth to others. You are in a period where you need to take a lower profile. There's more on this later.

The other headline this year is Jupiter's move into your 10th career house on August 11. You are very successful in your career. On top. In charge. Calling the shots. This could be another reason for all the seriousness now. Leadership is a heavy burden.

Uranus has been in your 5th house of fun and creativity for some years now and will be there for several more to come. Children or children figures in your life have been more difficult to handle. They seem more rebellious. They crave more freedom. You should give them as much as possible, so long as it isn't destructive.

Jupiter will be in your 9th house until August 11. Thus you are doing more of what you most love – travelling. This is a very nice transit for those of you who are higher students. There is success in your studies. Those applying to college or graduate school hear good news.

Your most important areas of interest this year are the body, image and personal pleasure (from January 1 to June 15 and from September 18 onwards); finance; home and family; children, fun and creativity; religion, philosophy, metaphysics, foreign travel and higher education (until August 11); career (from August 11 onwards); and spirituality (from June 15 to September 18).

Your paths of greatest fulfilment this year are religion, philosophy, metaphysics, foreign travel and higher education (until August 11); career (from August 11 onwards); and friends, groups and group activities (until November 13).

Health

(Please note that this is an astrological perspective on health and not a medical one. In days of yore there was no difference, these perspectives were identical. But now there could be quite a difference. For a medical perspective, please consult your doctor or health practitioner.)

Health becomes more delicate this year. Three long-term planets will be in stressful alignment with you. And, when they are joined by the short-term planets, your vulnerability to illness is increased.

There is another problem here as well. Your 6th house of health is basically empty this year. Only short-term planets will move through there briefly. You might not be paying as much attention to your health as you should. With the aspects as they are this year, you need more attention on health, not less. So you will have to force yourself, even when you don't feel like it, to pay attention. It will not come naturally, but you need to do it.

As our regular readers know, we understand the body to be a dynamic energy system. Change the energy and you change the physical chemistry and the physical components. Because this is so, the body is sensitive to the movements of the heavenly bodies, as they change the energy field of the body. If the planets are stressing the energy field, the body becomes more vulnerable to disease. It doesn't mean that disease has to happen, only that your vulnerability is increased. It means that a person has to increase his or her energy levels by artificial means.

So this is a year to rest and relax more, to pace yourself, to make sure you get enough sleep. It is a year where you need to focus on the really important things in your life and let the lesser things go. It will be a good year to spend more time at a health spa and to get regular massages. Anything that boosts your overall energy is good for you. This is vital – do your best to maintain high energy levels. Be business-like about your energy. Only invest it in important things.

In addition give more attention to the following areas: the heart; the liver and thighs; and the kidneys, throat and hips. These are the vulnerable areas in your chart, and their reflexes are shown in the diagram above. Attention here will prevent, or soften, potential problems.

The heart becomes important in the year ahead. Avoid worry and anxiety, the two emotions that are the root causes of heart problems.

Important foot reflexology points for the year ahead

Try to massage the whole foot on a regular basis, but pay extra attention to the points highlighted on the chart. When you massage, be aware of 'sore spots', as these need special attention. It is also a good idea to massage the ankles and the tops of the feet.

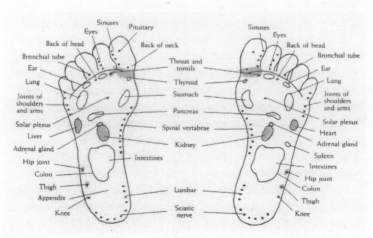

Heart action seems more sluggish this year – especially for those of you born early in the sign of Sagittarius, from November 22 to November 25. Acupuncture or acupressure treatment of the heart meridian will be beneficial.

The liver and thighs are always important areas for Sagittarius. Liver action too seems more sluggish, and acupuncture or acupressure treatments on the liver meridian will also be good. Liver detoxing is a good idea, as is regular thigh massage.

Another always beneficial treatment for Sagittarius is kidney detoxing. Regular neck and hip massage, craniosacral therapy, and acupuncture or acupressure treatments of the kidney meridian are all good this year.

Fast-moving Venus is your health planet. Thus there are many short-term trends in health that depend on where Venus is and the aspects she receives. These will be dealt with in the monthly reports.

Your most vulnerable health periods this year are from February 18 to March 20; May 21 to June 20; and August 23 to September 22. These are times when you need to rest more and pay more attention to your health and energy.

Saturn in your own sign is very good for weight-loss regimes if you need them. In general most of you will slim down this year, in natural kinds of ways.

Home and Family

Your 4th house became prominent in 2012 when Neptune moved in, and will remain so many years to come.

Neptune in the 4th house shows that the family as a whole is under intense spiritual influence. The family relationship is becoming more spiritual, more refined, more idealistic. Family members are more sensitive and more easily hurt and you need to be aware of this. Little things can set them off – body language or voice tone. Things that a few years back were not a big deal suddenly become huge.

Ever since Neptune moved into your 4th house the family (along with your financial life) has been the centre of your spiritual growth. It is Spirit's laboratory these days. This is where the books and the theories get tested in real life experience. You have the kind of aspects of someone who holds prayer or meditation services in the home. Or who invites spiritual teachers or speakers to the home. You seem open to volunteering the home for these purposes.

There seem to be some financial disagreements with the family, and especially with a parent or parent figure. There is no quick solution to this. It seems to deepen as the year goes by. Compromise will be necessary but neither you nor they seem satisfied.

You seem more practical this year, more down-to-earth and more bottom-line oriented, while the parent or parent figure seems more idealistic. And this seems the source of the conflict. It's going to take more effort to keep family harmony this year. However, if you (and they) put in the effort it can be done.

A move is not likely this year. Many of you have moved within the past two years so there is no need for this.

Parents or parent figures are not likely to move this year either. One of them is experiencing financial instability and uncertainty. The other is entering a period of prosperity from August 11 onwards. If the parent or parent figure is single, there is love and even marriage opportunity after August 11. If he or she is married, the marriage should improve and there will be increased social activity. One of them is experiencing career challenges.

Siblings or sibling figures are having a stable family year.

Children or children figures could have moved within the past two years, although the year ahead is quiet. Children or children figures are having fun this year. If they are of the appropriate age there are very nice job opportunities for them after August 11. Grandchildren of appropriate age seem prosperous this year and moves could happen after August 11. They also seem more fertile in the year ahead.

Finance and Career

Though your health and family situation could be better, the financial life seems good. Saturn's move into your sign brings the challenges that we have discussed, but it also brings prosperity and financial opportunity.

Money and financial opportunities will seek you out rather than vice versa. The causes were set in motion years ago and now they come to pass. There's nothing much you need to do; financial opportunity will find you. The money people in your life are on your side.

You are adopting the image of wealth this year. You dress expensively (though conservatively) and people see you as prosperous. You are showing your wealth, but in a restrained sort of way. You spend on yourself this year. You see yourself as the best investment there is – and there is some element of truth here.

For those of the appropriate age, you have the aspects of the celebrity, model, actor or athlete. You are known for how you look, for your physical attainments. Personal appearance seems very important in the career and hence the spending on the self – spending on the image. It's more of a business investment than a vanity thing. Even if you are not a model, actor or athlete, in the year ahead you are more of a celebrity in your own field.

The career is very successful in the year ahead and you are looking the part. You seem above everyone in your world. And even if you are not literally above them, you aspire to be and perhaps behave as if you are. Your ambition seems boundless.

For some years now you have been going deeper into the spiritual dimensions of wealth – learning the spiritual laws that govern these things and applying them. This trend continues in the year ahead. Though this tendency is less pronounced than it was over the past two years, it is still very much in effect. Pluto, your spiritual planet, is in your money house. (Your financial planet, Saturn, will spend three months in your spiritual 12th house too.) You are still very much in 'miracle money' mode. Your challenge is to access the spiritual sources of supply rather than the natural ones. Read all you can on the spiritual dimensions of wealth. There is much literature on the subject.

Pluto in your money house also shows other things. If you are of an appropriate age you are doing more estate planning this year. Many of you have had inheritances or have been named in someone's will. Taxes and tax implications are influencing many of your financial decisions – especially now with increased earnings happening.

Many of you are attaining financial independence in the next few years. And if not total financial independence, good progress is being made towards it. This seems the goal these days.

The business and corporate world is always good for you, but this year more so than is usual. You have a good feeling for traditional, blue chip companies as investments. Commercial real estate is also good.

Love and Social Life

Your 7th house of love is not prominent this year. So the tendency will be towards the status quo. Those of you who are married will tend to stay married and singles will tend to stay single.

Love is a bit more complicated than usual this year. Career – especially from August 11 onwards – seems all-consuming and this tends to distract from love issues. The beloved probably is not happy playing second fiddle to the career. But there are other complications too. Saturn in your sign can make people see you as cold, aloof and distant. You are not like this. Sagittarians are warm and loving people by nature, but Saturn's influence is there on a subconscious, energetic level. You are not as easy to approach as you used to be. Some people can feel intimidated by your presence. This is not conducive for love. It will take conscious effort on your part to project warmth and love to others. Make it a project this year. Those of you involved romantically with Sagittarius will need to understand this.

Fast-moving Mercury (the fastest moving planet after the Moon) is your love planet. So there are many short-term love trends in the year ahead that will depend on where Mercury is and the aspects that he receives. These trends are best covered in the monthly reports.

Singles working towards their first marriage will most likely not marry in the year ahead. However, with the 5th house of fun strong, there will be plenty of dating and plenty of love affairs (or opportunities for love affairs). You're not going to be sitting at home all alone.

Your most active love period this year will be from May 1 to June 21. This is a period where you could meet people who are marriage material – people you would consider marrying.

Singles working towards their second marriage have had beautiful aspects since July 2014. Marriage or a serious relationship is likely. You seem the instigator here. You go after this person. Those in or working towards their third marriage have a quiet year. While those in or working towards their fourth marriage have challenges. If they are married, the marriage gets tested. If single, marriage is not likely this year, nor advisable.

With Mercury as your love planet communication is very important in love. You gravitate to people who are easy to talk to, who have the gift of gab, who are smart. This is your trend by birth and it doesn't seem changed in the year ahead.

Romantic opportunities happen in educational settings – at lectures, seminars, or even in the library.

Self-improvement

As we mentioned earlier, Neptune, the most spiritual of all the planets, has been in your 4th house of home and family since 2012. Thus your spiritual life and growth is centred at home and in the family. Many people think that spiritual growth happens at the place of worship or in some far off spiritual retreat. Not necessarily, as you are learning these days. It is the application of spiritual principles in the day-to-day domestic affairs of life that brings spiritual growth. The mundane tasks at home can be converted to powerful rituals. Washing the dishes or cleaning the house can be elevated to an act of worship if it is done with the right attitude – for the glory of the Divine. For those of you on a spiritual path this would be a good year to read Brother Lawrence's classic work *Practising The Presence*.

Generally Sagittarius is comfortable with conventional religion. But these days you need to get your feelings engaged in the spiritual practice. There is a need to elevate the whole feeling nature – to raise it in vibration. Love and devotion – chanting, singing, reciting psalms or poems of praise, dancing and drumming – will be powerful for you. You already have a good intellectual and metaphysical understanding of things but now you've got to bring the feelings along for the ride. In a good mood, you will easily make contact with the Divine. In a bad mood, it will be very difficult.

Spirituality has been important for the past two years and becomes important again after August 11. Jupiter will make fabulous aspects with Pluto, your spiritual planet. Spirituality will not only play a role in your family and financial life, but in your personal appearance and body image. New techniques to mould and shape the body in spiritual ways will come to you. You will have more ability to do this.

Your intuition – in finance and other areas – becomes unusually good after August 11. You are receiving revelation from on high. You are receiving spiritual help in your career as well.

Month-by-month Forecasts

January

Best Days Overall: 6, 7, 8, 16, 17, 24, 25
Most Stressful Days Overall: 2, 3, 9, 10, 22, 23, 29, 30
Best Days for Love: 1, 2, 3, 11, 12, 13, 20, 21, 22, 29, 30, 31
Best Days for Money: 6, 7, 8, 16, 17, 18, 19, 24, 25
Best Days for Career: 1, 9, 10, 11, 12, 20, 21, 29, 30

You've had a birthday recently so your personal solar cycle is waxing (growing). Since the Winter Solstice, the universal solar cycle is also waxing. The planetary momentum is overwhelming forward this month (especially until the 21st). This is a powerful time to start a new activity or launch a new product into the world. From the 1st to the 5th and the 20th are the best days to do this, but, if you are rushed, anytime after the 21st is also good.

You begin your year with most of the planets below the horizon. At least 80 per cent (and sometimes 90 per cent) of the planets occupy the lower hemisphere of your chart. This is a time for focusing on your emotional wellness and the things that make for emotional wellness. The home and family need to be put in right order. You need to find and function from your point of emotional harmony. When emotional harmony is attained, career will take care of itself. The year ahead is going to be a very powerful career year – the inner preparation is necessary now. The more powerful the career, the more preparation is needed. This is what's happening now.

Most of the planets are still in the Eastern, independent sector of your chart. This will soon change, but in the meantime, take advantage of your enhanced personal power and create conditions that are pleasing to you. Your happiness is in your own hands now, not those of others. Take the steps necessary to create it. Your personal initiative is important now.

You entered a yearly financial peak late last year and this continues until the 20th. Your financial planet Saturn is just by your Ascendant and receiving good aspects. A prosperous month ahead. You seem comfortable with finance and the way you are earning. You seem in harmony with the money people in your life. Financial opportunity seeks you out. Money is chasing you: just show up and receive it.

Health and energy are good this month, although the days before the 20th are better than those after. You can enhance the health by giving more attention to the spine, knees, teeth and skeletal alignment until the 3rd. Back and knee massage is powerful then. From the 3rd to the 27th give more attention to the ankles and calves – massage them regularly and give the ankles more support. After the 27th give more attention to the feet. Foot massage is powerful then.

February

Best Days Overall: 3, 4, 13, 14, 21, 22
Most Stressful Days Overall: 5, 6, 7, 19, 20, 25, 26
Best Days for Love: 1, 2, 8, 9, 10, 11, 17, 18, 20, 21, 25, 26
Best Days for Money: 3, 4, 13, 14, 15, 16, 21, 22
Best Days for Career: 5, 6, 7, 8, 9, 17, 18, 25, 26

Finances are still good, but more challenging in the month ahead. Earnings happen but you have to work harder, overcome more obstacles, to achieve them. If you put in the work, prosperity will happen. Your financial planet is square to Neptune all month. This produces some financial disagreement with the family – with a parent or parent figure especially. Perhaps he or she is a financial burden, or sees you as a financial burden. More importantly this indicates clandestine, covert activity in the financial affairs. Things are not what they seem. You need to do more homework.

Health and energy are more delicate this month so be sure to get enough rest. So many problems are cured just by that – rest. Lack of energy is the primal disease. Enhance the health by giving more attention to the feet until the 20th. Spiritual healers and spiritual healing techniques will be powerful for you (especially from the 1st to the 3rd). After the 20th, give more attention to the head, face and scalp. Massage them regularly. Physical exercise is good after the 20th too.

The planetary power is now at its nadir (lowest point) in your Horoscope. You are, symbolically speaking, in the midnight hour of your year. This is a miraculous kind of period. All kinds of changes are happening on the invisible levels and you will see them later on in the year. At midnight the tone is set for the rest of the day ahead. So use it wisely.

This is also a period for emotional healing. It seems to us that we become nostalgic at this stage. The past is very much with us. The mind seems engaged with the past. But there is a cosmic logic to this – nature's psychological therapeutics. By bringing up old memories – things you have long forgotten or that seem irrelevant to you – the cosmos is showing you what needs to be resolved or reinterpreted in your life. We can't rewrite history, nor should we. But we can reinterpret it in a better way. We can take the sting out of it, absorb its lessons and be better prepared for the future.

If you are involved in therapy, there is good progress and many psychological breakthroughs this month.

On the 18th the planetary power begins to shift to the West – the social sector of your chart. The planetary power is moving away from you rather than towards you. Your period of personal independence is over with for now (it will come back later in the year). Now it is time to cultivate your social skills and start thinking of other people's interests rather than your own. Your good happens through others and not so much by personal initiative.

March

Best Days Overall: 2, 3, 12, 13, 20, 21, 29, 30, 31
Most Stressful Days Overall: 4, 5, 6, 18, 19, 24, 25, 26
Best Days for Love: 2, 3, 7, 8, 12, 13, 18, 19, 22, 23, 24, 25, 26, 29, 30, 31
Best Days for Money: 2, 3, 12, 13, 14, 15, 20, 21, 29, 30
Best Days for Career: 4, 5, 6, 7, 8, 18, 19, 29, 30, 31

Continue to pay more attention to the health until the 20th. Review our discussion of this last month. Until the 17th give more attention to the head, face and scalp. Face and scalp massage will be excellent. (The scalp has reflexes to the entire body and the face to many parts of the body.) Physical exercise is also important as you need good muscle tone. Craniosacral therapy would be good too. After the 17th focus more on the neck and throat. Don't allow too much tension to collect in the neck. Release it through massage. Health and energy will improve dramatically after the 20th.

There is a solar eclipse on the 20th. For most of you it is relatively benign. But, if you were born late in the sign of Sagittarius – from December 19 to December 20 – you will be powerfully affected. Everyone should take an easier schedule over this period, but especially those of you who fall into this category. Stay out of harm's way and avoid stressful activities. If you can, reschedule such things for another time. Foreign travel – your great love – is best avoided during this period. If you must travel, try to schedule your trip around the eclipse.

This eclipse occurs on the border of two houses, the 4th and the 5th, and so affects the affairs of both. Thus if there are flaws in the home or the family relationship, now is the time you find out about them. Family members will be more high strung and temperamental and could be undergoing dramatic personal experiences. Be more patient with them. Try not to make matters worse. Children and children figures are affected and they should be kept out of harm's way.

College students make changes to their educational plans. Perhaps they change establishments or subjects. Often there are changes in school policy that cause this. Sometimes the school that the student wanted and planned to attend doesn't accept them, and they wind up attending a different place. They are many such scenarios happening. There are upheavals and shake-ups in your place of worship, and perhaps dramas in the lives of worship leaders. Every solar eclipse tests your philosophic and religious beliefs. Flaws are revealed and over the next six months revisions are made. A good title for a solar eclipse in your Horoscope is 'crisis of faith'.

Once the dust settles from the eclipse, the month ahead is basically happy. You are in one of your yearly personal pleasure peaks from the 20th onwards. So there is much fun in the life. Personal creativity is also at a peak this month.

Finances are excellent from the 20th onwards. But your financial planet is goes retrograde on the 14th. I read this as prosperity that happens with delays involved – but it is happening.

April

Best Days Overall: 8, 9, 17, 18, 25, 26, 27
Most Stressful Days Overall: 1, 2, 15, 16, 21, 22, 28, 29
Best Days for Love: 1, 2, 8, 9, 13, 19, 20, 21, 22, 28, 29
Best Days for Money: 8, 9, 10, 11, 12, 17, 18, 25, 26, 27
Best Days for Career: 1, 2, 8, 9, 19, 20, 28, 29

A lunar eclipse on the 4th affects many areas of life but its effects are relatively benign for you. The impact will probably be stronger on the world at large.

It occurs in the sign of Libra, your 11th house of friends. Thus friendships get tested. Good ones will survive, flawed ones can break up – and this is as it should be. It is good that friendships get tested every now and then, although it's not pleasant when it happens.

Computers and high-tech equipment are also tested by the eclipse. Often repair or replacement is needed. Sometimes the disruptions are temporary and you might just need to uninstall some unwanted programs. It will be a good idea to have your important files backed up and to have your anti-virus, anti-hacking software up to date. Uranus, one of the planets affected by the eclipse, rules your 3rd house of communication, so cars and communication equipment also get tested. Be more careful driving at this time.

Siblings and sibling figures in your life (and neighbours) experience dramatic, life-changing events – perhaps near-death experiences. The impact on Pluto, which rules your 12th house, shows changes in your spiritual life – in your practice, attitudes and teachings that you follow. It often brings shake-ups in a spiritual or charitable organization that you are involved with and drama to the lives of spiritual mentors or teachers. Every lunar eclipse brings confrontations with death (although not literal physical death). Often there are dreams of death. Often you encounter death by reading of things in the newspapers or seeing things on TV. The dark angel is hovering around and letting you know of his existence. Basically it is a friendly reminder to get more serious about life and to focus on the really important things – your true purpose.

A lunar eclipse tends to bring financial change to the spouse, partner or current love and this one is no different. Usually the changes happen through some disturbance or crisis. But ultimately the changes will be good.

Your health and energy are basically good this month, but with two long-term planets stressing you out it would be good to enhance the health by giving more attention to the neck and throat (as discussed last month) until the 11th. After then, give more attention to the lungs, arms, shoulders and respiratory system. If you feel under the weather go out in the fresh air and just breathe. It's important to get enough oxygen during this period. Arm and shoulder massage is powerful too. The heart is especially important after the 20th. Physical exercise and good muscle tone is important all month.

The good news is that your 6th house of health and work is strong this month, so you are giving attention to health matters. This power in the 6th house is also excellent for job seekers. There are many job opportunities out there in the month ahead.

May

Best Days Overall: 5, 6, 14, 15, 23, 24
Most Stressful Days Overall: 12, 13, 18, 19, 25, 26, 27
Best Days for Love: 1, 2, 10, 11, 12, 13, 18, 19, 21, 22, 28, 29, 30, 31
Best Days for Money: 5, 6, 8, 9, 14, 15, 23, 24
Best Days for Career: 1, 2, 10, 11, 18, 19, 25, 26, 27, 28, 29

You are entering the full Moon stage of your solar cycle this month (and for some of you it happens next month). The universal solar cycle is also close to its full Moon phase. The planetary momentum is still mostly forward (although less so after the 14th) so this is an excellent time for starting new activities or launching new products into the world. The 1st to the 4th is best.

Sagittarians are not usually good with details. Their strength is in seeing the broad picture of things. But this month, especially until the 21st, you are better with details than usual. This is a good time to do those detail-oriented tasks that bore you, such as filing, your accounts, backing up computer files, etc. Last month, from the 20th onwards, was also good for this.

Your focus on health since April 20 will stand you in good stead after the 21st when health and energy become much more delicate. As always, the first line of defence is to get enough rest. Until the 7th pay attention to the lungs, arms, shoulders and respiratory system. Breathing exercises are good. Fresh air is good. After the 7th focus more on the stomach and the diet. Women should give more attention to the breasts. It would be good to schedule massages, reflexology or acupuncture treatments this month (especially after the 21st).

Though health and energy are not what they should be, many nice things are happening this month. On the 21st you enter a yearly love and social peak. Your 7th house is very powerful with half of the planets either there or moving through there this month. This shows an active love and social life. There are many romantic opportunities for singles. You seem to get on with all kinds of people. The only problem here is the retrograde of your love planet, Mercury, on the 14th. Yes, there are many opportunities, but don't jump into anything too serious just yet. Go slow in love. Observe. Get clear what you really want. Let time reveal the character of the people you are involved with. With Mars in your 7th house from the 12th onwards this might be difficult. You can be overly impulsive in love and this might not be wise.

You've had better financial periods than now and will have them again. Your financial planet has been retrograde since March 14 and receives stressful aspects. Earnings will happen but be prepared to work harder for them. The financial life seems slower, but this gives you an opportunity to review your financial goals and strategies. There's no need to rush major purchases or investments. This is a time for doing your homework on these things.

June

Best Days Overall: 2, 3, 10, 11, 20, 21
Most Stressful Days Overall: 8, 9, 15, 16, 22, 23
Best Days for Love: 1, 6, 7, 10, 11, 15, 16, 20, 21, 24, 25, 29, 30
Best Days for Money: 1, 2, 3, 4, 5, 10, 11, 19, 20, 21, 28, 29, 30
Best Days for Career: 6, 7, 15, 16, 22, 23, 24, 25

Last month on the 21st the planetary power made an important shift – from the lower to the upper half of your Horoscope. This is the time to start making your career push. This is the time for making those dreams, visions and fantasies, concrete realities. Now you pursue career goals in the 'regular' way – through concrete actions on the physical plane. If you used the past six months properly, found your point of emotional harmony and did the emotional healing that needed to be done, your actions will be powerful and successful. Now, emotional healing will come from doing right. Now the family is best served by being successful in the world.

For the astrologer a successful career and a successful home and family life are equal. We don't make judgements as to which is better. For us it depends on the stage of the cycle you are in. Now you are in a career cycle.

Health still needs attention until the 21st. Until the 5th enhance your health through right diet and by paying more attention to the stomach and breasts. Detox regimes have been powerful since May 7 and will be powerful for the rest of the month ahead. After the 5th, pay more attention to the heart. Examine your beliefs about health and disease too. These play a huge role in wellness and the ability to heal and be healed.

Health and energy should dramatically improve after the 21st. Saturn moves away (temporarily) from his stressful aspect on the 15th and the short-term planets later on. You should end the month with much better health than when it began.

Finances are much improved after the 21st as well. Saturn, your financial planet, is receiving better aspects. However, he is still retrograde, and your financial review should continue. Job seekers have wonderful opportunities from the 28th to the 30th. Friends seem financially helpful from the 5th to the 7th. Over the past two years you have made great progress learning about the spiritual dimensions of wealth, and it would be good to review your knowledge for the next few months. It seems very important on the financial level these days.

You are still in a yearly love and social peak until the 21st. This period should be better than last month. Mercury, your love planet, starts to move forward on the 11th. Social judgement and confidence is much better after that, and love choices and decisions should also be much better.

July

Best Days Overall: 8, 9, 17, 18, 26, 27, 28
Most Stressful Days Overall: 6, 7, 12, 13, 19, 20
Best Days for Love: 7, 8, 9, 12, 13, 17, 18, 26, 29, 30
Best Days for Money: 1, 2, 7, 9, 16, 18, 25, 27, 28, 29, 30
Best Days for Career: 7, 8, 17, 18, 19, 20, 29, 30

Your 8th house of transformation became powerful on June 21 and remains powerful until the 23rd. The spouse, partner or current love is in a yearly financial peak. He or she is more generous with you. You are more sexually active than usual, and love is expressed in that way. This is what allures you most (especially after the 8th), but other things are also important during this period.

Physical intimacy is important, but so is emotional intimacy. You gravitate to people who are easy to share feelings with. After the 27th, mental compatibility becomes more important. You want mental and philosophical sex. You gravitate to people you can learn from – mentor types. Religious and philosophical compatibility is important. The best sexual chemistry in the world will not save a relationship if you are not on the same page philosophically. Your love planet moves very fast this month, signalling confidence and someone who covers a lot of social territory.

We see a strong libido in other ways too. The Moon, your sexual planet, is full twice this month – a rare occurrence. The full Moon in your Horoscope, in particular, represents the height of libido.

Health and energy are good this month, but especially after the 23rd when the Sun enters Leo. You enter Sagittarius heaven. Your 9th house is the most powerful house. You are impelled to do the things that you most love to do – travel, study, and go deeper into religion and theology. For a Sagittarius any excuse to travel is enough for you, and in the month ahead this is even more true than normal. So you are travelling now. Religious and philosophical breakthroughs will happen. For students a powerful 9th house indicates success in their studies, and those applying to college or graduate school should hear good news. If you are involved in legal issues there is good fortune now.

When the 9th house is this powerful (and half of the planet are either there or moving through there this month) a good juicy theological discussion is more alluring than a night out on the town. The visit of a guru or minister is more important than the visit of the rock star or celebrity.

Be more patient in finances after the 23rd.

Children or children figures in your life should stay out of harm's way from the 14th to the 17th and from the 24th to the 27th. If you are involved in athletics or in an exercise regime don't push yourself so hard during these periods.

August

Best Days Overall: 4, 5, 13, 14, 23, 24, 31
Most Stressful Days Overall: 2, 3, 8, 9, 15, 16, 17, 29, 30
Best Days for Love: 5, 8, 9, 14, 15, 16, 23, 24, 26, 27, 31
Best Days for Money: 3, 5, 12, 15, 22, 25, 26, 30
Best Days for Career: 5, 15, 16, 17, 26, 27

Very important and happy changes are happening this month. Jupiter, the ruler of your Horoscope, makes a major move out of Leo and crosses the Mid-heaven on the 11th. He will be in your 10th house of career for the rest of the year ahead (and well into next year). This shows great career success, personal success. You are above (at least for a while) everyone in your world. You receive honours and recognition. A promotion in your job or in your profession is likely. You have almost celebrity status these days (and this will continue well into next year).

Aside from Jupiter's move, on the 23rd you enter a yearly career peak as well. For many of you it will be a lifetime peak; for others, a multi-year peak. The planetary power is now at its zenith (high point) of your Horoscope. It is noon, symbolically speaking, in your year. You are exerting more influence in your world now. Personal appearance seems very important careerwise. Who you are, how you look, is just as important (and perhaps more important) than your professional achievements.

There is tension with a parent or parent figure in your life. Neither you nor this person is right or wrong. You are just seeing things from opposite perspectives. Sometimes the parent figure is right, sometimes you are. If you can bridge the differences you can be very helpful to each other.

Your 9th house became very powerful on the 23rd of last month and is still powerful until the 23rd of this. Review our discussion of this last month. But there's something else that should be mentioned. Your career goals are high – stratospheric. Thus, this is a good time to take courses, higher degrees, or seminars in subjects related to the career. The higher the aspiration, the more preparation is needed. Bone up on any subject that helps the career.

All this ambition, this outer activity, makes the health more delicate after the 23rd. As always, make sure you get enough sleep. Pursue your career goals calmly and steadily, with plenty of rest periods thrown in. Delegate as much as possible. Avoid impatience (there are many planets retrograde this month). And, like last month, give more attention to the heart.

A very happy job opportunity occurs between the 3rd and the 6th, but study it carefully. You will have many happy opportunities in the coming year.

September

Best Days Overall: 1, 9, 10, 19, 20, 28, 29
Most Stressful Days Overall: 4, 5, 6, 12, 13, 26, 27
Best Days for Love: 1, 4, 5, 6, 9, 10, 14, 15, 19, 20, 24, 25, 28, 29
Best Days for Money: 2, 8, 12, 18, 19, 22, 23, 28, 30
Best Days for Career: 4, 5, 12, 13, 14, 15, 24, 25

Last month brought a lot of change, and this month brings even more. Two eclipses shake things up, both personally and in the world at large.

The state condemns buildings that are shaky or damaged. A shaky building is a danger to all around, not just the inhabitants of the building. Eclipses perform this kind of function in the cosmic world. The collapse of a shaky building is dramatic and unpleasant while it's happening – a scary kind of thing. But the end result is often good. Generally it is replaced with something superior. People and governments construct shaky buildings all the time – either physically or metaphorically. The foundations are weak, or the overall design is not right. So, periodically, they have to go. The cosmos is always seeking to express greater perfection. Sound, solid buildings (physical or metaphoric) are not touched by eclipses.

The solar eclipse of the 13th occurs in your 10th house of career. So, shaky career edifices (plans, projects or strategies) get demolished. For you this will be a very good thing – and you will see it is so when the excitement dies down. The barriers to your success and further progress are being brought low. Often heads roll in your company or industry. There are shake-ups in the corporate or industry hierarchy and important changes of policy. Dramatic events happen in the lives of people involved in your career and of bosses, parents or parent figures. Often the government agency in charge of your industry or profession changes the rules and major adjustments need to be made. Your career path is becoming cleared.

Since the Sun is the ruler of your 9th house every solar eclipse affects this area of life. Foreign travel is not advisable during this period; if you must travel, schedule your trip around it. Students make dramatic changes to their educational plans. Sometimes they change schools, sometimes they change courses, sometimes they must adapt to new rules or regulations. There are shake-ups and upheavals in your place of worship, too, and perhaps dramas in the lives of worship leaders or religious figures in your life. Make sure you have a nice easy relaxed schedule for a few days before and after the eclipse. You need to be taking it easier anyway until the 23rd, but especially over the eclipse period.

The lunar eclipse of the 28th (in the Americas it happens on the 27th) occurs in your 5th house and affects children or children figures in your life. They are redefining themselves over the next six months, changing their image and their look, reinventing their personalities. The spouse, partner or current love has a financial crisis or disturbance and is forced to make important changes. Dreams of death or encounters with death should not alarm you over much. These are love letters from the cosmos, urging you to get more serious in your life.

October

Best Days Overall: 6, 7, 8, 16, 17, 18, 25, 26
Most Stressful Days Overall: 2, 3, 9, 10, 23, 24, 29, 30
Best Days for Love: 2, 3, 8, 9, 11, 12, 13, 19, 20, 21, 22, 27, 28, 29, 30
Best Days for Money: 1, 6, 9, 10, 16, 19, 20, 25, 27, 28
Best Days for Career: 2, 3, 9, 10, 11, 12, 13, 21, 22, 29, 30

Technically your yearly career peak ended on the 23rd of last month. But your 10th house of career is still chock-full of beneficent planets.

Even Mars, not generally considered beneficent, is in your Horoscope as he is ruler of a beneficent house. So your career is going great guns. Much success is happening. You are working hard – career demands seem all consuming – but you're seeing the results. You seem to enjoy the hectic pace. Children and children figures in your life also seem successful these days and seem supportive of your career. Likewise your friends. Your good work ethic plays well with superiors.

Health still needs watching this month; happily you are on the case. Your health planet, Venus, spends most of the month in your 10th house so health is high on your agenda. You're seeing that the career goals you seek are impossible without good health. Good health is an important component of success. Good health impresses superiors. Enhance your health until the 8th by giving attention to the heart. After the 8th give attention to the small intestine. Good health for you (especially after the 8th) means a healthy career, not just 'no symptoms'. This is happening and this is a good signal for health.

The love life is reasonable this month. Mercury, the love planet, moves forward on the 9th and is in 'mutual reception' with Venus from the 8th onwards. This means that the two love planets in your chart, Mercury (actual) and Venus (generic) are co-operating with each other. Each is a guest in the house of the other. Thus friends are furthering romance. They are playing Cupid, making introductions, giving advice. Sometimes someone who was just a friend becomes more than that. Romantic opportunities happen as you get involved in groups and group activities. The online world is a source of romance too. There are some rough spots between the 22nd and 23rd and the 25th and 26th. Be more patient with the beloved on those days. Also, he or she should stay out of harm's way those days. Avoid risky kinds of activities.

Last month, on the 18th, Saturn, your financial planet, moved back into your sign. This brings money and financial opportunity to you. The message here is 'achieve your career goals and money will just follow'.

Avoid foreign travel from the 5th to the 7th and on the 11th and 12th.

November

Best Days Overall: 3, 4, 13, 14, 22, 30
Most Stressful Days Overall: 5, 6, 19, 20, 26, 27
Best Days for Love: 6, 7, 10, 11, 17, 18, 21, 26, 27, 30
Best Days for Money: 3, 5, 6, 12, 15, 16, 21, 24, 25, 30
Best Days for Career: 5, 6, 10, 11, 21, 30

On September 25 the planetary power made a decisive shift from the West to the East, from the social sector to the independent sector. Last month on the 8th, the shift became even stronger: 70 per cent (sometimes 80 per cent) of the planets are now in the East. It is time to look out for number one now. As the saying goes, 'If I am not for me, who will be?' Other people are always important, but you are no longer as dependent on them as you have been for many months this year. It's time to stand on your own feet and take responsibility for your happiness. The cosmos is supporting you and doesn't see you as selfish. You have the power to create conditions as you desire them to be and you should use it. Your way is the best way these days. This is a time for 'making karma' – creating circumstances. If you create properly, the karma will be good.

Career is important and going well, and is a lot less hectic than in the past few months. But things are winding down a bit. By the 22nd, the planetary power will shift to the lower half of the Horoscope and it will be time to give more attention to the family and to your emotional well-being. After the 23rd you start to prepare for the next career push, the next high, which will happen next year.

On the 22nd the Sun crosses your Ascendant and enters your 1st house. Thus you begin one of your yearly personal pleasure peaks. The body gets indulged with its desires. But it is also good to use this energy to get the body and image the way you want it to be. The focus is on the body. Foreign travel is likely during this period. Students find it easy to get into college. There's nothing special they need to do, colleges are seeking them.

Love is spiritual until the 20th. You are very idealistic this period (some would say impractical) and you care nothing about money or position. It is only the feeling of love that matters to you. Romantic (and social) opportunities happen in spiritual settings and with spiritual, creative kinds of people. Romance seekers should attend charity functions, meditation seminars or spiritual-type lectures. After the 20th, romance will find you wherever you are. Just go about your daily business.

Finance is good all month but becomes especially good after the 22nd. A nice windfall happens on the 29th or 30th.

December

Best Days Overall: 1, 10, 11, 19, 20, 27, 28, 29

Most Stressful Days Overall: 2, 3, 4, 17, 18, 23, 24, 30, 31

Best Days for Love: 7, 17, 18, 23, 24, 25, 26

Best Days for Money: 1, 2, 3, 4, 10, 12, 13, 19, 20, 21, 22, 27, 28, 30, 31

Best Days for Career: 1, 2, 3, 4, 12, 21, 22, 30, 31

A happy and prosperous month ahead. Enjoy!

The planetary power is now at its maximum Eastern position. You are at the peak of personal independence and personal power. Your personal goals have a lot of cosmic support (so long as they aren't destructive). You are having things your way these days and this is as it should be.

You are still in a yearly personal pleasure peak until the 21st. After that you enter a yearly financial peak – a period of peak earnings.

Though you have three long-term planets in stressful alignment with you, health and energy are good. The short-term planets are easing the stress. (Health would be even better if the long-term planets were leaving you alone.) Until the 5th you can enhance the health by giving more attention to the kidneys and hips. Regular hip massage would be good. From the 5th onwards give more attention to the colon, bladder and sexual organs. Herbal colonics might be a good idea this period. Safe sex and sexual moderation are also important. Detox regimes are more beneficial than usual. Good health, this period, is about getting rid of things that don't belong in the body, not about adding things to the body. Spiritual healing is powerful. If you feel under the weather a spiritual healer, or spiritual healing techniques, will be a big help. You respond well to this.

Love becomes more practical after the 10th. Wealth attracts you. You show love in material and financial ways and this is how you feel loved. Love and romantic opportunities happen as you pursue your normal financial goals and with people involved in your finances. There are opportunities for business partnerships or joint ventures.

Children and children figures in your life should stay out of harm's way from the 5th to the 12th. They should avoid confrontations, watch the temper and drive more carefully. A nice, easy, relaxed schedule is called for.

After your birthday, your personal solar cycle enters a waxing phase. The planetary power is mostly forward this month and the universal solar cycle will start to wax after the Winter Solstice. Thus (from the 21st onwards) you are in a very good period for starting new activities or releasing new products into the world.

Capricorn

♑

THE GOAT

Birthdays from
21st December to
19th January

Personality Profile

CAPRICORN AT A GLANCE

Element – Earth

Ruling Planet – Saturn
   Career Planet – Venus
   Love Planet – Moon
   Money Planet – Uranus
   Planet of Communications – Neptune
   Planet of Health and Work – Mercury
   Planet of Home and Family Life – Mars
   Planet of Spirituality – Jupiter

Colours – black, indigo

Colours that promote love, romance and social harmony – puce, silver

Colour that promotes earning power – ultramarine blue

Gem – black onyx

Metal – lead

Scents – magnolia, pine, sweet pea, wintergreen

Quality - cardinal (= activity)

Qualities most needed for balance - warmth, spontaneity, a sense of fun

Strongest virtues - sense of duty, organization, perseverance, patience, ability to take the long-term view

Deepest needs - to manage, take charge and administrate

Characteristics to avoid - pessimism, depression, undue materialism and undue conservatism

Signs of greatest overall compatibility - Taurus, Virgo

Signs of greatest overall incompatibility - Aries, Cancer, Libra

Sign most helpful to career - Libra

Sign most helpful for emotional support - Aries

Sign most helpful financially - Aquarius

Sign best for marriage and/or partnerships - Cancer

Sign most helpful for creative projects - Taurus

Best Sign to have fun with - Taurus

Signs most helpful in spiritual matters - Virgo, Sagittarius

Best day of the week - Saturday

Understanding a Capricorn

The virtues of Capricorns are such that there will always be people for and against them. Many admire them, many dislike them. Why? It seems to be because of Capricorn's power urges. A well-developed Capricorn has his or her eyes set on the heights of power, prestige and authority. In the sign of Capricorn, ambition is not a fatal flaw, but rather the highest virtue.

Capricorns are not frightened by the resentment their authority may sometimes breed. In Capricorn's cool, calculated, organized mind all the dangers are already factored into the equation – the unpopularity, the animosity, the misunderstandings, even the outright slander – and a plan is always in place for dealing with these things in the most efficient way. To the Capricorn, situations that would terrify an ordinary mind are merely problems to be managed, bumps on the road to ever-growing power, effectiveness and prestige.

Some people attribute pessimism to the Capricorn sign, but this is a bit deceptive. It is true that Capricorns like to take into account the negative side of things. It is also true that they love to imagine the worst possible scenario in every undertaking. Other people might find such analyses depressing, but Capricorns only do these things so that they can formulate a way out – an escape route.

Capricorns will argue with success. They will show you that you are not doing as well as you think you are. Capricorns do this to themselves as well as to others. They do not mean to discourage you but rather to root out any impediments to your greater success. A Capricorn boss or supervisor feels that no matter how good the performance there is always room for improvement. This explains why Capricorn supervisors are difficult to handle and even infuriating at times. Their actions are, however, quite often effective – they can get their subordinates to improve and become better at their jobs.

Capricorn is a born manager and administrator. Leo is better at being king or queen, but Capricorn is better at being prime minister – the person actually wielding power.

Capricorn is interested in the virtues that last, in the things that will stand the test of time and trials of circumstance. Temporary fads and fashions mean little to a Capricorn – except as things to be used for profit or power. Capricorns apply this attitude to business, love, to their thinking and even to their philosophy and religion.

Finance

Capricorns generally attain wealth and they usually earn it. They are willing to work long and hard for what they want. They are quite amenable to foregoing a short-term gain in favour of long-term benefits. Financially, they come into their own later in life.

However, if Capricorns are to attain their financial goals they must shed some of their strong conservatism. Perhaps this is the least desirable trait of the Capricorn. They can resist anything new merely because it is new and untried. They are afraid of experimentation. Capricorns need to be willing to take a few risks. They should be more eager to market new products or explore different managerial techniques. Otherwise, progress will leave them behind. If necessary, Capricorns must be ready to change with the times, to discard old methods that no longer work.

Very often this experimentation will mean that Capricorns have to break with existing authority. They might even consider changing their present position or starting their own ventures. If so, they should be willing to accept all the risks and just get on with it. Only then will a Capricorn be on the road to highest financial gains.

Career and Public Image

A Capricorn's ambition and quest for power are evident. It is perhaps the most ambitious sign of the zodiac – and usually the most successful in a worldly sense. However, there are lessons Capricorns need to learn in order to fulfil their highest aspirations.

Intelligence, hard work, cool efficiency and organization will take them a certain distance, but will not carry them to the very top. Capricorns need to cultivate their social graces, to develop a social style, along with charm and an ability to get along with people. They need to bring beauty into their lives and to cultivate the right social contacts. They must learn to wield power gracefully, so that people love them for it – a very delicate art. They also need to learn how to bring people together in order to fulfil certain objectives. In short, Capricorns require some of the gifts – the social graces – of Libra to get to the top.

Once they have learned this, Capricorns will be successful in their careers. They are ambitious hard workers who are not afraid of putting in the required time and effort. Capricorns take their time in getting the job done – in order to do it well – and they like moving up the corporate ladder slowly but surely. Being so driven by success, Capricorns are generally liked by their bosses, who respect and trust them.

Love and Relationships

Like Scorpio and Pisces, Capricorn is a difficult sign to get to know. They are deep, introverted and like to keep their own counsel. Capricorns do not like to reveal their innermost thoughts. If you are in love with a Capricorn, be patient and take your time. Little by little you will get to understand him or her.

Capricorns have a deep romantic nature, but they do not show it straightaway. They are cool, matter of fact and not especially emotional. They will often show their love in practical ways.

It takes time for a Capricorn – male or female – to fall in love. They are not the love-at-first-sight kind. If a Capricorn is involved with a Leo or Aries, these Fire types will be totally mystified – to them the Capricorn will seem cold, unfeeling, unaffectionate and not very spontaneous. Of course none of this is true; it is just that Capricorn likes to take things slowly. They like to be sure of their ground before making any demonstrations of love or commitment.

Even in love affairs Capricorns are deliberate. They need more time to make decisions than is true of the other signs of the zodiac, but given this time they become just as passionate. Capricorns like a relationship to be structured, committed, well regulated, well defined, predictable and even routine. They prefer partners who are nurturers, and they in turn like to nurture their partners. This is their basic psychology. Whether such a relationship is good for them is another issue altogether. Capricorns have enough routine in their lives as it is. They might be better off in relationships that are a bit more stimulating, changeable and fluctuating.

Home and Domestic Life

The home of a Capricorn – as with a Virgo – is going to be tidy and well organized. Capricorns tend to manage their families in the same way they manage their businesses. Capricorns are often so career-driven that they find little time for the home and family. They should try to get more actively involved in their family and domestic life. Capricorns do, however, take their children very seriously and are very proud parents – particularly should their children grow up to become respected members of society.

Horoscope for 2015

Major Trends

The ruler of your Horoscope, Saturn, will in your spiritual 12th house for most of the year ahead, and for the next two years. Thus you are in an intensely spiritual kind of period in your life. There is a lot of behind-the-scenes, interior growth happening. You are more open to spiritual teachings. This is unusual for a Capricorn as you are basically a down-to-earth, rational type of person. Should be interesting to watch.

Ever since Neptune moved into your 3rd house of communication, your taste in reading has also become more spiritualized. Spiritual books appeal to you. Poetry and other inspired writings also appeal to you.

The technological and online world has been very important for the past few years. It will still be important this year, but not as much. Your interests are shifting more to the spiritual side of things.

Pluto has been in your sign for many years now and will be there for many more. Thus a cosmic detox of the body and image – of your self-definition – has been going on. You are giving birth (a long-term process) to the person that you want to be. And this process often involves dramatic kinds of events – near-death experiences or encounters with death. Many of you have had cosmetic kinds of surgery recently and the trend continues in the year ahead.

Uranus has been in your 4th house of home and family for some years now and will be there in the year ahead. There has been much instability in the family. Family members seem prone to extreme mood swings. There have probably been multiple moves or renovations in the home over the past few years. These trends continue in the year ahead and there is more on this later.

Jupiter has been in your 8th house of transformation and regeneration since July 2014. This too shows more involvement with death and with estates. It reinforces the effect of Pluto in your sign and underscores what we have written above.

Jupiter's move into Virgo on August 11 brings foreign travel and overall prosperity to you. This is a very nice aspect for college-level students and they should be successful in their studies this year. Those applying to colleges will hear good news.

Your most important areas of interest this year are the body, image and personal pleasure; communication and intellectual interests; home and family; sex, death, life after death, debt and the repayment of debt (until August 11); foreign travel, religion, philosophy and higher education (from August 11 onwards); friends, groups, group activities (from June 15 to September 18); and spirituality (from January to June 15 and from September 18 onwards).

Your paths of greatest fulfilment in the year ahead are sex, death and rebirth, occult studies, debt and the repayment of debt (until August 11); foreign travel, religion, philosophy and higher education (from August 11 onwards); and career (until November 13).

Health

(Please note that this is an astrological perspective on health and not a medical one. In days of yore there was no difference, these perspectives were identical. Now there could be quite a difference. For a medical perspective, please consult your doctor or health practitioner.)

Pluto and Uranus have been in stressful aspect with you for some years now and they remain so during this year. However, during this period there have been years where the stresses have been much worse – when other planets were also stressing you. So if you reached 2015 with your health and sanity intact, you have done well. Health still needs watching this year, but you will see improvements after August 11.

Two powerful planets in stressful aspect is problem enough, but there will be periods in the year where the short-term planets also place stress and then your vulnerability is much increased. This year these periods are from March 21 to April 19, June 21 to July 23 and September 23 to October 23. It will be a good idea to rest and relax more during these times. If you can get away to a health spa or clinic in those periods it would be wonderful. If you can't, try to schedule massage, reflexology or acupuncture treatments then. You need to maintain high energy levels – the main defence against disease.

Another problem we see here is that your 6th house of health is basically empty. (Only short-term planets will move through there – and briefly.) Thus you might not be paying enough attention to your health. You need to force yourself to pay attention even if you don't feel like it.

It would also be good to give more attention to the following areas – the vulnerable areas in your chart: the heart; the spine, knees, teeth,

Important foot reflexology points for the year ahead

Try to massage the whole foot on a regular basis, but pay extra attention to the points highlighted on the chart. When you massage, be aware of 'sore spots', as these need special attention. It is also a good idea to massage the ankles and the tops of the feet.

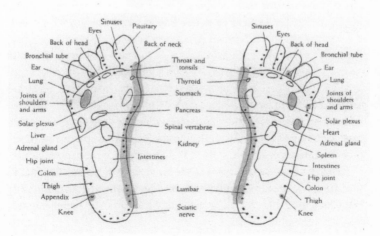

bones, skin and overall skeletal alignment; and the lungs, arms, shoulders and respiratory system. This will either prevent or soften any potential problems, and the reflex points for these areas are shown in the diagram above.

The heart has become important only in recent years. Acupuncture or acupressure treatments of the heart meridian will be helpful, and you should try to avoid worry and anxiety – the spiritual root causes of heart problems.

The spine, knees, teeth, bones, skin and overall skeletal alignment are always important for Capricorn. Regular back and knee massages will be good. Yoga, Pilates, the Alexander Technique and Feldenkrais are excellent therapies for the spine and regular visits to a chiropractor or osteopath will also be useful. Make sure you get enough calcium and vitamin K for the bones. If you're out in the sun use a good sun screen.

The lungs, arms and shoulders and the respiratory system are also areas that are always important for Capricorn. The arms and shoulders should be regularly massaged – tension tends to collect in the shoulders and needs to be released. Acupuncture or acupressure treatments of the lung meridian will also be good.

Pluto in your own sign is very good for detox regimes and for weight-loss programmes.

Your health planet, Mercury, is a very fast-moving planet. Only the Moon moves faster than he does. Thus there are many short-term health trends that depend on where Mercury is at any given time and the kinds of aspects he receives. These will be dealt with in the monthly reports.

Home and Family

As we have mentioned, this has been a turbulent area for some years now. Uranus has been in your 4th house for a while and will be there for several more years.

There has been many a crisis in the family unit these past few years. In many cases the family unit has broken up. In other cases there have been such dramatic change in the family and in family members that it is 'as if' the unit is broken.

You have the aspects for multiple moves or multiple renovations of the home. It's as if the home environment is constantly being upgraded. Every time you think you have things 'just right', a new idea or new concept comes and you change again. You are spending a lot of money on these things. This trend is very much in effect in the year ahead.

A parent or parent figure seems very restless and is travelling around from place to place. This person wants to explore his or her personal freedom and seems to resent any kind of obligation. He or she is going through life-changing kinds of dramas. The marriage of the parent figure is very stressed and this could be contributing to the problem. Marriages often survive this kind of testing, but it isn't easy. It takes much work and effort on both sides.

You have the aspects of someone who earns money from home or from a family business. You spend on the home and family but can earn from them as well. There's more on this later.

Siblings and sibling figures have a quiet home and family year. Children or children figures could have moved in the past year, but if not, it can still happen this year. Grandchildren, if you have them, are not likely to move this year, nor is it advisable. However, they will be travelling a lot and seem to be prospering.

Perhaps the most challenging part of this situation is the emotional instability – both within yourself and with family members. As we have mentioned, mood shifts can be swift and extreme and this is hard to handle. Your own mood shifts can be controlled with meditation, but this will not necessarily control the mood swings of family members. It will help you deal with them in a better way, though.

Renovations, construction and major repairs to the home are have good aspects all year, but especially from February 20 to April 20. Aspects for projects involving the beauty of the house – such as repainting or buying art objects for the home – are good from February 20 to March 17.

Finance and Career

Ever since Jupiter moved into Leo in July 2014 you have been in a cycle of prosperity. This continues until August 11. You are catching the lucky financial breaks. Though you are not a speculator, there is luck in these things. Capricorns are not usually at the casinos, but they take other kinds of risks – business risks – and these seem lucky these days. Assets that you already own – especially homes or residential real estate – go up in value. The family as a whole seems to prosper.

Jupiter is your spiritual planet. His positive aspects to your financial planet, Uranus, signal that your financial intuition is very good these days. It's just a matter of trusting it. Intuition is the short cut to wealth. Real intuition never violates logic; it just sees things that the logical mind does not yet see, and thus seems to violate logic. In hindsight, intuition is proved to be eminently logical. You will be exploring deeper into the spiritual dimensions of wealth this year. This began last year and continues.

By August 11 your important financial goals are achieved (if not completely, there has at least been good progress made towards them) and you can shift attention to other things. Good financial aspects will continue after August 11, but they seem less prominent. With Saturn making nice aspects to Uranus, you seem to be enjoying the act of money-making more. You seem comfortable with what you do.

With Uranus 'parked' in your 4th house of home and family you are spending on the home and family, but can earn from here as well. You are financially supportive of the family and they are supportive of you. A parent or parent figure is very involved in your finances. Family connections also seem important financially.

This is a wonderful aspect for buying or selling a home and for residential real estate in general. Generally you are a cautious, conservative investor. But these days you seem more of a risk-taker. Start ups – especially in the high-tech world or in real estate – are attractive. You are in a period – and this will go on for another few years – where you can achieve financial independence. This seems your goal.

With Uranus as your financial planet you tend to spend on new technology, and it seems a good investment. Your technological expertise is important regardless of the actual business you're involved with, and it's important to stay up-to-date with latest innovations.

Your best financial periods will be from March 21 to April 19, July 23 to August 23 and November 22 to December 21.

Jupiter in your 8th house of transformation until August 11 often indicates an inheritance, as we have mentioned. Sometimes it is a literal inheritance – someone dies and you inherit money or property – But often it is metaphorical. You are named in someone's will, or you are appointed to some administrative post in an estate. This transit shows the prosperity of the spouse, partner or current love and their generosity to you. It shows good fortune with either taking on or paying down debt – depending on your need.

Career brings fulfilment this year and you seem successful. But you will be even more successful in 2016 when Jupiter enters your career house. Your career is ruled by fast-moving Venus, and thus there are many short-term trends that are best dealt with in the monthly reports.

Love and Social Life

The past two years have been banner romantic years for you, Capricorn. Many of you married or entered into serious kinds of relationships. Perhaps they were not literal marriages but they were relationships that were 'like' a marriage. Social goals have been more or less attained and the romantic life is more or less stable. You seem basically content with the status quo. You have no pressing need to make changes. Those of you who are married will stay married; singles will most probably stay single. Current relationships will most likely continue.

Jupiter in your 8th house signals increased sexual activity during the first half of the year. While this is not the same as love, it does show interaction with the opposite sex. The sexual life seems happy this year. Whatever your age or stage in life, the libido seems stronger than usual.

If you are single and working towards your second marriage, there are wonderful opportunities after August 11, and well into 2016. You can meet this special someone at your place of worship, in an educational setting or as you get involved in charities or good causes. The person seems very spiritual. If you are working towards your third marriage you have better aspects than in the past two years. Love is in the air from August 11 onwards. If you are in your third marriage, the past two years have been a period of testing. Good marriages have survived, but flawed ones probably did not. Singles working towards their fourth marriages have better aspects for this next year.

Your love planet is the Moon, the fastest-moving of all the planets. She will move through your whole Horoscope every month. Thus there are many short-term trends in love that are best dealt with in the monthly reports.

Self-improvement

For the past year the main headline here has been your spiritual life.

Last year spiritual development was involved in the financial life. And this is so until August 11. You are to go deeper into the non-physical, non-material sources of supply, to learn the laws involved and to access these sources. Without this understanding, financial independence, which you are craving these days, cannot happen as it should. Wealth, like health or happiness, is a state of consciousness – a state of mind as some call it. If there are financial problems they are rooted in a disconnection from this state – the state we call affluence. The solution is to get back into this state as quickly as possible. Easier said than done, I know, but with meditation and a strong focus it can be achieved.

Everything we experience in life – without exception – is a reflection of our state of consciousness at a given time. The state of consciousness is the film and the outer life is the screen. If you don't like the movie that's playing it is useless to fiddle around with the screen – you must change the film. Change the film and a different movie will play – something more pleasing to you.

Your state of consciousness must express itself sooner or later. This is a spiritual law. So, if you are in the state of affluence, it must express itself in your world sooner or later. This is the spiritual way that we attain our financial goals.

This year as Saturn, the ruler of your Horoscope, is in your spiritual 12th house, you will learn how Spirit – your state of consciousness – impacts on the body and personal appearance. Your body too is only a reflection of your state of consciousness – the sum total of your thoughts, feelings and beliefs. Change the state of consciousness and the actual physical body will change. If you want a slimmer body, enter the consciousness of being slim and trim. If you want a more muscular physique, going to the gym might be a help, but changing your consciousness will help more. The results will be more permanent.

The body can be moulded and shaped according to your will. Your job is to enter the appropriate state of mind. The work will be done by a Higher Power – a great spiritual law. You need not concern yourself with 'how' this will happen. This is not your business. Your only job is to be in the appropriate state of mind – of what you want your body to look like.

Month-by-month Forecasts

January

> Best Days Overall: 9, 10, 18, 19, 27, 28
> Most Stressful Days Overall: 4, 5, 11, 12, 13, 24, 25, 31
> Best Days for Love: 1, 4, 5, 9, 10, 12, 13, 20, 21, 22, 29, 30, 31
> Best Days for Money: 6, 7, 8, 16, 17, 20, 21, 24, 25
> Best Days for Career: 1, 11, 12, 13, 21, 22, 31

You are unique among the signs in that your personal solar cycle coincides with the universal solar cycle, it moves more or less in lock-step with it. This is another reason that Capricorns tend to be successful in the world. You are in your personal new year, astrologically speaking, now. (With some of you it began last month.) With the planetary momentum strongly forward (90 per cent of the planets are in forward motion until the 21st) you are in a great period for initiating new activities or launching new products or ventures. The 20th is the best day to do this, but in a pinch after the 20th would also be good.

The month ahead is basically happy and successful. Health and energy are excellent. You are in a yearly personal pleasure peak until the 20th and afterwards you enter a yearly financial peak. You look good, have much charisma and tend to get your way in life.

Your money house is chock-full of planets this month – half of the planets are there or moving through there now. This indicates great focus and great financial support. Money comes in various ways and through a variety of people. There is a short-term financial disturbance from the 2nd to the 4th, but afterwards the coast is clear. By the end of the month you should be richer than when you began.

You begin your year with the Eastern, independent sector of the Horoscope dominant. In fact the planets are at their maximum Eastern position as the year begins. So the focus is on yourself and your personal goals and interests. You have to take responsibility for your happiness now and need not worry about the approval or disapproval of others. Your way is the best way as far as you are concerned. If you are happy others will also be happy. You have the power to create your life as you desire it to be, and now is the time to do just that. Later on in the planetary cycle it will be more difficult.

Last month, the planetary power shifted from the upper to the lower half of your Horoscope. Thus career goals are more or less achieved by now (or good progress towards them has been made) and it is time to focus on your emotional wellness. The home, family and domestic situation needs your attention. Career is always important for you and it is still important, but now it is better to approach it through interior action – the methods of night – rather than through overt ways. For the next six or so months, you will be creating the 'inner infrastructure' for future success.

February

    Best Days Overall: 5, 6, 7, 15, 16, 23, 24
    Most Stressful Days Overall: 1, 8, 9, 21, 22, 27, 28
    Best Days for Love: 1, 2, 8, 9, 10, 11, 17, 18, 20, 21, 27, 28
    Best Days for Money: 3, 4, 13, 14, 17, 18, 21, 22
    Best Days for Career: 1, 2, 8, 9, 10, 11, 20, 21

Students (especially below the college level) need to knuckle down and work harder this year. Happily, after the 18th they seem to be doing so and they should be successful in their studies this month. The same is true for those of you involved in sales, marketing and advertising. Success will happen but through more work.

Your money house is still powerful until the 18th. You are still in a yearly financial peak. Until the 18th (and this was true last month too) it will be good to detox the financial life. Eliminate waste and needless expense. Prosperity is not so much about earning more (which you will) but about getting rid of things that don't belong in the financial life. Get rid of possessions you don't use or need. Reduce the clutter in the home and in the financial life. Simplify your accounting. If you have good ideas, this is a good period to attract outside investors or outside capital; a good period too to pay down debt or to refinance debt in a better way. Those of you of the appropriate age will probably be doing more estate and tax planning now. In general there is more involvement with estates.

The love life goes better (in general) from the 1st to the 3rd and from the 18th onwards – as the Moon waxes. This is when your social magnetism will be strongest. You have some good love days until the 18th but they are not as good as the ones after that date. Love doesn't seem a major interest this month, compared with other areas of your life. The status quo prevails.

The month ahead is still an excellent time to start new activities or launch new products or ventures into the world. From the 18th onwards is best – 90 per cent of the planets are moving forward and the Moon will be waxing.

Your 3rd house of communication and intellectual interests is powerful from the 18th onwards. This is a good period to feed the mind – to give it the nutrition it needs. The mental body, though invisible, is a real body and it needs care and maintenance. This is a good period in which to catch up on your reading and to take courses in subjects that interest you.

Health is excellent this month. You have plenty of energy to achieve your goals. You can enhance it further in the ways mentioned in the yearly report. This month you can also enhance the health by giving more attention to the ankles and calves. Massage them regularly. You could also benefit from new, cutting-edge kinds of therapies.

March

Best Days Overall: 4, 5, 6, 14, 15, 22, 23
Most Stressful Days Overall: 1, 7, 8, 20, 21, 27, 28
Best Days for Love: 1, 2, 3, 10, 11, 12, 13, 18, 19, 20, 22, 23, 27, 28, 29, 30
Best Days for Money: 2, 3, 12, 13, 16, 17, 20, 21, 29, 30
Best Days for Career: 2, 3, 7, 8, 12, 13, 22, 23

The planetary power begins to shift on the 20th from the Eastern, independent sector to the social Western sector of the Horoscope. But this is just the beginning. Next month the shift will be more established. Your own needs and interests are important, but it is time now to give more attention to the needs of others. The planetary power is moving towards others and away from you. Hopefully you have made the changes that needed to be made during your period of independence since the beginning of the year. After the 20th it will be more difficult to make them. You will more or less have to adapt to things. Capricorns are very competent people, but soon this won't matter as much. It will be your ability to get on with others, to gain their co-operation that will matter. Social skills are now more important than personal competence.

Also on the 20th we have a solar eclipse that shakes things up. For most of you this eclipse is benign, but if you were born early in the sign of Capricorn – from December 21 to December 23 – it will affect you strongly. Take it nice and easy over that period. Generally the cosmos indicates when the eclipse period begins. Some strange event happens to you, or you hear of some weird event or see it on TV. This is your personal message to start taking it easy. This eclipse occurs on the border, the cusp, of your 3rd and 4th houses, which means that the affairs of both houses are affected. Hidden flaws in the home can be revealed. There can be dramas in the lives of family members – parents or parent figures, siblings or sibling figures. They should take it nice and easy this period too. It will be a good idea to drive more carefully. Cars and communication equipment could need repair or replacement.

Since the Sun, the eclipsed planet, rules your 8th house of transformation, there can be some financial crisis or disturbance in the finances of the spouse, partner or current love. He or she needs to make dramatic financial changes. If you are involved with estates or insurance claims, these move forward in a dramatic way – one way or another. (No matter what is happening now, these issues are fortunate this year and the end result should be good.) Often there are encounters with death. Perhaps you dream about it. Perhaps you encounter it in other ways. The purpose of these things is to spur you on to your true purpose in life.

Health and energy become more delicate after the 20th. Be sure to get enough rest. What's happening now is not the trend for the year ahead. Overall health is good, but this is not one of your best health periods. Until the 13th enhance the health by giving more attention to the ankles and calves. After the 13th pay attention to the feet. You respond very well to foot reflexology. Spiritual therapies will also be powerful then.

April

Best Days Overall: 1, 2, 10, 11, 12, 19, 20, 28, 29
Most Stressful Days Overall: 3, 4, 5, 17, 18, 23, 24
Best Days for Love: 1, 2, 8, 9, 13, 18, 19, 21, 22, 23, 24, 28
Best Days for Money: 8, 9, 13, 14, 17, 18, 25, 26, 27
Best Days for Career: 1, 2, 3, 4, 5, 13, 21, 22

Health and energy still need watching this month – especially around the lunar eclipse period of the 4th.

This eclipse affects you strongly, and impacts on many areas of your life. It occurs in your 10th house, announcing career changes. Sometimes people change their actual career and the career path. Most of the time, shake-ups in the corporate hierarchy, or in the industry, bring changes of policy that affect the career. Sometimes there are dramatic events in the lives of bosses, parents, parent figures or people involved in your career. Since your financial planet, Uranus, is affected here, there are some dramatic financial changes. Generally these come as a result of some crisis or disturbance. The eclipse's impact on Pluto indicates that friends are affected. Friendships get tested, which is a good thing. Often there are dramatic events in the lives of friends and this tests the relationship. Computer equipment and high-tech gadgetry get tested (and generally need repair or replacement). This might be a good time to upgrade your equipment. Computers are more vulnerable to hackers these days, so be sure your anti-hacking, anti-virus software is up to date. Back up important files too.

Every lunar eclipse tests the marriage or current relationship (the Moon is your love planet) and this one is no exception. Good relationships survive these things (you have this phenomenon twice a year and have been through it many times). Flawed relationships can dissolve. Be more patient with the beloved this period as he or she will most likely be more temperamental. It is good every now and then to clear the air with the beloved. It is good to see whatever hidden problems there are so that they can be dealt with. Often the eclipse of the love planet shows that a current relationship either goes forward or dissolves. Marriages or engagements often happen under this kind of eclipse.

Health and energy will improve dramatically after the 20th. In the meantime, you can enhance your health by giving more attention to the head, face and scalp until the 19th and to the neck and throat afterwards. Physical exercise is good until the 19th – the muscles need to be toned. Face and scalp massage, and craniosacral therapy will also be good until the 19th. Craniosacral therapy and neck massage will be good after that date as well.

Once the dust from the eclipse settles down the month ahead looks happy. On the 20th you enter one of your yearly personal pleasure peaks. You will have many opportunities for fun and leisure.

May

Best Days Overall: 8, 9, 16, 17, 25, 26, 27
Most Stressful Days Overall: 1, 2, 14, 15, 21, 22, 28, 29
Best Days for Love: 1, 2, 8, 9, 12, 13, 17, 18, 21, 22, 28, 29, 30, 31
Best Days for Money: 5, 6, 7, 10, 11, 14, 15, 23, 24
Best Days for Career: 1, 2, 12, 13, 21, 22, 28, 29, 30, 31

Your health planet, Mercury, goes retrograde on the 14th. Thus, if you are considering making important changes to your diet or health regime, do it before the 14th. Doctor's appointments, and medical tests, if they are elective, are best scheduled before the 14th as well. Overall health and energy are good this month, although you can enhance your health further by giving attention to the lungs, arms, shoulders and respiratory system. Regular arm and shoulder massage is good. Make sure you get enough fresh air. Breathing exercises are always good for you, but especially this month.

Until the 21st you are still in one of your yearly personal pleasure peaks. So you are exploring the rapture side of life. Capricorns in particular need this more than most. The tendency is to over-work and to be over-serious. Don't worry about lightening up for a time (you become more serious again after the 21st).

After the 21st your 6th house of health and work becomes powerful. This is a wonderful period to deal with health-oriented goals. The only problem is that Mercury's retrograde, so it might be better to wait until next month before you make important changes. It is a wonderful time for job seekers. There are many job opportunities happening now. Again the only problem is Mercury's retrograde, meaning that these job opportunities need studying carefully. Make sure you resolve all doubts before accepting anything. Things are not what they seem.

The love life is becoming more active this month. On the 7th Venus enters your 7th house. For singles this brings opportunities for love affairs, although not necessarily committed kinds of relationships. Her transit also shows meeting and mixing with socially and professionally prestigious people. It is the aspect for the office romance. Venus is your career planet. Her move into your 7th house signals that you can advance the career by social means during this period. But Venus is also announcing that dawn is soon to break in your year and that your next career push is starting to happen. On the 7th, she is the first short-term planet to move above the horizon. She is like the morning star announcing day break. It is still good to give more of your attention to the home and family, but very soon this will change.

Finances are good this month. Earnings should be strong. Uranus your financial planet is receiving good aspects from the 21st onwards. Enhance earnings in the ways mentioned in the yearly report.

June

Best Days Overall: 4, 5, 13, 14, 22, 23
Most Stressful Days Overall: 10, 11, 17, 18, 19, 24, 25
Best Days for Love: 1, 10, 11, 17, 18, 19, 20, 21, 29, 30
Best Days for Money: 2, 3, 6, 7, 10, 11, 20, 21, 29, 30
Best Days for Career: 1, 10, 11, 20, 21, 24, 25, 29, 30

Saturn, the ruler of your Horoscope, has been retrograde since March 14, so there has been much reviewing of your personal life and goals going on. Often one feels a 'lack of direction'. Sometimes we feel that we are going backwards instead of forward. But this is actually a good thing. Sometimes we need to 'back up' before going forward again. We need to review and gain mental clarity on personal goals. This is what is happening now.

The retrograde of the ruler of the Horoscope often indicates a lack of the usual self-confidence. But these days, with so many planets in the Western, social sector of the Horoscope, this too is a good thing. You don't need to assert yourself overmuch. Let others have their way, so long as it isn't destructive.

Saturn makes a move out of Sagittarius and back into Scorpio on June 15. He has been in Scorpio for the previous two years, which was an excellent transit for personal transformation and reinvention. These projects get 'rebooted' this month and seem successful. This aspect is very good for weight loss and detox regimes. Also it adds to the social nature of the month ahead.

The love and social life is the main headline this month. On the 21st you enter a yearly love and social peak. So there is going to be more dating, more parties and more attending of weddings. It also looks like a more sexually active kind of month.

Many planets in the 7th house (40 per cent of them are there or moving through there this month) indicates an ability to get on with all kinds of people – people of different types. For singles this can indicate too many romantic opportunities rather than too few – a nice problem to have.

The spouse, partner or current love prospers from the 21st onwards. Windfalls and financial opportunities come to him or her – without special effort.

Job seekers still have good opportunities until the 21st, and with Mercury moving forward on the 11th you have better judgement on these matters. It would probably be safer to accept a job offer after the 11th than before it.

Health and energy are more delicate after the 21st. Overall health is good and this is not a trend for the year, just not one of your better periods. Enhance the health in the ways mentioned last month.

July

Best Days Overall: 1, 2, 10, 11, 19, 20, 29, 30
Most Stressful Days Overall: 8, 9, 14, 15, 16, 22, 23
Best Days for Love: 6, 7, 8, 9, 14, 15, 16, 17, 18, 26
Best Days for Money: 3, 4, 5, 8, 9, 17, 18, 26, 27, 28
Best Days for Career: 8, 9, 17, 18, 22, 23, 26

You are still in the midst of a yearly love and social peak. Mars, your family planet, entered your 7th house on the 24th of last month and will be there all of this month. This signals more socializing with the family and perhaps socializing from home. It also shows a more aggressive attitude to love. You are more proactive. If you like someone, the person will know it. You're not playing games now. You seem direct and honest about your feelings and the family is playing Cupid this month. This transit often indicates the reappearance of an old love. This can be actual or metaphorical. You meet a person with similar personality patterns or appearance as the old love. You are reminded of the old love. This may or may not develop into something, but it is useful in other ways – it helps to resolve old love issues from the past. Its purpose is social healing.

Mercury enters your 7th house on the 8th, indicating an affinity for health professionals or for people involved in your health. There are romantic opportunities with co-workers and you socialize more at work. Mentors, ministers and foreigners become more alluring. There are romantic opportunities in your place of worship or at school.

Your health and energy will improve after the 23rd, but in the meantime get enough rest. Enhance the health in the ways mentioned in the yearly report, until the 8th. After the 8th give more attention to the stomach and the diet. Women should give more attention to the breasts. Avoid negative moods or negative emotional states after the 8th as they have a more dramatic impact on your physical health than usual.

Finances have been more stressful since the 21st of last month. Earnings are happening but through much more work and effort. This remains the case until the 23rd of this month. The good news is that the spouse, partner or current love is prospering and is more generous with you. He or she enters a yearly financial peak on the 23rd. Your personal finances also improve greatly after the 23rd but with some delayed reactions. Uranus, your financial planet, goes retrograde on the 26th. This indicates that it is time to review the finances, to gain mental clarity in this area and resolve any doubts. Earnings will happen – and they are larger than usual – but with delays and glitches. Be perfect in your financial transactions – make sure all the details are right. This will reduce any possible payment delays.

Last month, on the 21st, the planetary power began to shift into the upper half of your Horoscope. The shift is even stronger this month. It is time to start focusing more on the career again. You are in the early stages of a yearly career push. Let go of home and family concerns – downplay them – and focus on the career and outer goals.

August

Best Days Overall: 6, 7, 15, 16, 17, 25, 26
Most Stressful Days Overall: 4, 5, 10, 11, 12, 18, 19, 31
Best Days for Love: 4, 5, 10, 11, 12, 13, 14, 23, 24, 25, 31
Best Days for Money: 1, 4, 5, 13, 14, 15, 23, 24, 25, 27, 28, 31
Best Days for Career: 5, 14, 18, 19, 23, 24, 31

Your 8th house of transformation and regeneration has been strong all year, and last month it became stronger still. This remains is the situation until the 23rd of this month: 60 per cent of the planets are either in the 8th house or moving through there this month.

The 8th house is one of those mysterious, difficult to understand houses. It deals with the 'underworld' in ourselves – things we like to cover up. So when the 8th house is strong we find we are dealing more

with death and death issues, with estates and taxes. The sexual appe-
tite and libido are increased. We could be attending more funerals or
hearing about near-death kinds of experiences – and sometimes we are
involved in near-death experiences. In order to live properly – to fulfil
our true potential – it is important to understand death and come to
terms with it. Every year the cosmos brings you this opportunity.

The 8th house is called the house of death. But this is not literal
death (every year your 8th house becomes strong, and you are still
around to tell the story), more about 'encounters' with death. Your
spiritual planet Jupiter has spent the past year in your 8th house so you
have had spiritual revelation (either personal or though others) of what
death is all about.

If you are of the appropriate age, this is a great period for doing
estate and tax planning. Money can come to you from tax refunds or
insurance claims. It is also a great period to pay down debt or to refinance debt on better terms. Borrowing (if you need to) is also easier
this period. If you have good business ideas, this is a good period to
attract outside money for them.

The spouse, partner or current love is still in a yearly financial peak
until the 23rd.

Health and energy are good this month. You can enhance it further
by giving more attention to the heart until the 7th, the small intestine
after the 7th and the kidneys and hips from the 27th onwards. Kidney
detox might be a good idea then, as would hip massage.

Jupiter makes a major move into your 9th house on the 11th; the
Sun will enter on the 23rd. So there is travel in store this month.
University students (or applicants) are successful in their educational
goals now.

September

Best Days Overall: 2, 3, 12, 13, 22, 23, 30
Most Stressful Days Overall: 1, 7, 8, 14, 15, 28, 29
Best Days for Love: 1, 2, 3, 7, 8, 9, 10, 12, 13, 19, 20, 24, 28, 29
Best Days for Money: 1, 2, 9, 10, 12, 19, 20, 24, 25, 28, 29, 30
Best Days for Career: 1, 9, 10, 14, 15, 19, 20, 28, 29

An eventful month ahead. Two eclipses ensure that.

The solar eclipse of the 13th occurs in your 9th house (which is a strong house this month). Foreign travel is on the cards but try to schedule trips around this eclipse period. For students (at college level or above) this indicates changes in educational plans and strategy. They can change schools, or subjects, or courses they planned to take. Important changes in school policy could be behind this. An eclipse in the 9th house often brings a 'crisis of faith'. Your philosophical and religious belief system gets tested and will probably be revised or 'fine tuned' over the next six months. There are dramas in your place of worship and in the lives of ministers, priests, rabbis or imams. Like every solar eclipse, this one brings encounters with death. Sometimes this is via near-death experiences. Sometimes someone you know is diagnosed with an incurable illness. Often there are dreams of death. Often one reads of death and murder in the newspapers. The cosmos forces you to confront this issue and to come to terms with it better. If you are involved in estate, tax or insurance issues, these move forward now.

The lunar eclipse of the 28th (in the Americas it is on the 27th) affects you more strongly than the previous one. So take things nice and easy around the eclipse period. It occurs in your 4th house of home and family and brings dramas to family members, parents or parent figures. Hidden flaws in the family relationship get revealed so that they can be dealt with. Are there skeletons in the closet? Now is when you find out about them. The same is true with the physical home. If there are flaws there you find out about them now and you can take corrective action. Each lunar eclipse tests the marriage or current relationship and this one is no different. The beloved (as well as family members) is more tightly wound this period – more high strung. So be more patient with them. There's no need to make matters worse than they are.

Health and energy become delicate after the 23rd. Overall health is good though – this is just a temporary blip caused by short-term planetary transits. So make sure you get enough rest (especially around the eclipse period of the 28th). Enhance the health by giving more attention to the kidneys and hips. If you are scheduling medical check-ups or tests, it might be better to do them before the 17th. Your health planet Mercury starts to retrograde then.

On the 23rd you enter a yearly career peak.

October

Best Days Overall: 1, 9, 10, 19, 20, 27, 28
Most Stressful Days Overall: 4, 5, 11, 12, 13, 25, 26, 31
Best Days for Love: 2, 3, 4, 5, 8, 9, 12, 13, 19, 20, 22, 23, 27, 28, 29, 31
Best Days for Money: 1, 6, 7, 9, 10, 16, 17, 19, 20, 21, 22, 25, 26, 27, 28
Best Days for Career: 8, 9, 11, 12, 13, 19, 20, 27, 28

Though overall energy is not what it should be, or will be, many nice things are happening this month. There is much success.

You are still very much in a yearly career peak until October 23. Your career planet Venus travels with Jupiter from the 24th to the 27th bringing success and happy career opportunities. Your career is boosted by being involved in charitable functions during that period. Enhance the career by weeding out inessentials. Keep a laser-like focus. Don't get distracted by minutiae. There is probably career-related travel from the 8th onwards and your willingness to travel helps the career. It will also be good to take courses or seminars related to the career after the 8th. Outside investors seem willing to invest in your career. Mercury in your 10th house signals that your good work ethic boosts your career and is noticed by superiors.

Your 9th house is powerful this month and filled with mostly beneficent planets. This indicates foreign travel and travel opportunities coming to you. This is a beautiful period for students. There is success in their studies and in their educational ambitions.

Health needs some attention until the 23rd. As always, make sure you get enough rest. Lack of energy is the primal root cause of disease. Enhance the health by giving attention to the kidneys and hips again this month. Hip massage and kidney detox will still be beneficial. Mercury, your health planet, moves forward on the 9th, so important changes to the health regime, appointments and tests will go better after that date.

The finances are a bit stressful until the 23rd but these are short-term issues. Earnings will happen but there are more challenges involved. Your financial planet Uranus is still retrograde, so it is not advisable to draw conclusions from the temporary stress. It is still important to gain mental clarity in this area and it is happening. This is a time for research and reviewing options, not for making important financial decisions. Finances will improve after the 23rd.

On the 23rd the Sun enters your 11th house of friends. This is a strong social kind of period, although not necessarily romantic – it is more about friendship and group activities. This is a great period to expand your knowledge of technology, computers and software, and science, astrology and astronomy. Computer equipment gets tested from the 5th to the 7th and there could be drama in the life of a friend then too.

November

Best Days Overall: 5, 6, 15, 16, 24, 25
Most Stressful Days Overall: 1, 8, 9, 22, 28, 29
Best Days for Love: 1, 6, 7, 10, 11, 17, 18, 21, 26, 27, 28, 29, 30
Best Days for Money: 3, 4, 5, 6, 13, 14, 15, 16, 17, 18, 21, 22, 24, 25, 30
Best Days for Career: 6, 7, 8, 9, 17, 18, 26, 27

This month, by the 12th, the planetary power shifts back to the East from the West. This means that the planetary power is moving towards you, rather than away from you. Personal power and personal independence is getting stronger day by day. This shift began late in

September, but now it is confirmed. You are now in a different stage of your yearly cycle. It is time to look out for number one; time to be a little more selfish – that is, to focus on your self-interest; time to take personal responsibility for your happiness and to make the changes that produce it. Self-reliance, personal initiative and your personal abilities are what matter now. If conditions displease you, change them to something more pleasant. There's no need to seek the approval of others. They will more or less go along with you.

Though technically your career peak is over with, your 10th house seems very active this month. Venus enters the career house on the 8th, and Mars enters on the 12th. Venus in the 10th house indicates that children or children figures in your life are succeeding and being helpful in your career. If the children are very young they motivate you. If they are of an appropriate age they seem actively involved. This aspect shows that you succeed as you have fun – perhaps you make some important connection at the theatre or on the golf course or tennis court. Perhaps you are called on to entertain your clients or customers or people involved with your career. Mars in your 10th house shows the involvement of family members in your career. Family members are successful this month and seem helpful. A parent or parent figure can be overly controlling, but the motives seem benign. The family as a whole seems elevated in status.

Job seekers have a happy opportunity between the 24th and the 26th.

Health is good this month. But you could be overworking in your job, putting in longer hours to further your career and this could deplete your energy. You can enhance the health through detox regimes from the 2nd to the 20th. Give more attention to the colon, bladder and sexual organs. Colonic irrigation might be a good idea. Safe sex and sexual moderation are also important. After the 20th, give more attention to the liver and thighs. Thigh massage is beneficial then and liver detox would be effective. After the 20th you respond well to spiritual therapies – meditation, reiki, the laying on of hands – things of this nature. If you feel under the weather a spiritual healer will be very helpful.

Love, like last month, is more or less status quo. Social magnetism will be strongest from the 11th to the 25th as the Moon waxes. You have good love days outside this period, but they won't be as good as the ones within that period.

Finances are good all month but especially after the 20th. Keep in mind though that your financial planet Uranus is still going backwards.

December

Best Days Overall: 2, 3, 4, 12, 13, 21, 22, 30, 31
Most Stressful Days Overall: 5, 6, 19, 20, 25, 26
Best Days for Love: 1, 7, 10, 11, 17, 18, 20, 25, 26, 30, 31
Best Days for Money: 1, 2, 3, 4, 10, 11, 12, 13, 14, 15, 16, 19, 20, 21, 22, 27, 28, 29, 30, 31
Best Days for Career: 5, 6, 7, 17, 18, 25, 26

Mars is making dynamic aspects to Pluto and Uranus from the 5th to the 12th. Parents and parent figures should stay out of harm's way and avoid confrontations. There is some short-term financial disturbance from the 9th to the 12th – perhaps some unexpected expense in the home or with the family. You and a parent or parent figure are not in financial agreement. In spite of this short-term bump, finances will be good. The Sun will make very nice aspects to Uranus from the 7th to the 10th. You will have the wherewithal to handle the extra expense. Your financial planet will also start to move forward on the 26th and thus deals that previously seemed stuck now move forward. There should be more financial clarity then.

The planets are in their maximum Eastern position this month and next, and so you are at the maximum extent of your personal power and independence. You are getting your way in life. And you should. Make those changes that need to be made. Later on they will be more difficult.

Mars will be in your 10th house of career all month, signalling that you are putting in long hours, fending off the competition, and being more aggressive in career matters. It also shows the involvement of family members in the career and their support. The social connections are always important for you careerwise, but after the 5th even more so. It will be advantageous to be involved with groups and professional or trade organizations as this helps the career and boosts your status. Good to be up to date on the latest technology as well.

Many of you are having your personal new year this month. Many of you will have it next month. With your 12th house very strong (as it has been since November 22) it is a good time to review the past year, assess your achievements or failures, correct mistakes and set goals for the year ahead, which will begin on your birthday. From the astrological perspective your new year is your birthday, not January 1.

Health and energy are good this month, and get even better after the 21st. The liver and thighs are still important until the 10th, and so are spiritual therapies. After the 10th, give more attention to the spine, knees, teeth, bones, skin and overall skeletal alignment. These areas are always important for you but especially in this period. This is a very good month for detox regimes (after the 21st) and for weight loss. You enter a yearly personal pleasure peak from the 21st onwards, but you don't seem likely to over do it.

A happy job opportunity comes after the 10th.

Aquarius

~~~

THE WATER-BEARER

Birthdays from
20th January to
18th February

Personality Profile

AQUARIUS AT A GLANCE

Element – Air

Ruling Planet – Uranus
  Career Planet – Pluto
  Love Planet – Sun
  Money Planet – Neptune
  Planet of Health and Work – Moon
  Planet of Home and Family Life – Venus
  Planet of Spirituality – Saturn

Colours – electric blue, grey, ultramarine blue

Colours that promote love, romance and social harmony – gold, orange

Colour that promotes earning power – aqua

Gems – black pearl, obsidian, opal, sapphire

Metal – lead

Scents – azalea, gardenia

Quality – fixed (= stability)

Qualities most needed for balance – warmth, feeling and emotion

Strongest virtues – great intellectual power, the ability to communicate and to form and understand abstract concepts, love for the new and avant-garde

Deepest needs – to know and to bring in the new

Characteristics to avoid – coldness, rebelliousness for its own sake, fixed ideas

Signs of greatest overall compatibility – Gemini, Libra

Signs of greatest overall incompatibility – Taurus, Leo, Scorpio

Sign most helpful to career – Scorpio

Sign most helpful for emotional support – Taurus

Sign most helpful financially – Pisces

Sign best for marriage and/or partnerships – Leo

Sign most helpful for creative projects – Gemini

Best Sign to have fun with – Gemini

Signs most helpful in spiritual matters – Libra, Capricorn

Best day of the week – Saturday

Understanding an Aquarius

In the Aquarius-born, intellectual faculties are perhaps the most highly developed of any sign in the zodiac. Aquarians are clear, scientific thinkers. They have the ability to think abstractly and to formulate laws, theories and clear concepts from masses of observed facts. Geminis might be very good at gathering information, but Aquarians take this a step further, excelling at interpreting the information gathered.

Practical people – men and women of the world – mistakenly consider abstract thinking as impractical. It is true that the realm of abstract thought takes us out of the physical world, but the discoveries made in this realm generally end up having tremendous practical consequences. All real scientific inventions and breakthroughs come from this abstract realm.

Aquarians, more so than most, are ideally suited to explore these abstract dimensions. Those who have explored these regions know that there is little feeling or emotion there. In fact, emotions are a hindrance to functioning in these dimensions; thus Aquarians seem – at times – cold and emotionless to others. It is not that Aquarians haven't got feelings and deep emotions, it is just that too much feeling clouds their ability to think and invent. The concept of 'too much feeling' cannot be tolerated or even understood by some of the other signs. Nevertheless, this Aquarian objectivity is ideal for science, communication and friendship.

Aquarians are very friendly people, but they do not make a big show about it. They do the right thing by their friends, even if sometimes they do it without passion or excitement.

Aquarians have a deep passion for clear thinking. Second in importance, but related, is their passion for breaking with the establishment and traditional authority. Aquarians delight in this, because for them rebellion is like a great game or challenge. Very often they will rebel strictly for the fun of rebelling, regardless of whether the authority they defy is right or wrong. Right or wrong has little to do with the rebellious actions of an Aquarian, because to a true Aquarian authority and power must be challenged as a matter of principle.

Where Capricorn or Taurus will err on the side of tradition and the status quo, an Aquarian will err on the side of the new. Without this virtue it is doubtful whether any progress would be made in the world. The conservative-minded would obstruct progress. Originality and invention imply an ability to break barriers; every new discovery represents the toppling of an impediment to thought. Aquarians are very interested in breaking barriers and making walls tumble – scientifically, socially and politically. Other zodiac signs, such as Capricorn, also have scientific talents. But Aquarians are particularly excellent in the social sciences and humanities.

Finance

In financial matters Aquarians tend to be idealistic and humanitarian – to the point of self-sacrifice. They are usually generous contributors to social and political causes. When they contribute it differs from when a Capricorn or Taurus contributes. A Capricorn or Taurus may expect some favour or return for a gift; an Aquarian contributes selflessly.

Aquarians tend to be as cool and rational about money as they are about most things in life. Money is something they need and they set about acquiring it scientifically. No need for fuss; they get on with it in the most rational and scientific ways available.

Money to the Aquarian is especially nice for what it can do, not for the status it may bring (as is the case for other signs). Aquarians are neither big spenders nor penny-pinchers and use their finances in practical ways, for example to facilitate progress for themselves, their families, or even for strangers.

However, if Aquarians want to reach their fullest financial potential they will have to explore their intuitive nature. If they follow only their financial theories – or what they believe to be theoretically correct – they may suffer some losses and disappointments. Instead, Aquarians should call on their intuition, which knows without thinking. For Aquarians, intuition is the short-cut to financial success.

Career and Public Image

Aquarians like to be perceived not only as the breakers of barriers but also as the transformers of society and the world. They long to be seen in this light and to play this role. They also look up to and respect other people in this position and even expect their superiors to act this way.

Aquarians prefer jobs that have a bit of idealism attached to them – careers with a philosophical basis. Aquarians need to be creative at work, to have access to new techniques and methods. They like to keep busy and enjoy getting down to business straightaway, without wasting any time. They are often the quickest workers and usually have suggestions for improvements that will benefit their employers. Aquarians are also very helpful with their co-workers and welcome responsibility, preferring this to having to take orders from others.

If Aquarians want to reach their highest career goals they have to develop more emotional sensitivity, depth of feeling and passion. They need to learn to narrow their focus on the essentials and concentrate more on the job in hand. Aquarians need 'a fire in the belly' – a consuming passion and desire – in order to rise to the very top. Once this passion exists they will succeed easily in whatever they attempt.

Love and Relationships

Aquarians are good at friendships, but a bit weak when it comes to love. Of course they fall in love, but their lovers always get the impression that they are more best friends than paramours.

Like Capricorns, they are cool customers. They are not prone to displays of passion or to outward demonstrations of their affections. In fact, they feel uncomfortable when their other half hugs and touches them too much. This does not mean that they do not love their partners. They do, only they show it in other ways. Curiously enough, in relationships they tend to attract the very things that they feel uncomfortable with. They seem to attract hot, passionate, romantic, demonstrative people. Perhaps they know instinctively that these people have qualities they lack and so seek them out. In any event, these relationships do seem to work, Aquarian coolness calming the more passionate partner while the fires of passion warm the cold-blooded Aquarius.

The qualities Aquarians need to develop in their love life are warmth, generosity, passion and fun. Aquarians love relationships of the mind. Here they excel. If the intellectual factor is missing in a relationship an Aquarian will soon become bored or feel unfulfilled.

Home and Domestic Life

In family and domestic matters Aquarians can have a tendency to be too non-conformist, changeable and unstable. They are as willing to break the barriers of family constraints as they are those of other areas of life.

Even so, Aquarians are very sociable people. They like to have a nice home where they can entertain family and friends. Their house is usually decorated in a modern style and full of state-of-the-art appliances and gadgets – an environment Aquarians find absolutely necessary.

If their home life is to be healthy and fulfilling Aquarians need to inject it with a quality of stability – yes, even some conservatism. They need at least one area of life to be enduring and steady; this area is usually their home and family life.

Venus, the generic planet of love, rules the Aquarian's 4th solar house of home and family, which means that when it comes to the family and child-rearing, theories, cool thinking and intellect are not always enough. Aquarians need to bring love into the equation in order to have a great domestic life.

Horoscope for 2015

Major Trends

You have just had two very prosperous years. This year, with Saturn making stressful aspects to your financial planet Neptune, earnings will come, but with much more effort. If you put in the effort, you should prosper. More details later.

You are in the midst of a banner love and social period. It began last July and continues until August 11. Love is in the air these days and there's more on this later.

Though you will have to work harder for your finances, Saturn's move out of Scorpio, late last year, improves your overall energy tremendously. Health is much improved this year and you will have the energy you need to put into your financial life. Saturn is now making beautiful aspects to you and for the next two years.

Career has been very demanding these past few years. You had to succeed through earned effort – through old-fashioned hard work. But this year much of the stress leaves you.

Uranus, the ruler of your Horoscope, has been in your 3rd house of communication for some years now, and will be there in the year ahead. You are focused on communication and intellectual interests – much more so than usual. Jupiter is making fabulous aspects to Uranus for most of the year ahead and this shows travel and the good life. This is a very nice position for students – they should succeed in their studies this year.

Jupiter will move into your 8th house of transformation on August 11 and spend the rest of the year there. This signals a more sexually active kind of period.

Spirituality has been important for many years and the trend continues in the year ahead. It is high on your priorities and you should be successful here.

Your main areas of interest will be finance; communication and intellectual interests; love and romance (until August 11); sex, personal reinvention, occult studies, debt and repayment of debt (from August 11 onwards); career (from June 15 to September 18); friends, groups and group activities (from January 1 to June 15 and from September 18 onwards); and spirituality.

Your paths of greatest fulfilment in the year ahead will be love and romance (until August 11); sex, personal reinvention, occult studies, debt and the repayment of debt (after August 11); and religion, philosophy, foreign travel and higher education (until November 13).

Health

(Please note that this is an astrological perspective on health and not a medical one. In days of yore there was no difference, these perspectives

were identical. But now there could be quite a difference. For a medical perspective, please consult your doctor or health practitioner.)

Health, as we mentioned, is much improved this year. Saturn has for the most part left his stressful aspect to you (although he will spend three months from June back in his stressful aspect, but most of you won't feel it much – only those born later in the sign of Aquarius will be strongly affected – people born from February 17 to February 19). Jupiter will also move away from his stressful aspect to you on August 11. The other long-term planets are either making nice aspects to you or leaving you alone.

You will have all the energy you need to achieve whatever you want to achieve this year.

There will of course be periods in the year where health and energy are less easy than usual. These come from the transits of short-term planets. They are temporary blips though and not trends for the year – when they pass your normal health and energy return.

Important foot reflexology points for the year ahead

Try to massage the whole foot on a regular basis, but pay extra attention to the points highlighted on the chart. When you massage, be aware of 'sore spots', as these need special attention. It is also a good idea to massage the ankles and the tops of the feet.

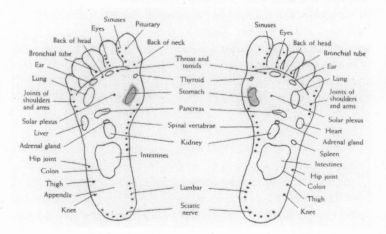

Given this situation it is understandable that your 6th house of health is mostly empty. There's no need to pay too much attention. You can sort of take good health for granted.

Good though your health is you can make it even better. Give more attention to the following areas: the ankles and calves; and the stomach and breasts. The reflex points for these vulnerable areas are shown above.

The ankles and calves are always important for you. It will be beneficial to massage them regularly and to give the ankles more support when exercising.

The stomach and breasts are also always important for you, and this year is no different. If you want to energize the breasts, massage the top of the foot, rather than the sole. Diet is always an issue for you and this should be checked by a professional. What you eat is important but *how* you eat is perhaps just as important. Eat slowly and chew your food well. Try to have nice, soothing music playing as you eat. Eat with right attitude. Give thanks for the food and bless it (in your own words). This will elevate the energy of the food and will also enhance the digestive system.

Emotional harmony is important for everyone, but for you more so than most, Aquarius. It is a health issue. Avoid depression and dwelling on negative things. Work to keep your moods positive and constructive. We were not designed to be victims of mood, but master of them. Meditation will be a big help here.

Family harmony is also very important – and it relates to what we have just said. If there is discord in the family it can impact on your physical health. Thus, should problems arise (God forbid), restore the family harmony as much as you can.

Home and Family

Your 4th house is not a house of power this year; home and family are not one of your priorities. This tends to be the status quo. The good news here is that you have more freedom to shape this area as you will. If you want to move or renovate your house, there's nothing stopping you. The problem is not freedom but lack of interest (compared with other things). Home and family issues will become important in a few years, but right now you seem basically content with the status quo.

You are travelling more this year, living in different places for long periods of time, but this is not really a move.

Fast-moving Venus is your family planet. In any given year she will move through all the signs and houses of your Horoscope. Thus there are many short-term family trends that are best covered in the monthly reports.

If you are planning major renovations or repairs to the home, April 1 to May 12 seems a good time. If you're planning to redecorate, to beautify the home in a cosmetic kind of way, to buy *objet d'art* or to repaint, March 17 to April 11 would be a good period to do this in.

The marriage of a parent or parent figure has been severely tested over the past two years. If the marriage has survived it will get even better in the year ahead. If it didn't survive, or if the parent or parent figure is single again, there is love this year – after August 11. This parent or parent figure could have moved last year, but if not a move or renovation is still signalled in the year ahead.

Siblings and sibling figures probably moved or renovated their homes in the past two years. This year they seem content with what they have.

Children or children figures in your life are likely to move in the next two years. The move seems happy. This sometimes shows renovations or the acquisition of additional homes. Children and children figures seem more fertile in the next two years as well.

Grandchildren, if you have them, are prospering from August 11 onwards. They could be involved in major repairs in the home.

Finance and Career

As we mentioned, the past two years have been very strong financial years. Earnings and overall net worth increased – each according to their status and stage in life.

Prosperity is still good for most of the year, especially until August 11, but there are more work and challenges involved. And, after August 11, even more work and challenge. You will have earnings, but you will definitely earn them. The lucky breaks are not there. You will have to create your own lucky breaks.

With Jupiter making wonderful aspects to the ruler of your Horoscope, Uranus, you are still living the high life. You are travelling, eating good foods and drinking fine wines. You are enjoying all the pleasures of the body. And, the universe is supplying the wherewithal for this.

However, Saturn's stressful aspect shows that there are some unpleasant revelations in store in the financial life, or perhaps with people involved in your finances. There is a lot of behind the scenes activity that you will learn about and have to handle. Things are not what they seem. More homework is needed when making important financial decisions or major purchases. The good news is that when the facts are known, you can make more realistic financial moves and plans. The truth might be unpleasant, but ultimately it is good. There is always a solution to every problem, but you have to know that the problem exists first. Jupiter will move into your 8th house on August 11 and spend the rest of the year there. Financially this indicates the prosperity of the spouse, partner or current love and his or her generosity with you. It is a period where debts can be easily paid or easily made – according to your need. If you have good business ideas, you have access to outside capital – either through banks or outside investors.

Often this aspect shows inheritance. Sometimes this can indicate being named in someone's will or being appointed to some administrative post in an estate. I have seen cases where the person didn't inherit money directly, but received gifts from people who had inherited money. It was 'as if' they had inherited. Those of you of the appropriate age are doing more estate planning in the year ahead.

There is good fortune with insurance claims in the year ahead. Money can come from tax refunds as well.

Jupiter in the 8th house will bring opportunities to profit from troubled companies or properties. They can be bought up cheaply. You have a good eye for this kind of thing these days.

Your financial intuition has been spot on for the past two years. It is still good, but it needs more verification this year. The intuition itself is good. But you could be interpreting the message wrongly. Allow time to get the message right.

Favourable financial numbers are 1, 12 and 18.

Career pressures are easing up this year. The past two years have been very demanding. In many cases these demands came from a boss who pushed you beyond your limits. In some cases it came from the demands of the career itself. Saturn is now mostly out of your career house. He will spend a few months there from June 15 to September 18, but the worst of the transit is over with.

Furthermore, Jupiter will start to make beautiful aspects to your career planet, Pluto, after August 11. Thus all the hard work of the past two years pays off. There are promotions and pay rises. Happy career opportunities will come to you – either within your present company or with another one. Your public and professional status will be elevated.

Many career trends that we have written of in past years are still in effect. You can advance your career by getting involved in charities and good causes. Authority figures look kindly on this. Often one makes important career connections through these activities. But in general these things will enhance your public and professional standing.

You have been idealistic about money and career for some years now, and this trend continues in the year ahead. You need to feel that you are helping the world as a whole. It's not just about making money and being successful.

Love and Social Life

You have been in a banner romantic period since July 2014, with Jupiter in your 7th house (where he remains until August 11). Those of you still unattached are likely to find a special someone this year. Marriage often happens with this aspect, but not always in a literal kind of way. Sometimes one enters a relationship that is 'like a marriage'.

In general the love life is happy. Sure, there will be periods in the year where love is less easy than usual. These come from the transits of the short-term planets. They are temporary issues and not trends for the year ahead.

Aquarians have a natural affinity for technology and the online world, and with Jupiter, the ruler of your 11th house of friends and groups, in your house of love, online activities are even more pronounced – especially when it comes to love. You would tend to have happy romantic opportunities through the various online dating services or social networking sites. You would tend to run the romance through texting and social networking.

This transit also shows that something that was perhaps just a friendship becomes more than that. Sometimes it shows that you meet that special someone through the introduction of friends or as you are involved in group activities. Friends enjoy playing Cupid this year.

Friendship is always important to you. This year it is an important factor in love. You want to be friends with your beloved, not just lovers. You want a relationship of peers – of equals. However you also like 'star quality' in a lover, and stars sometimes have a problem with 'equality'.

This year you are also attracted to foreigners – exotic types. And romance could happen in a foreign land too.

If you are single and working towards your first marriage, success is likely this year. If you are in or working towards a second marriage, the year ahead seems quiet and stable, though you will be dating more and attending more parties and gatherings. Singles will probably remain single and those who are married will probably remain married. If you are single and working towards your third marriage, patience is needed. Marriage is not likely and is probably not advisable. You will find romantic opportunities in spiritual settings – at meditation seminars, charity events, the yoga studio or prayer circle. If you are working towards your fourth marriage, romance is happening this year.

The romantic life is basically wonderful this year; the social challenges seem to be coming from friends. Friendships are getting 'stress tested'. This is not pleasant but is ultimately good. True friendships will weather the testing. Bad ones won't. Focus more on the quality of friendships rather than the quantity.

Self-Improvement

Saturn, as we mentioned, is now in your 11th house and will be there for the next two years. Friendship is very important to Aquarians. The tendency is to have many, many friends. In fact, Aquarius, you look on everyone as a friend or potential friend. These are wonderful qualities and make for great popularity. But now the cosmos is setting this area into right order. Too many friends – and especially the wrong kinds – is not healthy. A weeding out process is happening now. The wheat is being separated from the chaff. You are going to be more choosy in selecting your friends, more discriminating. The cosmos is doing this through stress testing your friendships. The testing will show who your real friends are and who can be discarded.

When times are good – and you've had a few years of easy times – we don't know who our real friends are. Success has many fathers, but failure is always an orphan. Success has many friends and followers, difficulty is a loner. So, it is good that this is happening. Truth is always good. You will find out who can be relied upon and how much, and who can't.

Saturn is your spiritual planet. Thus this year you need more spiritual type friends – and it will happen for you. Spiritual compatibility is probably the most important consideration in friendship this year. You need people who share your spiritual ideals and who foster your spiritual practice. Spiritual friendships tend to last longer than regular ones. They go on life after life. So the urge these days is for long, enduring kinds of friendships and this is what will happen.

Spirituality has been important to you for many years. On the financial level it is always important. But it has become even more so, ever since Pluto, your career planet, entered your 12th house. In many cases this transit shows a spiritual kind of career – a career with a non-profit organization or charity. In other cases it shows being involved with ministry, meditation groups or spiritual organizations. And, in others, as we have mentioned, it can show a worldly career but with much focus on charities and good causes. We could say that spiritual growth is the real career and everything else revolves around that. You will choose the career that best fosters spiritual growth.

Month-by-month Forecasts

January

Best Days Overall: 2, 3, 11, 12, 13, 20, 21, 29, 30
Most Stressful Days Overall: 6, 7, 8, 14, 15, 27, 28
Best Days for Love: 1, 6, 7, 8, 9, 10, 12, 13, 20, 21, 22, 29, 30, 31
Best Days for Money: 4, 7, 8, 14, 16, 17, 22, 23, 24, 25, 31
Best Days for Career: 9, 10, 14, 15, 18, 19, 27, 28

A happy and successful month ahead, Aquarius. Enjoy.

You begin your year with the planetary power mostly in the East – the sector of independence. In fact this month (and next) the planets are at their most Easterly position and you are in your greatest period of personal power and independence for the year. This won't happen again until this time next year. Now is the time to exercise personal initiative, to be more self-reliant and to take responsibility for your happiness. Other people don't really have much to say about your life these days. It's up to you. If conditions irk you, change them. It's time to create your personal paradise on Earth. You have the power to do it. You are having your way in life and this is as it should be.

The planetary power begins to shift this month (from the 20th onwards) to the lower half of your Horoscope. You are finishing your career push for the past year and are entering a stage of preparation for the next career push in six months' time or so. It is hard to say which is more important: the outer event or the preparation that precedes the outer event. One goes with the other. One is impossible without the other. It's merely a question of where you are in your cycle. Career takes a back seat now. This is a period to get the home, family and emotional life in right order. If these are in right order, the career will sort of take care of itself.

The planetary momentum is overwhelmingly forward this month. The universal solar cycle is waxing (growing) and on your birthday your personal solar cycle will start to wax. Thus you are in a wonderful period for launching new products or starting new activities – from your birthday onwards.

On the 20th you enter one of your yearly personal pleasure peaks. This is when the body gets indulged with its pleasures. But it's also a good time for getting the body and overall image in right shape.

Love is rocky from the 2nd to the 4th, but will straighten out later in the month. The beloved should stay out of harm's way during this period, drive more carefully, avoid confrontations and risky kinds of activities. Be more patient with the beloved at this time. On the 20th, as your love planet crosses the Ascendant, love seeks you out. You have love on your terms. There's nothing special you need to do, just go about your daily business.

Health is excellent.

February

Best Days Overall: 8, 9, 17, 18, 25, 26
Most Stressful Days Overall: 3, 4, 10, 11, 23, 24
Best Days for Love: 1, 2, 3, 4, 8, 9, 10, 11, 17, 18, 20, 21, 27, 28
Best Days for Money: 1, 3, 4, 10, 13, 14, 19, 20, 21, 22
Best Days for Career: 5, 6, 7, 10, 11, 15, 16, 23, 24

You are still in an excellent period for starting new activities or launching new products or projects into the world – even better than last month. After the 18th would be the absolute best time. You are also still in a yearly personal pleasure peak until the 18th. So there is lots of fun and sensual delight.

On the 18th, as the Sun enters your money house, you begin a yearly financial peak. Finances were stressed last month (they were slower coming in than usual) and you should see a big change from the 18th onwards. Half of the planets are either in or moving through your money house this month, which is a lot of financial power. It also shows that money can come in a variety of different ways and through many people. The spouse, partner or current love seems financially generous these days – last month too. He or she is very personally involved in your finances. A business partnership or joint venture could happen after the 18th (the 23rd to the 27th is a likely period for this). Family members are supportive until the 20th (and you are financially supportive of them). A parent or parent figure seems especially supportive from the 1st to the 3rd – but there could be some delays involved here. Mars in the money house until the 20th indicates earnings coming from sales, marketing or trading activities. Siblings, sibling figures and neighbours are supportive financially.

Love is still pursuing you until the 18th. Singles or the unattached will find love opportunities as they pursue their financial goals, or with people involved in their finances, after the 18th. Wealth and material gifts are romantic turn-ons after that date. Love is shown in material ways.

Health and energy are good all month. You can enhance the health further in the ways mentioned in the yearly report. If you are involved in detox regimes (and many of you are this month), the period from the 1st to the 18th will be best for these. If you're scheduling visits to the doctor or are having tests done, these would be better after the 18th.

March

Best Days Overall: 7, 8, 16, 17, 24, 25, 26
Most Stressful Days Overall: 2, 3, 9, 10, 22, 23, 29, 30, 31
Best Days for Love: 1, 2, 3, 10, 11, 12, 13, 18, 19, 20, 22, 23, 29, 30, 31
Best Days for Money: 1, 2, 3, 9, 10, 12, 13, 18, 19, 20, 21, 27
Best Days for Career: 4, 5, 6, 9, 10, 11, 14, 15, 22, 23

This is a wonderful year for love, but in the month ahead it gets tested by a solar eclipse on the 20th. It is good that love gets some testing. This is how we know whether or not it is real.

The solar eclipse of this month is basically benign for you. But it won't hurt to take it easy that period. It might not be so benign to others around you. The eclipse occurs on the border between the 2nd and 3rd houses and thus affects the affairs of both. There can be some financial disturbance that forces financial change on you – perhaps a financial scare or some flaw in your thinking or strategy. Cars and communication equipment get tested. It will be a good idea to drive more defensively at this time.

Siblings and sibling figure (and neighbours) can have dramatic, life-changing experiences. Students (below college level) can change schools or educational plans. There can be administrative or other kinds of shake-ups at school. The spouse, partner or current love should stay out of harm's way during this period too. He or she will be redefining him or herself over the next six months, changing the mode of dress, hair style and overall 'look'.

It will be a good idea to drive more carefully even before the eclipse – from the 9th to the 12th – too. Siblings or sibling figures in your life should reduce their schedule then too, and avoid confrontations and risky activities that period.

The month ahead is still a great time to start new projects or launch new products. After the 20th (let the dust settle from the eclipse first!) is excellent for this. The Sun in Aries is excellent starting energy.

In spite of the eclipse you are in a great financial period this month, especially until the 20th. Mercury in the money house from the 13th onwards shows luck in speculations. Speculations are especially favourable from the 17th to the 19th – though there might be delays involved. Children and children figures in your life seem very involved in your finances. If they are of an appropriate age they are supportive; if they are very young they are motivators for you. Foreigners and foreign companies also seem important.

April

Best Days Overall: 3, 4, 5, 13, 14, 21, 22
Most Stressful Days Overall: 6, 7, 19, 20, 25, 26, 27
Best Days for Love: 1, 2, 8, 9, 13, 18, 19, 21, 22, 25, 26, 27, 28
Best Days for Money: 6, 7, 8, 9, 15, 16, 17, 18, 23, 24, 25, 26
Best Days for Career: 1, 2, 6, 7, 10, 11, 12, 19, 20, 28, 29

You are still in an excellent period for starting new projects or launching new products this month; from the 1st to the 3rd and the 18th to the 20th are the best days.

The planetary power is now at the nadir (low point) in your Horoscope and Pluto, your career planet, goes retrograde on the 17th. Your 10th house of career is empty (except for the Moon's fleeting visit on the 6th and 7th) while your 4th house of home and family is chock-full of planets. A very clear-cut message. Let career issues go now, downplay them and give your attention to the home, family and domestic life. This is a month for emotional healing, rather than outer pursuits. If the home and domestic situation is right, the career will take care of itself in due course. With Pluto retrograde, the career is under review now.

A lunar eclipse on the 4th occurs in your 9th house of religion, philosophy and higher education. This eclipse is strong in that many planets, and many areas of life, are affected, so take an easy schedule over this period. Foreign travel is best avoided. College students will make changes to their educational plans. Sometimes they change schools, sometimes they change courses, and sometimes they pursue their academic goals in a different way. Often there are administrative shake-ups at their college. Often policies are changed. There will also be shake-ups in your place of worship, and dramas in the lives of the pastor, minister, priest, rabbi or imam. An eclipse in the 9th house indicates a crisis of faith. Religious and philosophical beliefs get tested and often need revision or fine tuning. This is a six-month process.

With the Moon as your health and work planet, every lunar eclipse brings job changes and instability at the workplace. Sometimes the job changes are within the same company, sometimes with a different one. The conditions of work change. There can be health scares too – but since your health is good this year, these are most likely just scares and nothing more. There are important changes in the health regime though.

Uranus, the ruler of your Horoscope, is affected by this eclipse. So, you will be redefining yourself, your image and personality over the next six months. You will be presenting a new look – a new image to the world.

Pluto, your career planet, will also be affected. There are important career changes happening at this time, although it will be too early just yet to see the eventual impact – this will unfold over the coming months. There are shake-ups and unrest in the corporate hierarchy or in your industry. Important policy changes are happening. Parents, parent figures and bosses should reduce their schedules over the eclipse period.

May

Best Days Overall: 1, 2, 10, 11, 18, 19, 28, 29
Most Stressful Days Overall: 3, 4, 16, 17, 23, 24, 30, 31
Best Days for Love: 1, 2, 8, 9, 12, 13, 17, 18, 21, 22, 23, 24, 28, 29, 30, 31
Best Days for Money: 3, 4, 5, 6, 12, 13, 14, 15, 21, 22, 23, 24, 30, 31
Best Days for Career: 3, 4, 8, 9, 16, 17, 25, 26, 30, 31

Aside from the strong eclipse last month, other important changes happened too. The planetary power began to shift from the independent East to the social West. The planetary power is now moving away from you and towards others. The cycle of personal independence is over with. Now your social skills become important. Your good happens through others and not because of personal merit or personal initiative. For the next five months or so it will be best to adapt to situations, rather than try to change them. Although they can be changed, it will only be through an awful lot of effort. Cultivate 'likeability'. Let others have their way, so long as it isn't destructive.

Health became more delicate last month too – from the 20th onwards – and now needs more attention until the 21st. Your overall health is good, but this is not one of your best periods. Just rest and relax more. From the 7th onwards pay more attention to the neck, throat, kidneys and hips. Neck and hip massage will be good. Work to stay positive and in a good emotional state. Negative moods and emotions have a stronger impact on health than usual. Family harmony is very important in general, but now it becomes a health issue. Visits to the doctor or medical tests are best arranged from the 1st to the 4th and from the 18th onwards. If you are involved in detox or weight-loss regimes, the 4th to the 18th is the best period for these.

On the 21st there is a dramatic resurgence of health and energy.

Love is nostalgic and sentimental this month, until the 21st (and this has been the case since April 21). It's as if you are trying to recapture happy memories and experiences from the past. There is more socializing from home and with the family this month. Love is found close to home. No need to travel far and wide. Love is basically happy this month but there are a few bumps on the road. Between the 22nd and the 24th there is a tendency to have spiritual and financial disagreements with the beloved. On the 30th and 31st there are more spiritual disagreements. But these don't affect your relationship too much.

On the 21st your love attitudes change. You are interested in fun. The person who can show you a good time attracts you. You want the fun aspects of love without the onerous duties that often come with it. And basically this is what happens.

On the 21st you enter another one of your yearly personal pleasure peaks. It's party time in your year.

June

Best Days Overall: 6, 7, 15, 16, 24, 25
Most Stressful Days Overall: 13, 14, 20, 21, 27, 28
Best Days for Love: 1, 6, 7, 10, 11, 15, 16, 20, 21, 27, 29, 30
Best Days for Money: 2, 3, 8, 9, 10, 11, 17, 18, 20, 21, 27, 28, 29, 30
Best Days for Career: 4, 5, 13, 14, 22, 23, 27, 28

This is a happy and prosperous month, Aquarius. Enjoy!

Your health and energy are wonderful now and you are still very much in a yearly personal pleasure peak, until the 21st. Get the partying out of your system now so you can focus on work issues later on.

This month you can enhance your health even further by giving more attention to the heart (from the 21st onwards) and to the head and face (from the 24th onwards). After the 24th, your health is enhanced by exercise regimes – good muscle tone is important.

Love seems happy and unserious until the 21st. Many of you are certainly involved in serious, committed kinds of relationships, but you're having fun these days. It's a kind of honeymoon period. After the 21st your love planet moves into your 6th house of health and work, and this gives all kinds of messages. For those of you still unattached (are there any of you left?) love and romantic opportunities happen at work or with co-workers. The workplace is very social these days. Love and social opportunities also happen as you pursue your health goals and with people involved in your health. Love attitudes become more serious than earlier in the month. Love is not just about fun and games but about practical service to the beloved. You show love by serving the beloved and this is how you feel loved. Emotional intimacy also seems important after the 21st.

Venus enters your 7th house on the 5th. The two beneficent planets of the zodiac, Venus and Jupiter, are now in the 7th house of love – a strong signal for romantic happiness. An old flame can come into the picture this month, either literally or allegorically. You could meet someone who is like the old flame, who has a similar appearance and personality to him or her. Whatever becomes of this there will be emotional healing and the resolution of old issues. Family members like to play Cupid during this period. Perhaps a parent or parent figure is too much involved in your love life – no doubt with good motives.

Your 6th house of health and work becomes powerful from the 21st onwards. This is a wonderful period for job seekers. There are many job opportunities out there. It is also good for those who employ others.

Though your financial planet Neptune goes retrograde on the 12th, the month ahead is very prosperous – especially after the 21st.

July

Best Days Overall: 3, 4, 5, 12, 13, 22, 23, 31
Most Stressful Days Overall: 10, 11, 17, 18, 24, 25
Best Days for Love: 6, 7, 8, 9, 14, 15, 16, 17, 18, 26
Best Days for Money: 6, 7, 9, 14, 15, 18, 24, 25, 27, 28
Best Days for Career: 1, 2, 10, 11, 19, 20, 24, 25, 29, 30

The month ahead is prosperous in spite of Neptune's retrograde. There can be delays and glitches, but prosperity will happen. You can alleviate things, speed things up, by being as perfect as you can be with your financial transactions. Make sure you date everything and keep all receipts. Make sure bills and payments are made out properly and the addresses are correct; double-check your accounts.

Your financial planet will be retrograde for some months, so put your financial life under review. Where can improvements be made?

What kind of savings or investment plan will bring you to your goals? The important thing, as with any retrograde, is to gain mental clarity on your finances. Things are not as they seem on the surface when a retrograde is in effect.

Love is really the main headline this month. On the 23rd the Sun, your love planet, moves into your 7th house of love and you begin a yearly love peak. (Mercury also moves into your house of love on the 23rd.) Your 7th house is chock-full of planets. Many of you are already in serious, committed relationships and this might be the time to take things further and to get engaged or to actually marry. The unattached are likely to meet someone special now. If you are as yet unattached you might not actually marry during this time, but you could meet people who are marriage material – people you would consider marrying.

If you're planning a wedding or engagement, do it before the 25th, as that is when Venus starts to retrograde.

Health and energy become more delicate after the 23rd. The short-term planets are making stressful aspects to you. Those of you born late in the sign of Aquarius – February 17–18 – have to really take it easy. Saturn moved back into Scorpio on the 15th of last month and remains there for the rest of the month ahead and on until mid-September. This is a stressful aspect for you. Enhance the health in the ways mentioned in the yearly report. Don't push yourself too far – if you're tired, rest. If you're involved in detox or weight-loss programmes, the period from the 1st to the 15th is best for these. If you're planning visits to the doctor or medical tests, the 15th to the 31st is best.

This month the planetary power begins to shift to the upper hemisphere of your chart. By now you should have attained a degree of emotional harmony. Family and domestic issues should be in relative order. Now it is time to focus on your career and outer goals. This is the beginning of your yearly career push.

August

Best Days Overall: 1, 8, 9, 18, 19, 27, 28
Most Stressful Days Overall: 6, 7, 13, 14, 20, 21, 22
Best Days for Love: 4, 5, 13, 14, 23, 24, 25, 31
Best Days for Money: 2, 3, 5, 10, 11, 15, 20, 21, 25, 29, 30
Best Days for Career: 6, 7, 15, 16, 20, 21, 22, 25, 26

Health and energy still need watching until the 23rd. This is especially so for those of you born late in the sign of Aquarius – on February 17 or 18. Review our discussion of this last month. The head and face should be given extra attention until the 9th. Scalp and face massage, and craniosacral therapy, will all be good. Physical exercise is also good.

Love is still the main headline this month. Your 7th house of love is very powerful, with 60 per cent of the planets either there or moving through there this month. For the unattached this shows many, many romantic possibilities – perhaps too many. It can be confusing. Still, it is a nice problem to have. However, serious decisions about love shouldn't be taken this month: Venus, the generic love planet, is retrograde all month. Let love develop as it will.

Finances become more stressful this month, especially after the 23rd. Neptune, your financial planet, is still retrograde all month, and after the 23rd he starts to receive stressful aspects. So, earnings will happen, but you'll have to work harder for them, and overcome more obstacles than usual.

The good news is that while your personal earning power is not at its best, the spouse, partner or current love is in a yearly financial peak. He or she takes up the slack. Jupiter's move into your 8th house on the 11th indicates that the beloved is going to have a prosperous year ahead. He or she seems lucky in speculations and in financial risk-taking. The beloved is going to be more generous with you too – a freer spender.

While finances might be temporarily challenging (things will improve in a month or so), your career seems very successful from the 11th onwards. Promotions can happen. Happy career opportunities come. Your professional achievements are appreciated. Friends seem very helpful in the career after Jupiter's move. Online activities are also helpful.

Your 8th house of transformation becomes very strong after the 23rd (and will be strong for the rest of the year). So you are in a more sexually active kind of period. Whatever your age or stage in life, the libido is more than usual. Detox and weight-loss regimes are good. It will be good to get rid of the clutter in your life too – possessions that you no longer need or use. Good to get rid of mental and emotional patterns that don't serve your interest.

September

Best Days Overall: 4, 5, 6, 14, 15, 24, 25
Most Stressful Days Overall: 2, 3, 9, 10, 17, 18, 30
Best Days for Love: 1, 2, 3, 9, 10, 12, 13, 19, 20, 24, 28, 29
Best Days for Money: 2, 7, 12, 17, 26, 27, 30
Best Days for Career: 2, 3, 12, 13, 17, 18, 20, 22, 23, 30

Two eclipses shake up the world this month, but you seem relatively unscathed.

The solar eclipse of the 13th occurs in your 8th house and can bring encounters with death (not literal death) or near-death kinds of experiences. Sometimes it signals surgery or the recommendation of surgery. People often have dreams of death. These are friendly reminders from the cosmos to get more serious about life and to do what you came here to do (if you don't know what this might be, it's worth taking the time to find out). Life on this planet is short and can end at any time. It is also the cosmos's way to help you come to terms with death. Fear of death is probably the main blockage to the attainment of one's dreams.

Your love life has been super the past two months (and all year as well), so it is good that the marriage or relationship gets a little testing now with the eclipse. Partnerships also get tested. If there are flaws in your relationship – perhaps things that were swept under the rug – you find out about them at this time and are in a position to deal with them. Good marriages and good relationships will easily survive, and get even better once the 'dirty laundry' is dealt with. But flawed relationships can end. The spouse, partner or current love should reduce their schedule over this period. He or she makes important financial changes, and these will be good. Usually these changes come about due to some financial crisis. Have no fear; the year ahead is very prosperous for them. (They have probably been unduly pessimistic in their financial planning and strategy.)

The lunar eclipse of the 28th (in the Americas it is on the 27th) occurs in your 3rd house of communication and is also relatively benign (although no eclipse is completely benign, it is all a matter of degree). Cars and communication equipment get tested and often need repair or replacement. Be sure to drive more carefully during that period. Siblings, sibling figures and neighbours have dramatic, life-changing experiences and there could be shake-ups in your neighbourhood as well. (I have seen major construction projects begin during eclipse periods which create traffic headaches for months. Or sometimes a grisly crime occurs in the neighbourhood, alarming everyone.) Siblings and sibling figures should take it nice and easy at this time.

Every lunar eclipse brings job changes and instability at the workplace. The job changes can be within the present company (a new assignment) or with another one. Those who employ others experience employee turnover. Sometimes a health scare happens (the Moon, of course, is your health planet). Over the next six months there will be important changes to the health regime. Aunts and uncles should reduce their schedule too.

October

Best Days Overall: 2, 3, 11, 12, 13, 21, 22, 29, 30
Most Stressful Days Overall: 1, 6, 7, 8, 14, 15, 27, 28
Best Days for Love: 2, 3, 7, 8, 9, 13, 19, 20, 22, 23, 27, 28, 29
Best Days for Money: 1, 4, 5, 9, 10, 14, 15, 19, 20, 23, 24, 27, 28, 31
Best Days for Career: 1, 9, 10, 14, 15, 19, 20, 27, 28

Saturn is now back in the sign of Sagittarius, away from its stressful aspect to you, and with the short-term planets making nice aspects to you (especially until the 23rd), health and energy are basically good this month. They are less good after the 23rd, but nothing serious. Detox and weight-loss regimes go better from the 1st to the 13th and from the 27th onwards. Doctor's visits or medical tests go better from the 13th to the 27th.

Your career planet, Pluto, went forward on September 25, and on the 23rd you enter a yearly career peak. The timing is beautiful. There is mental clarity in the career. You move forward with confidence.

Pluto is also receiving very nice aspects. So this is a successful month ahead. Pay rises and promotions could happen. You have good career support from the family and the spouse, partner or current love. The beloved also seems successful this month and is helping out. Your social skills and your ability to get on with others is important career-wise – perhaps just as important as your professional skills. This month the career is furthered by social means – by attending or hosting the right kind of parties or gatherings. Indeed, much of your socializing after the 23rd seems career-related.

Love is volatile and unstable until the 23rd, and especially so from the 5th to the 7th and on the 11th and 12th. Be more patient with the beloved then. He or she could be having some dramas of his or her own. (The beloved should stay out of harm's way on those particular days.) But things improve after the 12th. Until the 23rd singles find love opportunities in foreign lands or with foreigners. You find foreigners, the more exotic the better, alluring during this period. There are romantic opportunities in religious and educational settings as well. People in your place of worship are playing Cupid. You gravitate to highly educated and refined people – to mentor types.

After the 23rd, as your love planet enters Scorpio, sexual magnetism seems the most important attraction for you. But also you gravitate to people of power and prestige, to people who can help you careerwise. There are romantic opportunities with bosses and with people involved in your career.

You have favourable aspects to receive a new car or communication equipment between the 15th and the 19th. A sibling or sibling figure has a nice payday, and a parent or parent figure has a nice payday between the 24th and the 27th. Nice things come to you for the house.

November

Best Days Overall: 8, 9, 17, 18, 26, 27
Most Stressful Days Overall: 3, 4, 10, 11, 24, 25, 30
Best Days for Love: 1, 3, 4, 6, 7, 10, 11, 17, 18, 21, 22, 26, 27, 30
Best Days for Money: 5, 6, 10, 15, 16, 19, 20, 24, 25, 28
Best Days for Career: 5, 6, 10, 11, 15, 16, 24, 25

Finances have been stressed over the past few months but you should see some improvement this month. Neptune, your financial planet, is starting to move forward on the 18th, bringing mental clarity, confidence and sound financial judgement. Many of the stressful aspects to Neptune are removed now. You are still in a yearly career peak until the 22nd, so success is still happening here. Pluto, your career planet, receives stressful aspects this month from the 12th onwards. This doesn't stop your success but it does force you to work harder and overcome more obstacles.

Health needs more attention this month, especially until the 22nd. This is nothing serious. Overall your health is good, it's just not one of your best health periods. Make sure you get enough rest. Health and energy will improve after the 22nd. This is not a good period for scheduling doctor's appointments or medical tests. When your energy is low these tests can seem worse than they really are. If you have to do these things wait until after the 22nd.

Love is excellent all month and especially from the 22nd onwards. Until the 22nd many of the trends we wrote of last month are still in effect. You mix with the high and mighty. You are attracted to people of power and position. Perhaps you are too practical about love – you see it as just another career choice. The sexual magnetism is unusually important. You have romantic (and sexual) opportunities with bosses and people involved in your career. However, after the 22nd the love needs and desires change. Power and prestige are not that important now. Instead you want a relationship with your peer. You want friendship with the beloved. There are romantic opportunities online and as you are involved with groups and group activities. Friends play Cupid now. There is a romantic opportunity with someone older, a spiritual-type person, on the 29th or 30th.

A parent or parent figure should stay out of harm's way from the 19th to the 24th. Let him or her take it easy over that period and avoid stressful activities. Foreign travel is not advisable then. Be more patient with this person now. You don't seem in synch.

The planetary power begins to shift this month to the independent Easter sector, from the West. From now until the end of the year (and beyond) the planetary power moves towards you, rather than away from you. Thus personal power and independence is increasing. It is easier for you to have your way in life. You are not as dependent on others as you have been for the past six months or so.

December

Best Days Overall: 5, 6, 14, 15, 16, 23, 24
Most Stressful Days Overall: 1, 7, 8, 9, 21, 22, 27, 28, 29
Best Days for Love: 1, 7, 10, 11, 17, 18, 20, 25, 26, 27, 28, 29, 30, 31
Best Days for Money: 2, 3, 4, 7, 8, 12, 13, 17, 18, 21, 22, 25, 26, 30, 31
Best Days for Career: 2, 3, 7, 8, 9, 12, 13, 21, 22, 30, 31

Venus, your family planet, crosses the Mid-heaven and enters your 10th career house on the 5th. You have excellent family support for your career goals. You might even be doing more work from home. The family as a whole seems more elevated now. A parent or parent figure is successful this month and helping your career. He or she seems financially supportive from the 10th to the 12th. A foreign, business-related trip is likely.

Last month, as we mentioned, the planetary power began to shift to the East. This shift gets stronger after the 5th and next month will become even stronger. So it is time to be more self-reliant and to focus on your personal interests. Your interest is as important as anyone else's. It is time to take personal responsibility for your own happiness. Day by day your personal power and independence grows. If conditions irk you, change them to your liking. There is less need to adapt to situations. Your way is the best way (at least for you) these days.

Health and energy are good this month. There is only one short-term planet in stressful aspect to you. You have all the energy you need to achieve whatever you set your mind to. If you're scheduling doctor's appointments or medical tests, this is a good month for them (from the 11th to the 25th is best). If you're involved in detox or weight-loss regimes, the 1st to the 11th and from the 25th onwards are the best days.

Until the 22nd you are in Aquarian heaven. Your 11th house of friends is powerful, and the cosmos impels you to do the things you most love to do and what you're best at. Friends, groups and group activities are always enjoyable, but this month (until the 22nd) they are also the source of romance and romantic opportunity. This is a great period to increase your knowledge of computers and technology, and to upgrade your equipment if necessary. It is also wonderful for increasing your knowledge of astrology, astronomy, mathematics and science.

After the 22nd you enter a more spiritual kind of period. If you find yourself craving more solitude this period, there's nothing wrong with you. This is just natural when your spiritual 12th house is strong. This is a great period to involve yourself in charities or good causes, to go on spiritual retreats, attend meditation seminars or lectures and to grow spiritually. These kinds of settings become the venue for romance after the 22nd.

Be more careful driving from the 5th to the 12th. Siblings or sibling figures should stay out of harm's way that period. They need to watch the temper and avoid confrontations.

Pisces

THE FISH

Birthdays from
19th February to
20th March

Personality Profile

PISCES AT A GLANCE

Element – Water

Ruling Planet – Neptune
   Career Planet – Jupiter
   Love Planet – Mercury
   Money Planet – Mars
   Planet of Health and Work – Sun
   Planet of Home and Family Life – Mercury
   Planet of Love Affairs, Creativity and Children – Moon

Colours – aqua, blue-green

Colours that promote love, romance and social harmony – earth tones, yellow, yellow-orange

Colours that promote earning power – red, scarlet

Gem – white diamond

Metal – tin

Scent – lotus

Quality – mutable (= flexibility)

Qualities most needed for balance – structure and the ability to handle form

Strongest virtues – psychic power, sensitivity, self-sacrifice, altruism

Deepest needs – spiritual illumination, liberation

Characteristics to avoid – escapism, keeping bad company, negative moods

Signs of greatest overall compatibility – Cancer, Scorpio

Signs of greatest overall incompatibility – Gemini, Virgo, Sagittarius

Sign most helpful to career – Sagittarius

Sign most helpful for emotional support – Gemini

Sign most helpful financially – Aries

Sign best for marriage and/or partnerships – Virgo

Sign most helpful for creative projects – Cancer

Best Sign to have fun with – Cancer

Signs most helpful in spiritual matters – Scorpio, Aquarius

Best day of the week – Thursday

Understanding a Pisces

If Pisces have one outstanding quality it is their belief in the invisible, spiritual and psychic side of things. This side of things is as real to them as the hard earth beneath their feet – so real, in fact, that they will often ignore the visible, tangible aspects of reality in order to focus on the invisible and so-called intangible ones.

Of all the signs of the zodiac, the intuitive and emotional faculties of the Pisces are the most highly developed. They are committed to living by their intuition and this can at times be infuriating to other people – especially those who are materially, scientifically or technically orientated. If you think that money, status and worldly success are the only goals in life, then you will never understand a Pisces.

Pisces have intellect, but to them intellect is only a means by which they can rationalize what they know intuitively. To an Aquarius or a Gemini the intellect is a tool with which to gain knowledge. To a well-developed Pisces it is a tool by which to express knowledge.

Pisces feel like fish in an infinite ocean of thought and feeling. This ocean has many depths, currents and undercurrents. They long for purer waters where the denizens are good, true and beautiful, but they are sometimes pulled to the lower, murkier depths. Pisces know that they do not generate thoughts but only tune in to thoughts that already exist; this is why they seek the purer waters. This ability to tune in to higher thoughts inspires them artistically and musically.

Since Pisces is so spiritually orientated – though many Pisces in the corporate world may hide this fact – we will deal with this aspect in greater detail, for otherwise it is difficult to understand the true Pisces personality.

There are four basic attitudes of the spirit. One is outright scepticism – the attitude of secular humanists. The second is an intellectual or emotional belief, where one worships a far-distant God-figure – the attitude of most modern church-going people. The third is not only belief but direct personal spiritual experience – this is the attitude of some 'born-again' religious people. The fourth is actual unity with the divinity, an intermingling with the spiritual world – this is the attitude of yoga. This fourth attitude is the deepest urge of a

Pisces, and a Pisces is uniquely qualified to pursue and perform this work.

Consciously or unconsciously, Pisces seek this union with the spiritual world. The belief in a greater reality makes Pisces very tolerant and understanding of others – perhaps even too tolerant. There are instances in their lives when they should say 'enough is enough' and be ready to defend their position and put up a fight. However, because of their qualities it takes a good deal to get them into that frame of mind.

Pisces basically want and aspire to be 'saints'. They do so in their own way and according to their own rules. Others should not try to impose their concept of saintliness on a Pisces, because he or she always tries to find it for him- or herself.

Finance

Money is generally not that important to Pisces. Of course they need it as much as anyone else, and many of them attain great wealth. But money is not generally a primary objective. Doing good, feeling good about oneself, peace of mind, the relief of pain and suffering – these are the things that matter most to a Pisces.

Pisces earn money intuitively and instinctively. They follow their hunches rather than their logic. They tend to be generous and perhaps overly charitable. Almost any kind of misfortune is enough to move a Pisces to give. Although this is one of their greatest virtues, Pisces should be more careful with their finances. They should try to be more choosy about the people to whom they lend money, so that they are not being taken advantage of. If they give money to charities they should follow it up to see that their contributions are put to good use. Even when Pisces are not rich, they still like to spend money on helping others. In this case they should really be careful, however: they must learn to say no sometimes and help themselves first.

Perhaps the biggest financial stumbling block for the Pisces is general passivity – a *laissez faire* attitude. In general Pisces like to go with the flow of events. When it comes to financial matters, especially, they need to be more aggressive. They need to make things happen, to create their own wealth. A passive attitude will only cause loss and missed opportunity. Worrying about financial security will not provide that security. Pisces need to go after what they want tenaciously.

Career and Public Image

Pisces like to be perceived by the public as people of spiritual or material wealth, of generosity and philanthropy. They look up to big-hearted, philanthropic types. They admire people engaged in large-scale undertakings and eventually would like to head up these big enterprises themselves. In short, they like to be connected with big organizations that are doing things in a big way.

If Pisces are to realize their full career and professional potential they need to travel more, educate themselves more and learn more about the actual world. In other words, they need some of the unflagging optimism of Sagittarius in order to reach the top.

Because of all their caring and generous characteristics, Pisces often choose professions through which they can help and touch the lives of other people. That is why many Pisces become doctors, nurses, social workers or teachers. Sometimes it takes a while before Pisces realize what they really want to do in their professional lives, but once they find a career that lets them manifest their interests and virtues they will excel at it.

Love and Relationships

It is not surprising that someone as 'otherworldly' as the Pisces would like a partner who is practical and down to earth. Pisces prefer a partner who is on top of all the details of life, because they dislike details. Pisces seek this quality in both their romantic and professional partners. More than anything else this gives Pisces a feeling of being grounded, of being in touch with reality.

As expected, these kinds of relationships – though necessary – are sure to have many ups and downs. Misunderstandings will take place because the two attitudes are poles apart. If you are in love with a Pisces you will experience these fluctuations and will need a lot of patience to see things stabilize. Pisces are moody, intuitive, affectionate and difficult to get to know. Only time and the right attitude will yield Pisces' deepest secrets. However, when in love with a Pisces you will find that riding the waves is worth it because they are good, sensitive people who need and like to give love and affection.

When in love, Pisces like to fantasize. For them fantasy is 90 per cent of the fun of a relationship. They tend to idealize their partner, which can be good and bad at the same time. It is bad in that it is difficult for anyone to live up to the high ideals their Pisces lover sets.

Home and Domestic Life

In their family and domestic life Pisces have to resist the tendency to relate only by feelings and moods. It is unrealistic to expect that your partner and other family members will be as intuitive as you are. There is a need for more verbal communication between a Pisces and his or her family. A cool, unemotional exchange of ideas and opinions will benefit everyone.

Some Pisces tend to like mobility and moving around. For them too much stability feels like a restriction on their freedom. They hate to be locked in one location for ever.

The sign of Gemini sits on the cusp of Pisces' 4th solar house of home and family. This shows that Pisces likes and needs a home environment that promotes intellectual and mental interests. They tend to treat their neighbours as family – or extended family. Some Pisceans can have a dual attitude towards the home and family – on the one hand they like the emotional support of the family, but on the other they dislike the obligations, restrictions and duties involved with it. For Pisces, finding a balance is the key to a happy family life.

Horoscope for 2015

Major Trends

There are a lot of exciting things happening in the coming year – at work, in love and in finance. It looks like an active kind of year and you will need to watch your energy more.

The main headline this year is Saturn's move into Sagittarius, which began in December 2014. It is a stressful aspect that you will face for the next two years. It shows that you are working very hard on your career. You are earning your success through sheer merit and not because of political pull or favouritism. This extra work forces you to watch your energy. Health will be OK, but more delicate than last year. More details on this later.

Jupiter moved into your 6th house of health and work in July of last year and he will be there until August 11. This is wonderful news for job seekers. Dream jobs could have already manifested, and if not, can still manifest themselves in the year ahead. Those suffering from health problems should hear good news this year.

On August 11 Jupiter will move into your 7th house of love. So this is going to be a banner romantic year and it will last well into next year. More details later.

Pluto has been in your 11th house of friends for some years now and will be there for several more years. Friends have been undergoing surgery and perhaps near-death kinds of experiences. Many a friendship is being tested these days.

Neptune, the ruler of your Horoscope, has been in your own sign since 2012. Spirituality is always important to you and these days more than ever. Your challenge will be to keep your feet on the ground now – especially when you are involved in your daily outer affairs.

Uranus has been in your 2nd money house for some years now, and remains there for some time. This indicates major and dramatic financial changes happening. Financial highs are higher than usual, but the lows can be ultra low. Dealing with financial instability is a major lesson for you these days.

Your most important areas of interest this year are the body, image and personal pleasure; finance; health and work (until August 11); love and romance (from August 11 onwards); religion, philosophy, foreign travel and higher education (from June 15 to September 18); career (from January 1 to June 15 and from September 18 onwards); and friends, groups and group activities.

Your paths of greatest fulfilment this year are health and work (until August 11); love and romance (from August 11 onwards); and sex, personal reinvention, occult studies, debt and the repayment of debt (until November 13).

Health

(Please note that this is an astrological perspective on health and not a medical one. In days of yore there was no difference, these perspectives were identical. But now there could be quite a difference. For a medical perspective, please consult your doctor or health practitioner.)

Saturn's move into Sagittarius is a stressful aspect for you as we mentioned, and health is more delicate than last year. The good news is that your 6th house is very strong for most of the year, and so you're paying attention here. The danger would be in ignoring things.

Jupiter will also move into stressful aspect to you after August 11, so there will be two long-term planets in stressful aspect. By itself this is not enough to cause health problems, but when the short-term planets join in, you become more vulnerable. This year these periods will be from May 21 to June 20, August 23 to September 22, and November 22 to December 21. Of these three periods the last one seems the most

Important foot reflexology points for the year ahead

Try to massage the whole foot on a regular basis, but pay extra attention to the points highlighted on the chart. When you massage, be aware of 'sore spots', as these need special attention. It is also a good idea to massage the ankles and the tops of the feet.

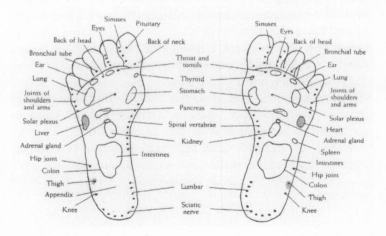

important. Be sure to rest and relax more. Get enough sleep. Try to spend time at a health spa, or schedule massages, reflexology or acupuncture treatments. Do your best to maintain high energy levels. High energy, as our regular readers know, is the first (and perhaps most important) line of defence against health problems.

Your health can be enhanced by giving more attention to these vulnerable areas of your chart: the feet; the heart; and the liver and thighs. This will either prevent or lessen potential problems.

The feet are always important for you, and you respond well to foot reflexology – see our chart above – foot baths and foot whirlpools. As always make sure your shoes are comfortable and fit correctly. Better to sacrifice fashion for comfort, but if you can have both that's all to the good. Regular visits to a podiatrist might also be a good idea.

The heart is also always another important area for you. Your health planet is the Sun which rules the heart and the reflex point is shown in the diagram above. It's very beneficial to have acupuncture or acupressure treatments along the heart meridian. As always, avoid worry and anxiety – the root causes (according to many spiritual healers) of heart problems.

The liver and thighs have only become important since July 2012. Regular thigh massage is beneficial and liver detoxing is a good idea this year (especially until August 11). Acupuncture or acupressure treatments of the liver meridian will also be good this year.

Your career planet, Jupiter, spends most of the year in your 6th house of health. Thus problems in the career – loss of reputation or a perceived loss of professional standing – can impact on your health if you allow it. You shouldn't. Without good health there will be no career to speak of, so de-couple these things in your mind. Health is health and career is career.

The Sun, as we mentioned, is your health planet. He is a fast-moving planet and in the course of a year he will move through all the signs and houses of your Horoscope. So there are many short-term health trends that depend on where the Sun is and the aspects he receives. These are best dealt with in the monthly reports.

Home and Family

Your 4th house of home and family is not a house of power this year. As our regular readers know, this tends towards the status quo. It is true that you will have more freedom and latitude in domestic matters this year – if you choose to move or renovate or make changes, there is nothing holding you back. You are free. But generally, without a cosmic push we seldom make major changes. I read this as a good signal. You are basically content with the way things are and have no pressing need to make dramatic changes.

There is another issue here too. Many of you have moved, renovated or acquired additional homes in the past two years. So you seem pretty much settled in now.

If you plan to renovate – to do major repairs or construction around the home – June 12 to July 24 is a good time. If you plan to redecorate or beautify the home, or to buy art objects for the home, April 11 to May 8 is a good time.

A parent or parent figure seems bossy and demanding this year. On the one hand he or she is serving your interest and seems very helpful, but on the other there is an element of control here too. This parent figure seems to be prospering this year, especially until August 11. He or she is not likely to move in the year ahead (any move could have been made in the past two years). But another parent figure is likely to move after August 11. (Move, renovate or acquire an additional home.)

Siblings or sibling figures could move this year (and this could have happened last year too). If they are of childbearing age they are very fertile these days. Their personal family circle expands in the year ahead. Children and children figures are prospering this year, but a move doesn't seem on the cards. Grandchildren of appropriate age (if you have them) are struggling financially this year. They are getting help from their parents though. They could move in the year ahead. If they are of childbearing age they are more fertile than usual.

Your family planet, Mercury, is the fastest moving of all the planets except for the Moon. Thus in a given year there will be many short-term family trends, depending on where Mercury is and the aspects he receives. These are best dealt with in the monthly reports.

Finance and Career

Uranus, as we have mentioned, has been in your money house for some years now. You are in a very exciting and frenetic financial cycle. You tend to be a risk-taker in finance by nature, but these days even more so. You are throwing out all the rule books, all the conventional wisdom, and learning through trial and error what works for you.

This is good. This is how new knowledge is gained. However it does introduce some instability into the finances. Since you are breaking new ground, you are never sure of the outcome of your experiments. When your experiments work out, earnings will soar – beyond your imagination. When they don't work out, earnings can be ultra low.

But don't be dismayed about this. It is natural. For every new and exciting product that is developed in the laboratory there can be an explosion or two. This goes with the territory.

In general you should work to smooth out your earnings. Put aside money from the good times (and there will be very good times) to cover the low periods (and these will also certainly happen). Just because earnings soar for a while doesn't mean that they will continue to do so.

Uranus rules the technological world, astronomy and astrology. All these things are important financially to you. They are good as investments and businesses. Also the good use of technology is important. Whatever your business, it is important to stay up to date with the latest technology. Online businesses or activities are important this year.

Most of you won't become practising astrologers in the year ahead, but astrology can give you financial insights. If you are having financial problems, it could be a good idea to consult with your personal astrologer.

Uranus is your spiritual planet. And, this gives us many messages. Intuition is important in financial matters. And your financial intuition is excellent – especially until August 11. Financial guidance can come to you while you are meditating, in dreams, or through psychics, ministers or spiritual channels.

The spiritual planet in the money house shows that you are going deeper into the spiritual dimensions of wealth. This has been going on for many years now and the trend continues in the year ahead. You already have much understanding of this, but one can always go deeper. Read all you can on the subject and, more importantly, put what you read into practice.

Job seekers have beautiful opportunities this year. A dream job could have already been landed by you, but if not, it is still likely in the year ahead.

Career seems stressful this year. Saturn will spend the year on or very near your Mid-heaven. This doesn't mean failure – on the contrary it often brings success – but it comes the hard way, through work and merit. Sometimes this aspect shows a demanding boss or restrictive rules in your business or industry. The best way to deal with this is to give the boss more than is asked for. Exceed their expectations. Don't shirk the work or responsibility.

Your career planet Jupiter is in Leo until August 11. Thus, perhaps, you want to have fun in your career. But this doesn't seem likely. Learn to enjoy the work itself. Make your work fun.

After August 11 your career planet moves into your 7th house of love and social activities. This signals that you can advance the career through social means – by attending or perhaps hosting the right kinds of parties or gatherings. You will be mixing socially with people who can open career doors for you. All very useful, but keep in mind that although social connections can open doors, ultimately (and especially over the next two years) you have to do the work.

Love and Social Life

On the love front the year starts slowly; nothing special one way or another – a static kind of period. But, as we mentioned, on August 11 Jupiter enters your 7th house and things start to heat up. You enter one of the most socially active periods in your life. The last time Jupiter was in your 7th house was twelve years ago, so it's been a while since you've had this kind of aspect.

As our regular readers know, Jupiter in the 7th house is a classic love indicator. In many cases it shows literal marriage, but not always. Sometimes you enter a relationship that is 'like' a marriage: something committed and serious. In general, there will be more parties, weddings and social invitations happening.

What I like here is that you are meeting influential kinds of people, people above you in social and professional status. This seems a romantic turn-on in the year ahead. Love is more practical now. You want the good provider, the person who can help you careerwise, the person of power, and there is nothing wrong with that. However, one needs to be careful not to get involved in marriages or relationships of convenience. Love should be the most important consideration.

Aside from love, the year ahead seems more sexually active than usual. Perhaps too much so. Excess, not lack, is the problem here.

If you are single, working towards your first, second or third marriage, marriage or a serious relationship is on the cards. If you are already married the marriage should be more romantic than usual.

Romantic opportunities happen at work or as you pursue your health goals, with co-workers or people involved with your health. You have the aspects for an office romance this year. As we mentioned, love is more practical this year. Love is shown through serving the interests of the beloved – doing for the beloved. This is how you show love; this is how you feel loved.

Romance can also happen in religious or educational settings (especially after August 11) – at your place of worship, or college or graduate school. Elders, parents or parent figures and bosses are playing Cupid in the year ahead.

Your love planet is Mercury. Only the Moon moves faster than him. Thus there are many short-term love trends in the year ahead, depending on where Mercury is and the aspects he receives. These are best dealt with in the monthly reports.

Self-improvement

Spirituality is always important to you, but these days there are certain aspects of it that are most important.

Neptune, the ruler of your Horoscope, has been in your own house since 2012. This reveals the refinement and spiritualization of the body. The body is becoming ever more sensitive to spiritual vibrations. Thus, as we have mentioned in previous years, one will feel vibrations as if they were physical things. If you are around someone with heart problems, for example, you are likely to feel that your own heart is hurting or not in rhythm. It will feel real, but is not what you think it is. The reverse is also true. If you are around uplifting kinds of people, you will feel these vibrations physically as well. You might feel giddy – high – even though you are completely sober. With training, you will be able to hold an object and sense all kinds of things about its owner. Don't take physical sensations too seriously. Be aware of them, but don't identify with them. This will save a lot of heartache.

It is said that the reason behind old age and physical deterioration is the slowing down of the physical energy vibrations. If the vibrations are raised, the body will become more youthful. Many of you will experience this kind of thing now.

The enhanced sensitivity of the body means that you should be very moderate in your use of alcohol and drugs. The body can overreact to these things.

In the spiritual perspective, the body is not seen as a cause for anything. The body is the side effect – the visible manifestation – of unseen causes. Thus if one knows how to change the dimension of causes – through meditation, affirmation and right attitude – the body can be moulded and shaped according to one's will. You have unusual ability to do this now.

The other area of spiritual growth which has been going on for some years now is that of finance. Undoubtedly much progress has been made here. You are seeing that just as your body is a side effect of spiritual causes – the same is true for finance. Financial problems always have their origins on other, more subtle levels. If we want to clear a negative financial condition we must clear the spiritual root cause of the problem. Otherwise the financial problem will recur again and again and again. Sure there are rational solutions that can alleviate some financial distress, such as better money management, living within one's means, and creating savings and investment plans. But these will not be enough if the spiritual root causes are not dealt with. Generally these causes are misunderstandings about the nature of wealth and where it comes from. These misunderstandings can be very subtle and are often instilled in childhood. Spiritually speaking this is where the thrust of your financial work needs to be.

Month-by-month Forecasts

January

Best Days Overall: 4, 5, 14, 15, 22, 23, 31
Most Stressful Days Overall: 2, 3, 9, 10, 16, 17, 29, 30
Best Days for Love: 1, 9, 10, 12, 13, 20, 21, 22, 29, 30, 31
Best Days for Money: 2, 3, 7, 8, 14, 16, 17, 22, 23, 24, 25, 31
Best Days for Career: 7, 8, 16, 17, 24, 25

You begin your year with 80 per cent (and sometimes 90 per cent) of the planets in the independent Eastern sector of your Horoscope. You have great personal power and independence now and you need to put it to good use. Make those changes in your life that need to be made. There is no need to consult with others or seek their approval (if this involves your personal situation). The cosmos supports you and others will go along with you. You have strong leadership skills now. Your way is the best way as far as your life is concerned. Independent action is always 'karma-creating', but if you build well the karma should be good. Personal initiative matters now, not your social connections.

The planetary power is still mostly above the horizon. So it is good to focus on your outer goals and career. This will soon change, but this is the trend for this month. Career is hectic and there are many challenges to overcome. You just have to work harder. Your career planet Jupiter is retrograde this month, thus it is a good time to review your career and its direction. Career opportunities need more study.

Saturn is stressing you out this month, but most of the other planets are in harmonious aspect or leaving you alone. Health should be good. You can enhance it further by giving more attention to the spine, knees, teeth, bones, skin and overall skeletal alignment until January 5. Regular back and knee massage and regular visits to a chiropractor or osteopath will be beneficial. After the 5th give more attention to the ankles and calves. Massage them regularly and give the ankles more support.

The month ahead is prosperous. On the 12th your financial planet, Mars, crosses the Ascendant and enters your 1st house, heralding a wonderful financial period. Windfalls happen and there's not much you need to do. Money comes to you – financial opportunity as well. You look rich (more than usual) and feel rich. People see you that way. More windfalls and financial opportunities come from the 16th to the 20th, as Mars travels with Neptune. Your financial intuition is excellent that period. The spiritual dimensions of wealth are always important to you but especially this month: Mars is in your spiritual 12th house until the 12th and then in your own sign after that date. It is a period for 'miracle' money rather than natural money.

The spiritual dimensions of love are also important this month. Mercury, your love planet, is in your 12th house from the 5th onwards, turning retrograde on the 21st. So put the love life under review and don't make any major love decisions. Things are not as they seem. Study things further.

Your 12th house is your most powerful house this month – especially after the 20th. Half of the planets are either there or moving through there. This shows more contact with the invisible realms. For you the challenge will be to keep both feet on the ground. It's OK to have your head in the clouds, but keep your feet firmly planted on the earth.

February

Best Days Overall: 1, 10, 11, 19, 20, 27, 28
Most Stressful Days Overall: 5, 6, 7, 13, 14, 25, 26
Best Days for Love: 1, 2, 5, 6, 7, 8, 9, 10, 11, 17, 18, 20, 21, 25, 26
Best Days for Money: 1, 2, 3, 4, 10, 11, 13, 14, 20, 21, 22
Best Days for Career: 3, 4, 13, 14, 21, 22

The planetary power begins to shift this month. On the 18th the upper half of the Horoscope becomes weak and the bottom half becomes dominant. You have just finished a yearly career push. Career is still important and will be important for years to come, but now you take a bit of a breather. Now you need to focus on the inner conditions, the psychological infrastructure that makes success possible. The home, family and emotional life need to be put in right order. It is time to fill up the emotional gas tank that will make future career success possible. Symbolically speaking, night has fallen in your year. The affairs of the day are finished. The activities of night begin.

On the 18th, as the Sun crosses the Ascendant and enters your 1st house, you begin one of your yearly personal pleasure peaks. This is the time to indulge the body and enjoy the sensual delights. Since the Sun rules your 6th house of health and work, this will be a great period for health regimes. Overall health is excellent this month, in spite of Saturn's stressful aspect. You have plenty of energy to achieve what you want.

Job seekers have excellent aspects all year, but especially after the 18th. Job opportunities are seeking you out. There's no need to pound the pavements or do online searches. These opportunities will find you.

Your personal power and independence are now at their maximum extent for the year this month (and will be next month too), so make those changes that need to be made. Have life on your terms. If there are mistakes here you will learn about them in the coming months and experience the consequences. But if your terms are not destructive the consequences will be pleasant. The cosmos supports your personal happiness now. Your personal interests are important and a little self-ishness is called for.

The love life is improved over last month. The love planet Mercury moves forward on the 11th, bringing social confidence. You look exceptionally good. The presence of the Sun and Mars in your 1st house brings charisma and sex appeal. Neptune in your 1st house brings glamour and other worldly beauty. So you are attractive to the opposite sex now. The love planet spends the month in your spiritual 12th house and this is the venue for romance. Spiritual lectures, spiritual retreats and charity events bring romantic opportunities. You are especially idealistic about love now. Your standards are very high. You don't care about money or position – only the feeling of love matters to you.

This is a happy and prosperous month, Pisces. Enjoy!

March

Best Days Overall: 1, 9, 10, 18, 19, 27, 28
Most Stressful Days Overall: 4, 5, 6, 12, 13, 24, 25, 26
Best Days for Love: 2, 3, 4, 5, 6, 7, 8, 12, 13, 18, 19, 22, 23, 29, 30, 31
Best Days for Money: 2, 3, 12, 13, 20, 21, 30, 31
Best Days for Career: 2, 3, 12, 13, 20, 21

A solar eclipse on the 20th occurs in your own sign. All of you will feel it to some degree, but those of you born late in the sign of Pisces (from March 18 to 20) will feel it very strongly. It is always a good idea to reduce your schedule during a solar eclipse, but especially if you fall in this latter group.

This eclipse occurs on the border of your 1st and 2nd houses and will impact on the affairs of both. Thus over the next six months you will be redefining your personality, image and overall demeanour. You will be presenting a new look to the world. There are also dramatic financial changes happening over this period. By now, after a few years of Uranus in your money house, you are used to dramatic financial changes, but more are on the way. Your financial thinking and strategy need to become more realistic. The eclipse will reveal where the flaws are and you will be able to make the adjustments.

Every solar eclipse brings job changes – the Sun is the ruler of your 6th house. These job changes should be good ones, but they will be disruptive. (Good things can be just as disruptive as bad things.) The job changes can be within your present company (a new assignment) or with another company. Sometimes there are health scares, but your health is good these days and most probably they will be nothing more than scares. However, the overall health regime will change (dramatically) over the next six months.

Those who employ others will experience instability in the workplace and employee turnover in the coming months. But this too seems good. There seems no problem in attracting high quality employees these days.

Many of you will experience financial changes and disruptions before the eclipse begins. Your financial planet Mars will make dynamic aspects with Uranus and Pluto from the 9th to the 12th. These are all short-term problems though; overall prosperity is good.

Health (as we mentioned) is good, in spite of the eclipse. You can enhance it further by giving more attention to the feet until the 20th, and to the head and face afterwards. Foot massage is more powerful than usual until the 20th. Head and face massage is beneficial from the 20th onwards. If you feel under the weather before the 20th, a spiritual healer might be helpful. After the 20th more physical exercise and better muscle tone will help.

On the 20th you enter a yearly financial peak. The eclipse might cause some extra expenses, but you will have the money to cover them.

Mercury's move into your sign on the 13th is wonderful for love. The current spouse, partner or love interest is very devoted. Singles will find that love pursues them – it is right where you are.

April

Best Days Overall: 6, 7, 15, 16, 23, 24
Most Stressful Days Overall: 1, 2, 8, 9, 21, 22, 28, 29
Best Days for Love: 1, 2, 8, 9, 13, 19, 20, 21, 22, 28, 29
Best Days for Money: 1, 2, 8, 9, 10, 11, 12, 17, 18, 19, 20, 25, 26, 28, 29
Best Days for Career: 8, 9, 17, 18, 25, 26

Your yearly financial peak continues this month until the 20th. The financial life is exciting, with many highs, lows and everything in between. Money can come to you in surprising ways and when you least expect it. Job opportunities can happen in surprising ways too. There can be sudden expenses from the 4th to the 7th, but the money comes to cover them. Good sales, marketing and PR – good use of the media – is important in your finances this month. Family support is good. Family connections also play a big role.

We have a powerful lunar eclipse on the 4th. It is powerful in the sense that many planets – and thus many areas of life – are affected. Take it nice and easy during that period. The eclipse occurs in your 8th house of transformation and regeneration. Thus there can be near-death experiences or encounters with death. The cosmos forces you to look deeper here. The spouse, partner or current love is forced to make important financial changes – usually due to some crisis. If you are involved in estate, tax or insurance issues, these things move forward now.

Every lunar eclipse affects children and children figures in your life and they should be kept out of harm's way during this period. There is no need for them to indulge in stressful or daredevil-type activities. This eclipse indicates that they are redefining themselves, redefining the personality and self-concept. Generally this results in wardrobe changes and changes in hair style and overall demeanour. There can also be dramatic, life-changing experiences in their lives. The same can be said for grandchildren (if you have them).

Since Pluto is affected here, there are shake-ups in your place of worship and dramas in the lives of worship leaders. College students make important changes to their educational plans. Sometimes they change colleges, sometimes they change courses. Often there are shake-ups in the establishments – changes in the hierarchy and changes of policy. Often there is a 'crisis of faith'. Religious and philosophical beliefs get tested and need either to be scrapped or more finely tuned. Along with this, there are changes in the spiritual life (seems to me that one is connected with the other). These can be changes in your spiritual practice, your attitudes and even teachings. Often people are introduced to new teachings or teachers that attract them. There are shake-ups in a charity or spiritual organization that you're involved with.

Now that you've had your birthday, your personal solar cycle is waxing. The universal solar cycle started to wax at the Winter Solstice. The Sun is in Aries until the 20th. Most of the planets are moving forward. You are in the optimum period for starting new activities or launching new products into the world, and the 1st and 2nd and the 18th and 19th are the best days to do this.

May

Best Days Overall: 3, 4, 12, 13, 21, 22, 30, 31

Most Stressful Days Overall: 5, 6, 7, 18, 19, 25, 26, 27

Best Days for Love: 1, 2, 10, 11, 12, 13, 18, 19, 21, 22, 25, 26, 27, 28, 29, 30, 31

Best Days for Money: 5, 6, 9, 14, 15, 18, 19, 23, 24, 28, 29

Best Days for Career: 5, 6, 7, 14, 15, 23, 24

The planets are approaching the nadir (low point) of your chart this month. Symbolically speaking, you are entering the midnight hour of your year. Mighty events happen at midnight, but we don't see them. They happen on the internal levels. They become visible in the morning. So it is with you. At this apparently inactive point, the forces for the next career push are being aligned and readied. This is a month – from the 21st onwards – for emotional healing and cleansing. It is a time for coming to terms with traumas (especially if they are still active) from the past, and for resolving old memories and experiences. The interpretation that you put on an event when you were a child is probably not correct, especially when the event is viewed from your present standpoint. Sometimes we have to go backwards (look at the past) in order to go forwards.

Health and energy are stressed this period, especially from the 21st onwards. So, as always, make sure you get enough rest. It is especially stressful for those of you born early in the sign of Pisces – February 18 to 20. Pushing yourself when you're tired usually doesn't speed things up. There are more mental mistakes and you just have to redo your work. It is better to rest and work when you have your full energy. This month enhance your health through neck massage until the 21st, and with arm and shoulder massage after then. Give more attention to the lungs, bronchial tubes and respiratory system. Make sure you're breathing properly and getting enough air. If you feel under the weather, get out in the fresh air and do some deep breathing. Do your best to keep your mood positive and constructive. Family harmony is good for its own sake, but this period (after the 21st) it contributes to your health.

Job seekers have good aspects this year, but this month they are better after the 21st than before. Jobs are found close to home. Family or family connections are especially helpful.

The love and social life also seem centred on the family this month. Love is close to home. Family members are most likely playing Cupid. Family connections seem important too. You seem more nostalgic in love this month. You are trying to recapture high romantic moments from the past. Sometimes an old flame comes into the picture with these aspects. This contributes to the emotional healing we discussed earlier. Emotional intimacy seems just as important as physical intimacy this month. Mercury, your love planet, goes retrograde on the 14th, so avoid making important love decisions (one way or another) from the 14th onwards. Things are not what they seem. Time will bring clarity to the matter.

June

Best Days Overall: 8, 9, 17, 18, 19, 27, 28

Most Stressful Days Overall: 2, 3, 15, 16, 22, 23, 29, 30

Best Days for Love: 1, 6, 7, 10, 11, 15, 16, 20, 21, 22, 23, 24, 25, 29, 30

Best Days for Money: 2, 3, 8, 9, 10, 11, 17, 18, 19, 20, 21, 27, 28, 29, 30

Best Days for Career: 2, 3, 10, 11, 20, 21, 29, 30

Health still needs watching but we see improvements over last month. Saturn is temporarily moving away from his stressful aspect on the 15th, and on the 21st the Sun also moves away from his stressful aspect. By the 24th you should feel a resurgence of energy. In the meantime, enhance the health in the ways mentioned last month. Until the 21st regular arm and shoulder massage will be powerful. Fresh air and breathing exercises are good. Reflexology or acupressure treatments of the lungs and bronchial tubes are good. From the 21st onwards give more attention to the stomach and digestive system. Women should give more attention to the breasts. Right diet becomes important then.

You are still in a period for emotional healing until the 21st. Review our discussion of this last month. After the 21st you enter one of your yearly personal pleasure peaks. Now it is fun and games; it's about recreation and recharging your batteries. See how your health improves when you are enjoying yourself. A night out on the town is not only fun in its own right, but it improves the overall health.

Job seekers find job opportunities as they are having fun, or when they are involved in leisure pursuits. Those who already have jobs are enjoying their work more – finding ways to enjoy their work. A very nice job opportunity comes at the end of the month.

Last month, the planetary power began to shift once again. The Western, social sector of your chart became powerful. Your period of personal independence is over with. You are in a new stage of your yearly cycle. With the planetary power now moving towards others and away from you, your way is probably not the best way. Others probably have better ideas now. Your personal attainments and merits are less important now: it's your social skills and likeability that count. Downplay self-interest and focus more on the needs of others. Your own needs will be met naturally and easily by the karmic law.

Personal creativity will become very strong after the 21st. And those of you in the creative arts will find your work more marketable from the 24th onwards.

Finances are good this month. Until the 24th the family and family connections are important. Many of you will be working more from home, earning from the home. Investors should explore residential real estate, restaurants and hotels. The telecommunications and transportation sectors of the market also seem good.

July

Best Days Overall: 6, 7, 14, 15, 16, 24, 25
Most Stressful Days Overall: 12, 13, 19, 20, 26, 27, 28
Best Days for Love: 7, 8, 9, 17, 18, 19, 20, 26, 29, 30
Best Days for Money: 6, 7, 8, 9, 14, 15, 16, 18, 24, 25, 27, 28
Best Days for Career: 9, 18, 26, 27, 28

Continue, like last month, to put others first. It is good to take a vacation from oneself every now and then. Many problems in life come from too much self focus. Your self-interest is important but now it happens through the good graces of others.

Finances are good this month but there are some short term bumps along the road. With Mars in your 5th house of fun and enjoyment all month, there is luck in speculations. Money is earned in happy ways. You are spending on leisure and fun-type activities. You are enjoying the wealth that you have – and not everyone can say this. Be more careful in financial matters from the 14th to the 17th – extravagance can be a problem. There is some short-term financial disturbance from the 24th to the 27th – perhaps an unexpected expense or turn of events. Avoid speculations during those two periods. Your financial intuition needs verification from the 24th to the 27th.

Your financial planet in the sign of Cancer all month is basically a harmonious aspect for you. But there are some down sides to it. You can be too moody. Your spending and investing depend on your mood. If your mood is negative mistakes can be made. If there are major decisions to be made, sleep on things more. Make the decisions when you are in a state of peace and harmony.

On the 23rd the Sun moves into your 6th house of health and work. This is an excellent period for making doctor's appointments or having tests or screenings done, as well as for getting involved in health regimes. This will stand you in good stead next month when the health becomes more delicate. If you employ others, this is an excellent time for interviewing and hiring workers. Job seekers have excellent prospects this period too.

Retrograde activity increases this month. We are in the maximum level for the year from the 25th onwards. Things are slowing down in the world. But in your love life, things are moving fast. Your love planet Mercury is moving very fast, through three signs and houses this month. This signals social confidence – someone who makes rapid social progress. Until the 8th Mercury is in your 4th house of home and family, and you are attracted by emotional intimacy and the sharing of feelings. From the 8th to the 23rd emotional intimacy is still important to you, but you want fun too. You are attracted to the people who can show you a good time. If you are in a relationship you are having more fun in that relationship. From the 23rd onwards you seem more practical. Service is love in action. You are attracted to those who serve your interests in practical ways.

Be more patient with the beloved from the 15th to the 20th. He or she should stay out of harm's way that period. Avoid risky or stressful activities.

August

Best Days Overall: 2, 3, 10, 11, 12, 20, 21, 22, 29, 30
Most Stressful Days Overall: 8, 9, 15, 16, 17, 23, 24
Best Days for Love: 5, 14, 15, 16, 17, 23, 24, 26, 27, 31
Best Days for Money: 3, 4, 5, 13, 15, 23, 24, 25, 31
Best Days for Career: 5, 15, 23, 24, 25

The main headline this month is the love life. Your 7th house of love becomes very powerful from the 11th onwards. Jupiter makes a major move from your 6th to your 7th house then. Mercury, your love planet, moves in on the 7th, the Sun will enter on the 23rd. You are in a yearly (and perhaps multi-year) love and social peak now. In the coming months many of you will marry or enter into relationships that are 'like' marriage. (And this could happen next year too.) There is a very happy love and social month and year ahead.

Love still seems very practical this month, with both your career planet (Jupiter) and your work planet (the Sun) in your 7th house. Moreover, your love planet is in practical Virgo from the 7th to the 27th too. Forget about moonlit walks on the beach, flowers and music. Love is very down to earth. You are attracted to people of high status, the good providers, the people who serve your interests in practical ways, the people who can help you careerwise. Flowers and moonlit walks and the whisper of sweet nothings are all ephemeral. Practical service endures. So, this is the kind of month (and year) where the beloved shows his or her love by fixing your computer or changing a flat tyre, or giving career support. This is how you feel loved and this is how you show it.

This month you have the classic aspects for an office romance. This can be with a co-worker or with a boss or superior – or with someone involved in your career. Power and prestige are mighty aphrodisiacs this month (and in the year ahead).

Even your health is affected by your love life after the 23rd. It will be important to maintain harmony with the current love or partner. Health and energy are good until the 23rd but need more attention afterwards. Until the 23rd give attention to the heart (always important for you). After the 23rd the small intestine becomes important. Reflexology, acupuncture or acupressure treatments along the small intestine meridian will be very helpful. Most important, as always, is to get enough rest. Low energy is the primal disease and the primal cause of disease.

Jupiter is your career planet. His move on the 11th shows important career changes happening. The spouse, partner or current love is very involved in your career and supportive. It is good now to advance the career by social means – through networking and through attending or hosting the right kinds of parties. Your personal merits are important but your ability to get on with others is perhaps more important careerwise. (This is not just for now with the planets in the Western sector of the Horoscope, but is a trend for the rest of the year and well into next year too.)

September

Best Days Overall: 7, 8, 17, 18, 26, 27
Most Stressful Days Overall: 4, 5, 6, 12, 13, 19, 20
Best Days for Love: 1, 4, 5, 9, 10, 12, 13, 14, 15, 19, 20, 24, 25, 28, 29
Best Days for Money: 1, 2, 9, 10, 12, 20, 28, 29, 30
Best Days for Career: 2, 12, 19, 20, 30

Last month brought many changes and the month ahead brings even more. This is a tumultuous kind of month. Just read the newspapers and you'll see what we're talking about.

There are two eclipses this month and these are causing all the ruckus. The solar eclipse of the 13th affects you very strongly, so take it nice and easy that period. You should be taking it easy until the 23rd anyway, but especially so during the eclipse period. It occurs in your

7th house of love, triggering dramatic changes in the love life. The ground is being prepared for love and a lot of impurities and obstructions need to be cleared away. Only the best will do for you. Lesser loves or imperfect relationships tend to fail now. Good marriages and good relationships will survive this testing – they always do. It is the flawed ones that are in danger.

As the Sun is your work planet, every solar eclipse brings job changes. The change can be within your present company or situation or with another one. The conditions of work are changing, the rules and environment. Sometimes there are health scares too. With health more delicate this period, health scares could happen this month. But don't leap into any kind of action just yet. Let the dust settle from the eclipse first and get a second opinion. Health and energy improve dramatically after the 23rd and the diagnosis can be revised. Over the next six months you will be making important changes to the health regime.

The lunar eclipse of the 28th (in the Americas it is on the 27th) occurs in your money house and announces major financial changes. Generally these changes happen as a result of some crisis or disruption. Your financial thinking, opinions and strategy could be flawed and the eclipse reveals this to you. While this is usually not pleasant, it is good. You are in a position to make corrections. These changes long needed to be made, and now the cosmos forces the issue. It is for your own good.

As with every lunar eclipse, children and children figures in your life are affected. They should reduce their schedule and stay out of harm's way for a few days before and after the 28th. Cosmically speaking, this is like a violent storm happening. While the storm rages, it is best to stay indoors and out of trouble. They can experience dramatic, life-changing kinds of events. They are forced, by circumstances, to redefine their image and personality – their whole perspective on themselves. This leads to a new wardrobe, hair style and image as time goes on.

October

Best Days Overall: 4, 5, 14, 15, 23, 24, 31
Most Stressful Days Overall: 2, 3, 9, 10, 16, 17, 18, 29, 30
Best Days for Love: 2, 3, 8, 9, 10, 11, 12, 19, 20, 21, 22, 27, 28, 29, 30
Best Days for Money: 1, 9, 10, 19, 20, 25, 26, 27, 28
Best Days for Career: 1, 9, 10, 16, 17, 18, 19, 20, 27, 28

Last month the planetary power shifted once again. The upper, objective half of the Horoscope became powerful, and this month it is stronger still. You are beginning your yearly career push. You are not yet at your peak – not for another month or so – but the energy and interest is happening. You can safely let go of home, family and emotional issues and focus on your career and your outer objectives in life. It is mid-morning, symbolically speaking, in your year. The activities of the day are prominent. Last month too, Saturn re-crossed your Mid-heaven and re-entered your 10th house of career. So, like earlier in the year, you succeed now by sheer merit, by being the best at what you do. Jupiter, your career planet, is getting plenty of positive stimulation.

Mars, your financial planet, travels with Jupiter from the 15th to the 18th. This brings a nice payday and often a pay rise. Your good career reputation brings earnings. A parent or parent figure is generous. You have the financial favour of bosses, elders, parents or parent figures. Venus travels with Jupiter from the 24th to the 27th. This brings social connections that help the career and signals good communication with bosses, elders, parents and parent figures. They seem very open to your thinking that period.

All these things are nice, but the main headline this month is the love life. Technically your yearly love peak ended last month on the 23rd. But your 7th house is still very powerful this month. The two beneficent planets of the zodiac, Venus and Jupiter, are there, and all in all, nearly half of the planets are either in or moving through your 7th house at this time. So love is in the air now. Romance blooms. The social life sparkles. The social connections are also helping the career. Singles have many opportunities and options this month but it is the money people, the power people, who seem most alluring to you. Your love planet Mercury is retrograde until the 9th. So don't be in a rush to make any important love decisions. Clarity will come after the 9th.

With your financial planet in your 7th house all month, there are opportunities for business partnerships and joint ventures. Social connections and social skills are not only important in the career, but financially as well. Who you know is probably more important than how much you actually have.

Health is delicate this month. As always, make sure you get enough rest. Enhance the health by giving more attention to the kidneys and hips until the 23rd and to the colon, bladder and sexual organs afterwards. Hip massage and kidney detox will be helpful until the 23rd. And detox regimes are powerful after that.

November

Best Days Overall: 1, 10, 11, 19, 20, 28, 29
Most Stressful Days Overall: 5, 6, 13, 14, 26, 27
Best Days for Love: 5, 6, 7, 10, 11, 17, 18, 21, 26, 27, 30
Best Days for Money: 5, 6, 7, 8, 15, 16, 17, 18, 21, 22, 24, 25, 26, 27
Best Days for Career: 5, 6, 13, 14, 15, 16, 24, 25

Your health and energy improve after the 12th but become more delicate again towards the end of the month. Enhance the health through detox regimes and paying more attention to the colon, bladder and sexual organs until the 23rd. If you feel under the weather a colonic might be a good idea. Safe sex and sexual moderation are also important. With your love life so intense these days, this might be hard to achieve. Reflexology, acupuncture or acupressure treatments along the meridians of the large intestine, bladder and conception vessel will also be very helpful. After the 23rd give more attention to the liver and thighs. Thigh massage will be beneficial. Liver detoxing (by herbal means) will also be good.

Many love and social goals have been achieved over the past few months and the focus now is on the career. On the 22nd you enter a yearly career peak. Your social connections have certainly helped you in the career – doors have been opened for you – but with Saturn and the Sun, the ruler of your 6th house of work in your career house this month, you still have to perform. You are succeeding the old-fashioned way, through merit and a good work ethic. The only problem is overwork. You might be overdoing things and this can impact on your health. Succeed by all means, but do schedule rest periods. It might be necessary to let go of lesser things in your life this month and just focus on your career and on getting enough rest.

You have had the aspects for an office romance for many months and this month, after the 20th, they are even more pronounced. Power and prestige are certainly the most alluring factors in love these days.

The planetary momentum is forward this month. From the 18th onwards, 90 per cent of the planets are moving forward (which is unusual). This indicates rapid progress towards your goals. Events in the world and in your life move quickly.

Drive more carefully between the 19th and the 24th. Siblings and sibling figures should stay out of harm's way during that period and take a more relaxed schedule. There's no need for risky, stressful activities.

A happy romantic or social meeting happens between the 24th and the 26th.

December

Best Days Overall: 7, 8, 9, 17, 18, 25, 26
Most Stressful Days Overall: 2, 3, 4, 10, 11, 23, 24, 30, 31
Best Days for Love: 1, 2, 3, 4, 7, 12, 17, 18, 21, 22, 25, 26, 30, 31
Best Days for Money: 2, 3, 4, 5, 6, 12, 13, 14, 15, 16, 19, 20, 21, 22, 23, 24, 30, 31
Best Days for Career: 2, 3, 4, 10, 11, 12, 13, 21, 22, 30, 31

Continue to watch your health this month until the 22nd. You are ambitious and this is good, but be careful of overworking. Pursue the career calmly. Delegate tasks wherever possible. Continue to pay attention to the liver and thighs until the 22nd. After then, enhance your health by giving more attention to the spine, knees, teeth, bones, skin and overall skeletal alignment. Regular back and knee massages will be good. Regular visits to a chiropractor or osteopath will also be good. And it might be a good idea to schedule a visit to the dental hygienist. Health and energy will improve after the 22nd.

In your career, social connections and your social skills are still very important (especially until the 10th), but so are hard work and personal merit. The past year did not bring much honour or recognition, but this month (and late last month) you had more than usual.

This is not a year for instant, overnight success. (And the same is true for the next two years.) It is a period of steady, methodical, step-by-step career growth. And this is happening now. No, all your career goals will probably not be achieved, but you will see solid progress made. The long-term view is needed now.

Finances are good this month, but you will need to work harder and overcome more obstacles after the 22nd. Your financial planet Mars spends the month in your 8th house of transformation and regeneration. Thus you seem very involved in the finances of the spouse, partner or current love. He or she seems an important factor in earnings. This is a good month to detoxify the financial life. It is not more money that you need; you need to get rid of the waste and redundancies in your financial life. If you do this, you will find that you have ample resources. Are you paying needless interest on your credit cards? Perhaps loans could be consolidated, reducing payments and interest charges. Do you have overlapping cable, phone and internet bills? Perhaps these too can be consolidated and the payments reduced. Is your house cluttered with items you don't use or need? Get rid of them. Sell them or give them to charity. This is a month for clearing out the material clutter. Extra cash should be used to pay down debt. Often loans or mortgages can be refinanced on more favourable terms – this is a good month to explore this.

The financial interest of others should come first this month. You don't ignore your own interest, but give it a back seat. You prosper as you prosper others this period.

There are some short-term financial disruptions from the 5th to the 12th. Important changes need to be made. If you make them, the financial life straightens out once again.